KU-685-319

Study and Revise from one book

You may be starting – or part of the way through – your Key Stage 3 Science course. You may be in year 9 and getting close to your National Test in Science. Wherever you are in your course, this book will help you. It will improve your scientific knowledge and your skills in answering Test questions.

The Science National Curriculum explained

First, the technical information! The Science National Curriculum is divided into four *Attainment Targets*. These are called:

Sc1 Experimental and investigative science
Sc2 Life processes and living things
Sc3 Materials and their properties
Sc4 Physical properties

Each Attainment Target is divided up into *level descriptions*, numbered from level 1 to level 8. (There is also a top level called Exceptional performance.) These level descriptions tell you what you should know and be able to do at each level.

By the end of Key Stage 3, the majority of pupils should be between levels 3 and 7. A typical Key Stage 3 pupil will be around levels 5 and 6.

Exceptional performance ●	} considerably better than the expected level
Level 8 ●	
Level 7 ●	} better than the expected level
Level 6 ●	} expected level for 14 year olds
Level 5 ●	
Level 4 ●	
Level 3 ●	} working towards the expected level
Level 2 ●	
Level 1 ●	
Age **14 years**	

Typical 14 year olds get a level 5 or 6 in the Science National Test. This book will show you where you are and help you move up the Levels.

What's in the Science National Test?

The National Test papers for Science that you will sit in May of year 9 have questions that cover Sc2, 3 and 4. Your teacher assesses *Experimental and investigative science* (Sc1) from your coursework.

You sit two Test papers. Both papers include biology, chemistry and physics questions.

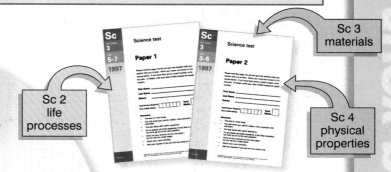

Sc 3 materials

Sc 2 life processes

Sc 4 physical properties

LEVEL 3	LEVEL 4	LEVEL 5	LEVEL 6

	LEVEL 5	LEVEL 6	LEVEL 7

			LEVEL 8

There are two tiers of test papers – Tier 3–6 and Tier 5–7. There is an Extension paper that covers level 8 (and above).

The Test papers are available at two different *tiers*. The first tier covers National Curriculum levels 3–6 and the second tier covers levels 5–7. Everybody has to take their tests in one of these tiers. Your teacher will decide which tier of papers is best for you to show what you know and understand about science.

The questions for levels 5 and 6 are the same in both tiers. You have to take two Test papers. Each Test lasts one hour. Both Tests start with the easier questions and get harder as you work through.

An optional Extension paper has questions that cover level 8 and the 'Exceptional performance' work.

The first book to show you, level-by-level, what you need to know for your Tests.

This book covers the topics that are described in the level descriptions for each Attainment Target at levels 4–8. At each level – 4, 5, 6, 7 and 8 – there is a section on *Life processes and living things*, one on *Materials and their properties*, and one on *Physical properties*.

Each section has three short topic chapters. Some of the topics at the higher levels build on earlier work. Every chapter starts by telling you *What you should already know*.

The chapters at levels 4 and 5 also have introductions, which are a fun way of reminding you what you should already know.

This tells you what you should already know.

This tells you the National Curriculum level.

This tells you the Attainment Target.

This tells you the topic.

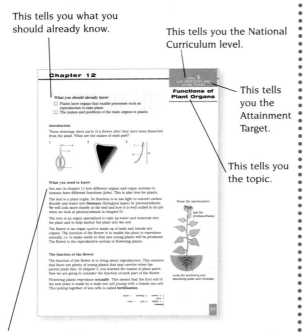

This tells you what the chapter is about.

Before you start a chapter, we tell you what you should already know. And some chapters have word games and puzzles to remind you.

This book's level-by-level structure makes it really easy to use for your study and revision.

We have written the book to be used in two different ways …

You can learn about everything at one Test level

If you are near the start of your Key Stage 3 course, this may be the best way to use the book. You will probably use chapters 4 and 5 in year 7 and then move through the other chapters as you move up into years 8 and 9.

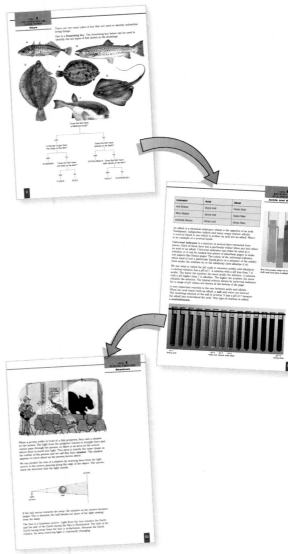

Be confident with everything at one level before you move on.

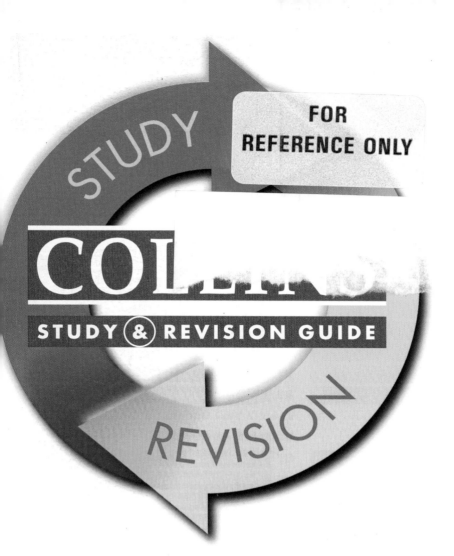

STUDY

COLLINS

STUDY & REVISION GUIDE

REVISION

SCIENCE

National Tests Key Stage 3

▶ Ian Richardson
▶ Steve Goldsmith

▶ Series Editor: Jayne de Courcy

Collins Educational

An Imprint of HarperCollins*Publishers*

Contents

You can follow a topic across all Test levels

This is very useful if there is a topic that you know you need more help with.

It's also an excellent way to plan your Test revision.

For example, you might be looking at the *Reproductive Organs of Plants* at level 4, then move on to *Functions of Plant Organs* (level 5) and the details of *Cell Structure* (level 6). You can then progress to level 7 work on *Specialised Cells* and level 8, *Cell Structure and Life Processes*. You may well reach a point where you find the chapter or the questions too difficult. If you have tried all of the questions and worked through the Tutorials, you should check with your teacher.

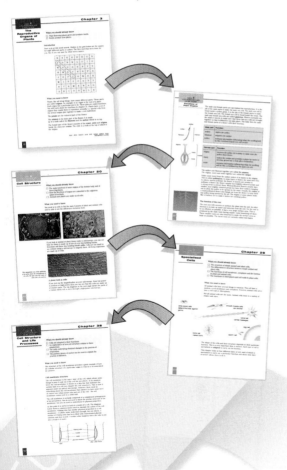

Follow one topic through all of the levels.

You will find that you can reach a higher level on some topics than others, even within the same Attainment Target. Don't worry about this – we are all better at some things than at others!

Testing yourself

This book is full of questions – many different sorts – but for all of them we have given you the answers and tutorials to help out.

Check yourself

At the end of every chapter there is a *Check yourself* section that consists of several short questions that will let you see if you have understood the chapter. The questions are always written down the middle of the book with the answers on the outside, so you can use the flaps on the cover to hide the answers as you work.

Tutorial help – you're never left stranded!

Each answer has a *Tutorial* to go with it. This provides some extra help if you are having trouble getting an answer or if your answer is wrong. These *Tutorials* have been written by people who work with your Tests and they tell you about some of the common errors that pupils make when answering questions. Look out for the hints!

This is the Tutorial.   This is the answer.

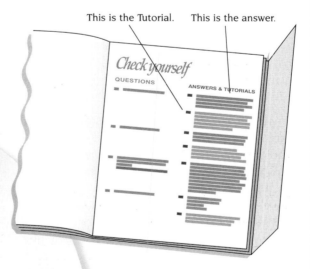

The *Check yourself* questions test that you have understood the chapter. Every *Question* has help from the examiner in a *Tutorial*. Cover up the answers while you work!

v

Practise *real* Test questions

At the end of the chapters at each level, you will find some Test questions from previous years' papers. These test your understanding of the big ideas from across the whole level.

This is the level.

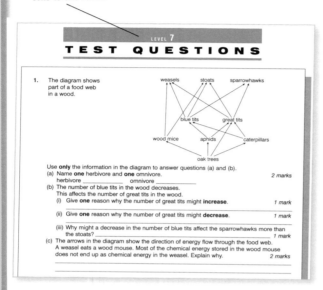

The Test questions are from real National Test papers, so you know what to expect.

On your real Test paper, there is plenty of space for you to write on the paper itself. We have had to change some of the answer spaces to fit in this book, so you do not always have space to write in your book. But always look at the number of marks available for each part of a question. This is a good indication of how much you should write.

If you are using the book for **revision**, you might want to start by trying some of these real Test questions. If you are entered for the level 5–7 tier, try some of the questions at level 5. If you have problems with some of them, work through the chapters and try the questions again. Once you're confident about your answers to the level 5 questions, you could move on to level 6, and so on.

If you are using the book for **study**, you may prefer to work through the chapters and *then* use the Test questions to double-check your understanding of topics.

Help with the Test questions

The answers to the real Test questions are at the back of the book. Every answer has E*xaminer's comments* with it. This shows you the best way to answer the question and where you might have gone wrong if you did not get the right answer.

Answers to Test questions plus Examiner's comments are at the back of the book.

Boosting your confiden – and your Test level

Using this book will help you to enjoy your Key Stage 3 Science course because you will *understand* your science.

If you use this book throughout your course and in planning your revision, you will have a better chance of achieving the best possible level. Perhaps better than you, your parents or your teacher would ever have thought possible!

Chapter 1

What you should already know

☐ Living things can be grouped according to their features.
☐ How to sort living things into groups according to what they look like.
☐ An explanation of the reasons for these groupings.

Introduction

Look carefully at the six figures below. They can be sorted into groups by looking at any features they have in common. For example, you could sort the figures into two groups by looking at their shape. A, C and E are all squares, but B, D and F are not squares. By looking at *another* feature, sort the figures into two groups of three, making sure that each figure in that group has that particular feature. When you have done this successfully, try it once more using a different feature.

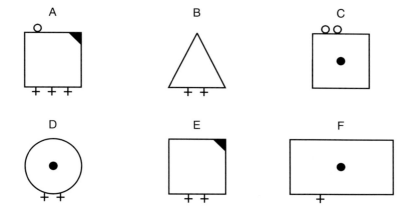

What you need to know

If you want to identify an animal or a plant, what can you do to find out its name? One way would be to ask your science teacher, but your teacher may not know. There are so many kinds of living thing that it is impossible to know them all. There are, for example, about 750 000 different kinds of insects in the world.

You might try to match the plant or animal with photographs in books. However, it would take an awfully long time even if you had all the books you needed.

A better way is to use a **key**. A key used for identification is a series of questions that have two possible answers. The questions start by being fairly general, but they have to be more specific as the choice of living things narrows down.

Your groups should have been:
- B, D and E have two crosses   A, C and F do not have two crosses
- C, D and F all have a dot in them   A, B and E do not have a dot

Keys

There are two main types of key that are used to identify unfamiliar living things.

One is a **branching key**. The branching key below can be used to identify the six types of fish shown in the drawings.

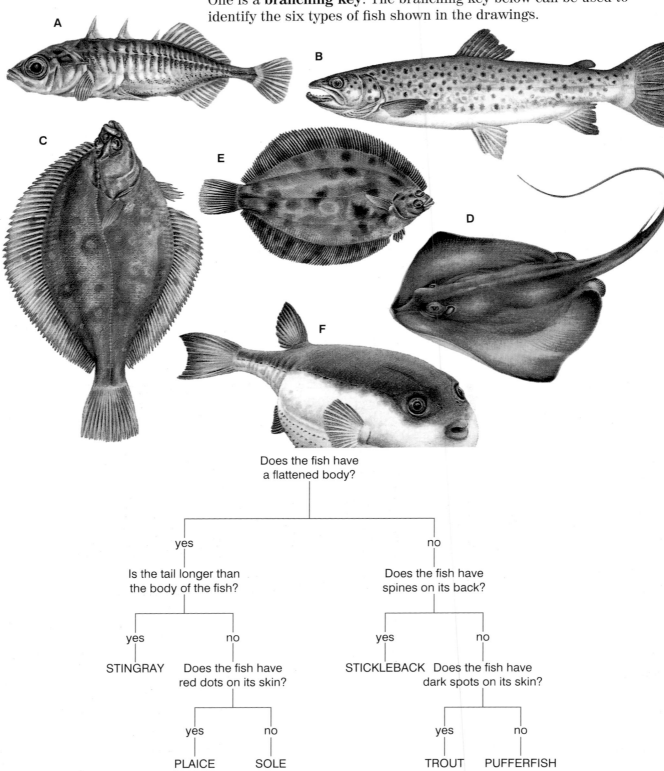

Does the fish have
a flattened body?

yes

Is the tail longer than
the body of the fish?

yes

STINGRAY

no

Does the fish have
red dots on its skin?

yes

PLAICE

no

SOLE

no

Does the fish have
spines on its back?

yes

STICKLEBACK

no

Does the fish have
dark spots on its skin?

yes

TROUT

no

PUFFERFISH

Look at fish A: it <u>does not</u> have a flattened body; it <u>does</u> have spines on its back. Fish A is a STICKLEBACK.

Look at fish B: it <u>does not</u> have a flattened body; it <u>does not</u> have spines; it <u>does</u> have dark spots on its skin. Fish B is a TROUT.

Look at fish C: it <u>does</u> have a flattened body; it <u>does not</u> have a long and thin tail; it <u>does</u> have red dots on its skin. Fish C is a PLAICE.

Look at fish D: it <u>does</u> have a flattened body; it <u>does</u> have a long and thin tail. Fish D is a STINGRAY.

Look at fish E: it <u>does</u> have a flattened body; it <u>does not</u> have a long and thin tail; the skin <u>does not</u> have red dots. Fish E is a SOLE.

Look at fish F: it <u>does not</u> have a flattened body; it <u>does not</u> have spines on its back; it <u>does not</u> have dark spots on its skin. Fish F is a PUFFERFISH.

A second type of key uses pairs of statements or questions. You must read the first pair and decide which is true for the living thing you are trying to identify. This then tells you which pair of questions or statements to look at next.

We can use the pairs of statements to name all six fungi shown in the photographs. Fungi are living things that are not animals but do not have chlorophyll like plants do. Examples of fungi include moulds, mildew, mushrooms and toadstools.

1   Fungus has an obvious stem   go to 2
     Fungus does not have an obvious stem   go to 4

2   Fungus is brightly coloured .... FLY AGARIC
     Fungus is not brightly coloured   go to 3

3   Fungus has a waxy body with a rim that curls up .... BUTTER CAP
     Fungus has long, domed cap with dark lower rim . SHAGGY INK CAP

4   Fungus is orange .... ORANGE PEEL
     Fungus is not orange   go to 5

5   Fungus has outer lobes forming a star shape .... EARTH-STAR
     Fungus has dark upper surface and white gills .. OYSTER FUNGUS

Look at fungus A: it does have an obvious stem (go to 2); it is brightly coloured. Fungus A is a FLY AGARIC.

Look at fungus B: it does have an obvious stem (go to 2); it is not brightly coloured (go to 3); it has a waxy body with a rim that curls up. Fungus B is a BUTTER CAP.

Look at fungus C: it does not have an obvious stem (go to 4); it is not orange (go to 5); it does have outer lobes forming a star shape. Fungus C is an EARTH-STAR.

Look at fungus D: it does not have an obvious stem (go to 4); it is orange. Fungus D is ORANGE PEEL FUNGUS.

Look at fungus E: it does not have an obvious stem (go to 4); it is not orange (go to 5); it has dark upper surface and white gills. Fungus E is an OYSTER FUNGUS.

Look at fungus F: it does have an obvious stem (go to 2); it is not brightly coloured (go to 3); it has a long, domed cap with dark lower rim. Fungus F is a SHAGGY INK CAP.

Check yourself

ANSWERS & TUTORIALS

A1   **A key is a set of questions or statements used to identify living things.**

T1   A common mistake is to not focus on the feature asked about. Pay careful attention to detail.

QUESTIONS

Q1   **What do we mean by the word 'key'?**

QUESTIONS

Q2 What are the two most common types of keys that scientists use?

Q3 Use the key below to identify the six plants shown in the photographs, all of which can be found in the British countryside.

1	Flowers are white	go to 2
	Flowers are not white	go to 4

2	Flowers have coloured veins	WOOD SORREL
	Flowers do not have coloured veins	go to 3

3	Has large, pointed oval leaves	LILY OF THE VALLEY
	Flowers have small, narrow leaves	SNOWDROP

4	Flowers are purple	BLUEBELL
	Flowers are yellow	go to 5

5	Flowers are small on shrub-like stems	GORSE
	Flowers have about eight petals with heart-shaped leaves	LESSER CELANDINE

ANSWERS & TUTORIALS

A2 Branching keys; pairs of questions or statements.

T2 A common mistake with pairs of questions or statements is to not go to the question or statement indicated. Check the number of the next question or statement that you need to go to.

A3
A BLUEBELL
B WOOD SORREL
C GORSE
D LILY OF THE VALLEY
E SNOWDROP
F LESSER CELANDINE

T3 It is important that you choose a flower and then follow the statements through carefully for that flower. Do not be tempted to choose a flower and then try to guess the name without using the key. Even if you think you know the flower, you should always work through all the statements of the key to make sure you are correct.

Body Systems

What you should already know

- [ ] Living things feel, grow and reproduce.
- [ ] Humans have skeletons made up of many bones.

Introduction

Written below are the jumbled names of nines organs found in the human body. Unscramble the letters and write the correct name of the organs in the grid. When you have completed the grid, you should see the name of another organ written down the page.

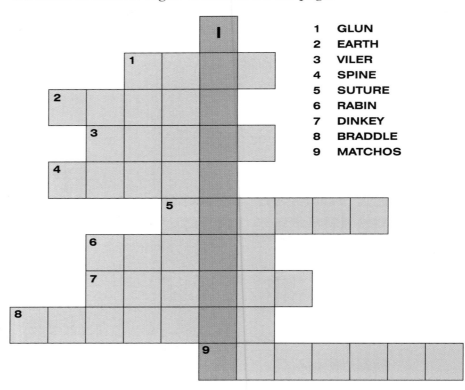

1	GLUN
2	EARTH
3	VILER
4	SPINE
5	SUTURE
6	RABIN
7	DINKEY
8	BRADDLE
9	MATCHOS

What you need to know

Inside our bodies there are many different **organs**, such as the heart and the lungs. Each organ has a special job (function) to do. In chapter 11 you will learn about the functions of some organs.

Some of the organs in the human body work together and are part of an **organ system**. An example of an organ system is the digestive system. This contains all of the organs which enable you to digest your food, from the moment you put food in your mouth until the waste leaves your body through your anus.

The hidden word is INTESTINES.

Answers to Introduction

1 LUNG   2 HEART   3 LIVER   4 PENIS   5 UTERUS
6 BRAIN   7 KIDNEY   8 BLADDER   9 STOMACH

The table lists some of the organs that are part of the four main organ systems of your body and the function of each system. The position of these and other organs in the human body are shown in the diagram that follows.

Name of organ system	Function of the organ system	Some of the organs in the system
Digestive system	digestion of food	stomach, intestines
Reproductive system	production of babies	uterus (female), penis (male)
Circulatory system	circulation of blood	heart, arteries, veins
Respiratory system	taking in and giving out gases	lungs

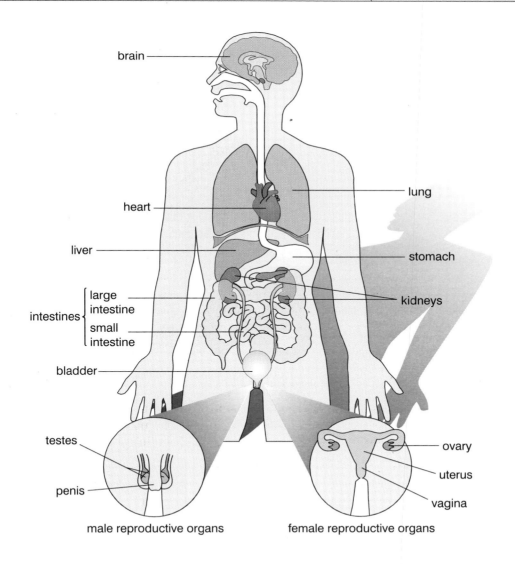

male reproductive organs   female reproductive organs

Check yourself

ANSWERS & TUTORIALS

A1 An organ is a part of the body that has a
particular job to do (function).

T1 All you need to know at this stage are the names
of the major organs of the body, which system
they are part of and their position in the body.

A2 An organ system is the name given to a number
of organs that work together to enable a
particular process to take place.

T2 Remember that an organ system is made up of
two or more organs. Each organ has a job to do
(function) and contributes to the functions of the
system. Try not to confuse an organ with the
system it is part of.

A3 The circulatory system.

T3 The system contains a number of organs.
The heart is an organ but is only *part* of the
circulatory system, not the system itself.

A4 Correct answers include stomach and intestines.

T4 You may have learned more detail but at
this stage you do not need to know more
details of the digestive system.

QUESTIONS

Q1 What is an organ?

Q2 What is an organ system?

Q3 What is the name of the organ system
responsible for the circulation of the blood?

Q4 Give the names of two organs that are part of
the digestive system.

QUESTIONS

Q5 Identify the organs labelled A–E in the diagram.

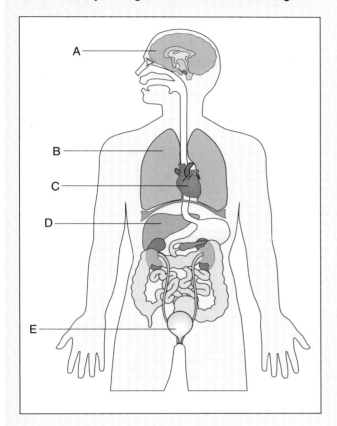

ANSWERS & TUTORIALS

A5 A   Brain
        B   Lung
        C   Heart
        D   Liver
        E   Bladder

T5 If you have trouble locating any of the organs,
        look again at the diagrams shown on page 7.
        It will help you to learn if you try to sketch the
        outline from memory and draw in the position of
        the organs.

Chapter 3

The Reproductive Organs of Plants

What you should already know

- [ ] That flowering plants grow and produce seeds.
- [ ] Seeds produce new plants.

Introduction

Have a go at this word search. Hidden in the grid below are the names for eight different parts of a plant. The first word has been done for you. See if you can spot the other seven names.

R	E	K	B	O	H	U	X
F	O	S	N	L	C	I	O
W	A	O	G	E	S	Y	V
N	M	E	T	S	N	P	A
J	G	F	L	O	W	E	R
M	I	P	F	C	E	T	Y
S	T	A	M	E	N	A	G
A	S	I	D	O	Q	L	E

What you need to know

Plants, like all living things, have many different parts. These parts are called **organs**. An example of an organ is the root of a plant. Each organ has a particular job to do. These jobs are called functions. You will learn about the functions in chapter 12. Plants have a set of organs that enable them to reproduce sexually, i.e. special cells from the sexual organs join together to make a new individual.

The **petals** are the coloured part of the flower.

The **stamen** is the male part of the flower. It is made up of a stalk called the **filament** and the **anther** which is on top.

The female part of the flower consists of the **ovary**, **style** and **stigma**. Inside the ovary are **ovules**. The style is a stalk at the top of which is the stigma.

Each of these parts of the flower are labelled on this diagram.

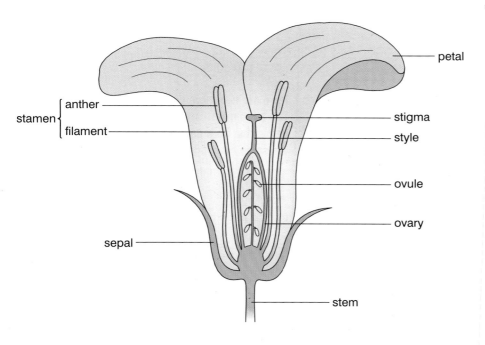

Check yourself

QUESTIONS

Q1 Here is a photograph of a flower. Complete the labels by putting in the word for each part (organ).

Which of these are male organs and which are female organs?

ANSWERS & TUTORIALS

A1 a petal
b stigma
c stamen
d ovary
e stem

The stamen is the male organ. The stigma and ovary are the female organs.

T1 The most common mistake is made in naming of male and female organs in the flower; the stigma is the female part and the stamen is the male part. The stigma sits on top of a stalk that is called the style and connects it to the ovary. Try to draw the flower from memory as a way to remember the names and positions of the organs.

ANSWERS & TUTORIALS

A2

T2 When drawing labelling lines always use a ruler. You need to be very careful to finish the labelling line exactly on the part you are labelling. Do not leave a gap between the line and the part it labels.

Take care to identify one of the stigmas and not one of the anthers that surround them.

If you did not get the labels correct, have another look at the pictures in the **WHAT YOU NEED TO KNOW** section.

QUESTIONS

Q2 Here are two more photographs of flowers. The two flowers are different in shape and colour, but both have the same organs with the same functions.

Draw a labelling line on each flower to show the position of a stigma.

Chapter 4

States of Matter

What you should already know

☐ Matter exists in three different states: solid, liquid and gas.
☐ Some changes to a particular substance are reversible and some are not.

Introduction

Look at the picture below. The numbers in the picture represent states of matter and changes that can occur with heating. Identify these words and use them to complete the crossword.

What you need to know

Matter is the word used to describe everything that exists. Every substance is made of a different kind of matter. Substances can exist in three different **states**. These states of matter are called **solid**, **liquid** and **gas**. Water in the solid state is called ice. Water in the gaseous state (gas) is called steam. Steam is often referred to as water vapour. Other substances do not have different names for their different states. Mercury, for example, is a metal which is liquid at 20 °C (room temperature). If it is cooled to −38 °C, it becomes a solid. If mercury is heated to 357 °C, it becomes a gas. The three different states of mercury are described by their states, i.e. liquid mercury, solid mercury and gaseous mercury (or mercury vapour).

When a substance changes state, we say a **physical change** takes place. A physical change is reversible. If a solid substance is heated to produce a liquid, the liquid can be cooled to return it to its original

Answers:
1 GAS 2 EVAPORATION 3 MELTING 4 SOLID 5 LIQUID

Chapter 5

LEVEL 4
MATERIALS AND
THEIR PROPERTIES

Acids and Alkalis

What you should already know

☐ Materials can be sorted into groups according to their properties.

☐ Mixing some materials can cause them to change.

Introduction

Look at the foods and drinks shown in the picture. Which of them do you think contain acid?

What you need to know

What do you think of when you hear the word **acid**? A liquid that will eat through metal? A liquid that will burn your skin? Some acids do these things, but we also come across some acids in our food. Some fruits such as lemons and grapefruit contain acids and have a sour taste. Vinegar also contains acid and many foods that contain vinegar also have a sour taste. The sour taste is a property of all the acids in our food. Tasting other liquids, which do not come from familiar foods, is not a good idea and should never be done.

In your science lessons you will have come across hydrochloric acid, sulphuric acid and perhaps even nitric acid. These have similar properties and react in the same ways with materials such as metals and alkalis. For example, many metals react with acids and give off hydrogen. Substances like marble (calcium carbonate) and washing soda (sodium carbonate) react with acids and give off carbon dioxide.

You can tell if a substance is an acid by using a chemical called an **indicator**. These can be made from dyes extracted from plants, e.g. litmus. Test papers can be used to tell if a liquid is an acid, an alkali or a neutral liquid. The table below shows what happens to the different types of litmus paper when they are used to test for acids and alkalis.

Answer: They all contain acid!

Indicator	Acid	Alkali
red litmus	stays red	turns blue
blue litmus	turns red	stays blue
neutral litmus	turns red	turns blue

An alkali is a chemical substance which is the opposite of an acid.
Toothpaste, indigestion tablets and many soaps contain alkalis.
A neutral liquid is one which is neither an acid nor an alkali. Water
is an example of a neutral liquid.

Universal indicator is a mixture of several dyes extracted from
plants. Each of these dyes has a particular colour when put into either
an acid or an alkali. Universal indicator can either be used as a
solution, or it can be soaked into pieces of absorbent paper to make
test papers like litmus paper. The colour of the universal indicator
when used to test a particular liquid gives us a measure of the acidity
(how acidic the solution is) or the alkalinity (how alkaline it is).

We use what is called the pH scale to measure acidity and alkalinity.
A neutral solution has a pH of 7. A solution with a pH less than 7 is
acidic. The lower the number, the more acidic the solution. A solution
with a pH higher than 7 is alkaline. The higher the number, the more
alkaline the solution. The typical colours shown by universal indicator
for a range of pH values are shown at the bottom of the page.

A very important reaction is the one between acids and alkalis.
When the acid reacts with an alkali, a **salt** and water are formed.
The resulting solution of the salt is neutral. It has a pH of 7 because
the alkali has neutralised the acid. This type of reaction is called
a **neutralisation**.

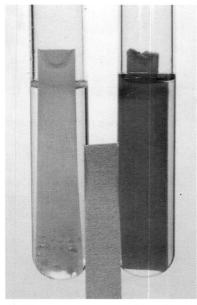

*Red litmus paper stays red in acids
(left) and turns blue in alkalis (right)*

pH 1:
strong acid

pH 6:
weak acid

pH 7:
neutral

pH 8:
weak alkali

pH 14:
strong alkali

Check yourself

ANSWERS & TUTORIALS

A1 Any two from: lemon, orange, lime, grapefruit.

T1 These fruits contain citric acid.

A2 An indicator is a substance that changes colour when added to an acid or an alkali. Indicators can be used to show which liquids are acids and which are alkalis.

T2 Indicators are made from plant extracts. They react to the presence of an acid or an alkali by changing colour. Universal indicator is a mixture of indicators and it changes to a colour that depends on the strength of the acid or alkali being tested.

A3 Blue litmus turns red in an acid solution.

T3 Remember red is the colour produced by acid conditions in the presence of an indicator.

A4 Neutral litmus turns blue in an alkaline solution.

A5 Universal indicator turns green in a neutral solution.

T5 Neutral solutions are neither acidic nor alkaline.

A6 A strong alkali will have a pH of 14.

T6 The bigger the number on the pH scale, the stronger the alkali.

A7 Carbon dioxide.

T7 Carbon dioxide gas is given off when an acid reacts with a carbonate.

A8 A neutralisation reaction.

T8 The acid and alkali react to produce a salt dissolved in water. The solution is neutral.

QUESTIONS

Q1 Give the names of two fruits which have a sour taste.

Q2 What is an indicator?

Q3 What colour does blue litmus turn when added to an acid solution?

Q4 What colour does neutral litmus turn when added to an alkaline solution?

Q5 What colour does universal indicator turn in a neutral solution?

Q6 What is the pH value of a strong alkali?

Q7 What gas is produced when hydrochloric acid reacts with washing soda?

Q8 What name is given to the reaction between an acid and an alkali?

Chapter 6

Separation Methods

What you should already know

- ☐ A mixture is made up of two or more different substances.
- ☐ Some substances dissolve in water and some do not.
- ☐ Some changes such as dissolving, boiling and condensing can be reversed.

Introduction

For each of the labels on the left draw a line that links the word with its correct definition.

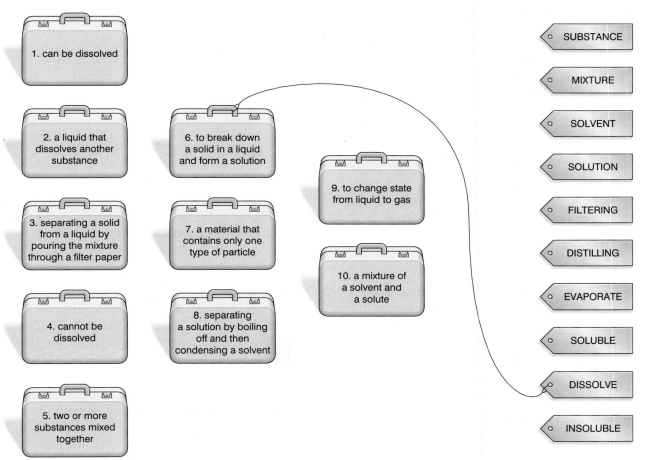

1. can be dissolved
2. a liquid that dissolves another substance
3. separating a solid from a liquid by pouring the mixture through a filter paper
4. cannot be dissolved
5. two or more substances mixed together
6. to break down a solid in a liquid and form a solution
7. a material that contains only one type of particle
8. separating a solution by boiling off and then condensing a solvent
9. to change state from liquid to gas
10. a mixture of a solvent and a solute

SUBSTANCE
MIXTURE
SOLVENT
SOLUTION
FILTERING
DISTILLING
EVAPORATE
SOLUBLE
DISSOLVE
INSOLUBLE

What you need to know

Substances often need to be separated from other parts of a mixture before they can serve a useful purpose. There are four important methods of separating substances from mixtures: filtration, evaporation, distillation and chromatography.

Filtration is used to separate an insoluble solid from a liquid. The insoluble material stays in the filter paper and the liquid goes through the paper into the beaker. The solid is then washed, dried and removed from the filter paper.

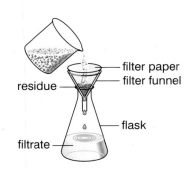

filter paper
filter funnel
residue
flask
filtrate

Answers:
1 soluble,   2 solvent,   3 filtering,   4 insoluble,   5 mixture,
6 dissolve,   7 substance,   8 distilling,   9 evaporate,   10 solution

19

Separation Methods

*Copper sulphate crystals formed by
evaporation of copper sulphate solution.*

Evaporation is used to separate a soluble solid from a liquid. If the solution is left in a shallow container in a warm place, the liquid evaporates leaving the solid behind in the container.

Distillation is used to separate and collect a liquid from a solution of a soluble solid. The flask in the diagram below is heated and the liquid boils. The vapour produced goes into the condenser where it is cooled and condenses (forms a liquid). This pure liquid solvent (called the distillate) collects in the beaker.

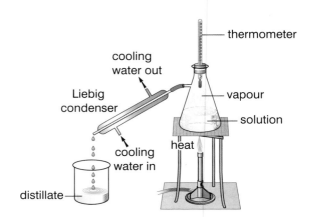

Fractional distillation is a special type of distillation used to separate a mixture of liquids. The liquids boil at different temperatures. The one with the lowest boiling point evaporates first, then the next lowest and so on. Oil refineries use this method to separate the substances contained in crude oil.

Chromatography is used to separate dyes in a colour mixture. A horizontal line is drawn in pencil near the bottom of a piece of chromatography paper. Dots of the mixture of coloured dyes are put onto the paper along that line. The bottom of the paper, below the pencil line, sits in solvent. The start line is drawn in pencil because it is insoluble and will not be affected by the solvent. As the solvent rises up the paper, the dyes are dissolved and move up the paper. Each dye in the mixture will move up the paper until it cannot remain in solution. At this point a coloured spot is formed on the paper. As each dye forms a coloured spot at a different place, the separate dyes can be identified on the paper.

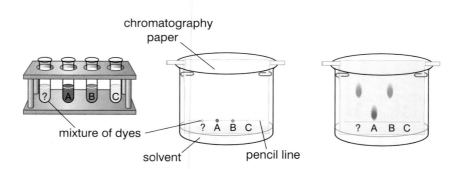

Check yourself

QUESTIONS

Q1 What are the names of the four important methods of separating mixtures?

Q2 Which method would you use to separate the following mixtures:
a   a mixture of different coloured dyes;
b   crude oil;
c   to capture the water from salt and water;
d   sand and water;
e   to collect solid copper sulphate from copper sulphate solution?

Q3 Draw a simple flow chart to show the main steps in separating salt from a mixture of sea water and sand.

ANSWERS & TUTORIALS

A1 filtration
evaporation
distillation
chromatography

T1 Evaporation and distillation can be confused. Check through this chapter again to avoid confusing the methods. Distillation involves condensing the vapour to form a liquid. In evaporation, the liquid turns to vapour but is not collected.

A2 a   **chromatography**
b   **fractional distillation**
c   **distillation**
d   **filtration**
e   **evaporation**

T2 Think carefully about the sorts of substances to be separated. Ask yourself questions like: is the solid soluble; does the mixture contain two liquids; which part of the mixture do you want to collect when the separation is complete?

A3   sea water + sand
↓
filter ———————→ sand
↓
evaporation ———————→ water
↓
salt

T3 Sand does not dissolve in sea water so it can be filtered out of the mixture.

Evaporating the sea water solution will drive off the water leaving the salt behind in the container.

Chapter 7

**LEVEL 4
PHYSICAL PROCESSES**

Shadows

What you should already know

- [ ] Objects that give out light are called luminous sources.
- [ ] Luminous sources include light bulbs, the Sun and other stars.
- [ ] Light cannot pass through some materials.
- [ ] A narrow beam of light is called a ray.
- [ ] Light travels much faster than sound.

Introduction

Look carefully at the picture below. Write down the names of three sources of light and three things that are good at reflecting light.

What you need to know

A material that does not allow light to pass through it is described as **opaque**. Wood and iron are opaque materials. Some other materials, such as plain glass, are described as **transparent**. Transparent materials allow most light to pass through them.

Materials, such as grease-proof paper, are described as **translucent**. Translucent materials allow some light to pass through them.

When light rays are stopped by something opaque, a shadow is formed. Shadows form because light travels in straight lines and cannot bend around corners.

Answers:
Sources of light include: Sun, stars, torch bulb, car lights.
Reflectors of light include: Cats'eyes, warning triangle, reflective jacket, moon.

When a person walks in front of a film projector, they cast a shadow on the screen. The light from the projector travels in straight lines and cannot pass through the person, so there is an area on the screen where there is much less light. This area is exactly the same shape as the outline of the person and we call this their **shadow**. The shadow appears to move about as the person moves about.

We can predict the size of a shadow by drawing lines from the light source to the screen passing along the edge of the object. The arrows show the direction that the light travels.

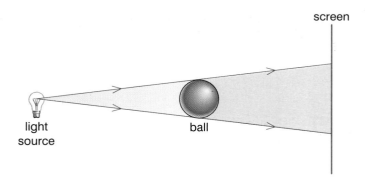

If the ball moves towards the lamp, the shadow on the screen becomes larger. This is because the ball blocks out more of the light coming from the lamp.

The Sun is a luminous source. Light from the Sun reaches the Earth and the side of the Earth facing the Sun is illuminated. The side of the Earth facing away from the Sun is in darkness. Because the Earth rotates, the area receiving light is constantly changing.

When our part of the Earth is facing away from the Sun, no light from the Sun reaches us and it is dark. This period of darkness is called night.

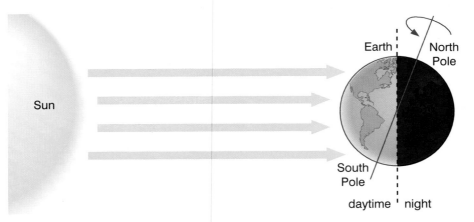

You will learn more about the effects of the Earth moving in relation to the Sun in chapter 18.

Check yourself

ANSWERS & TUTORIALS

A1 Opaque materials do not allow light to pass through them.
Translucent materials allow some light to pass through them.
Transparent materials allow most light to pass through them.
A shadow is a dark area formed because light has been stopped by an opaque object.

T1 Remember to write these answers in complete sentences.
Some materials that appear to be translucent are not really. Think of woven cloth. This lets some light through, but the light is passing through the gaps in the weave.
Clear materials such as plain glass do not let all of the light through but they do let most through.
Make sure that you answer the question and describe the meaning of the word 'shadow' and not just how a shadow is formed.

QUESTIONS

Q1 Write one sentence to explain the meaning of each of the following words:
opaque
translucent
transparent
shadow

QUESTIONS

Q2

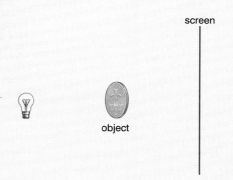

a **Draw two rays of light onto the diagram above to show how a shadow is formed on the screen. Indicate on the diagram which parts of the screen will be lit and which part will be a shadow.**

b **How is the shadow of the coin formed?**

c **How could the shadow of the coin be made smaller?**

d **The shadow is seen clearly as soon as the lamp is turned on. What does this tell you about the speed of light?**

ANSWERS & TUTORIALS

A2   a

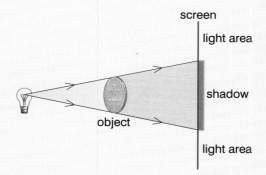

b **Light travels in straight lines and it cannot pass through the coin.**

c **Either by moving the coin away from the lamp so that it is closer to the screen, or by moving the screen closer to the coin.**

d **The speed of light is very fast.**

T2   a Always use a pencil and ruler to draw rays of light as straight lines and do not forget an arrow on each ray to show the direction in which the light is travelling. Remember to label the shadow.

b Remember that light cannot pass through opaque objects and that it always travels in straight lines. This means that light is stopped when it reaches the coin. An area where there is no light is a shadow.

c The size of the shadow depends on the distance between the object and the screen. The smaller the distance, the smaller the shadow and the bigger the distance, the bigger the shadow.

d A common mistake here is to give the answer that it is faster than sound. This is true, but it does not answer the question. The important point is that light travels at a very high speed (300 million metres every second).

Circuit Components

What you should already know

☐ A complete circuit, including a battery or power supply, is needed to make electrical devices work.

☐ Electrical devices can be represented by symbols and electrical circuits can be represented by circuit diagrams using these symbols.

Introduction

Look at the table below. Draw a line from each component to its name and then draw a line from each name to its symbol.

Component	Name of component	Symbol for component
	open switch	
	bulb	
	closed switch	
	battery	

What you need to know

Switches are used to control bulbs in a circuit. The bulb in the circuit below will not light up because the switch is open. This means there is a break in the circuit and that electricity cannot flow because the circuit is not complete.

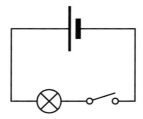

If the switch is closed the circuit is complete, so electricity will flow and the bulb will light.

To find out whether a bulb will light you need to follow the circuit from the battery, through the wires to the bulb, back through the wires to the battery. If there is no break in the circuit then the bulb will light (as long as the battery, wires and bulbs are not faulty!).

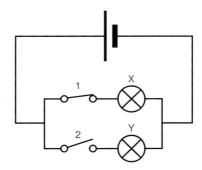

In the circuit above, bulb X will light, because it is part of a complete circuit, but bulb Y will not light, because switch 2 is not closed.

Check yourself

ANSWERS & TUTORIALS

A1 **a** **A and B**
    b **A and C**

T1 Follow the circuit from the left side of the battery through bulb A. If switch 1 is closed, there is a complete circuit back to the right side of the battery and so A and B will light. Bulb C will not light because it is not part of a complete circuit when switch 2 is open.

Bulb C is now included in the complete circuit but bulb B is not because of the open switch 1.

A2 **a** **2**
    b **3**
    c **2 and 3**

T2 The bulb is always lit in circuit 2. It is in a complete circuit, so the electricity will flow through it.

In circuit 3, the motor will always be on. The switch only controls the bulb.

In circuits 2 and 3, electricity can still flow through the motor even when the bulb is broken. The motor is still part of a complete circuit (the switch needs to be closed in 2).

The symbol —(M)— represents a motor.

QUESTIONS

Q1 **a** **Which of the bulbs light up if switch 1 is closed?**

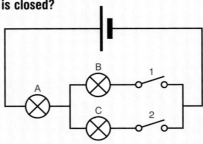

    b **Which bulbs light if just switch 2 is closed?**

Q2 **a** **In which of these circuits will the bulb be lit?**
    b **In which circuit does the switch control the bulb only?**
    c **In which circuits would the motor still work if the bulb is broken?**

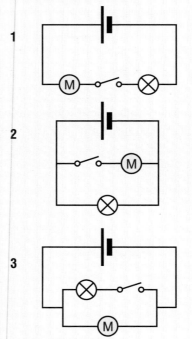

QUESTIONS

Q3 Fill in the table to show which bulbs will be lit when the switches are closed in each of the four circuits shown.

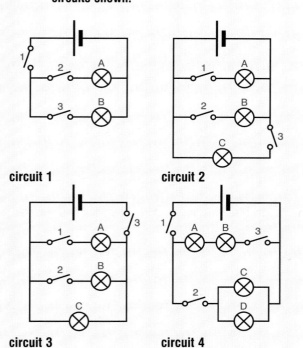

circuit 1   circuit 2

circuit 3   circuit 4

switches closed	bulbs lit in circuit 1	bulbs lit in circuit 2	bulbs lit in circuit 3	bulbs lit in circuit 4
1				
2				
3				
1 and 2				
2 and 3				
1 and 3				
1, 2 and 3				

ANSWERS & TUTORIALS

T3   **Circuit 1**
Neither bulb A or B will light unless switch 1 is closed as well as the switch alongside each of the bulbs.

Circuit 2
Switch 3 only controls bulb C. Closing either of switches 1 and 2 will complete that branch of the circuit and the bulb will light.

Circuit 3
Switch 3 controls all of the bulbs in the circuit. When switch 3 is closed, bulb C will light. If bulbs A and B are to light, switch 3 needs to be closed when either of switches 1 and 2 are also closed.

Circuit 4
Switch 1 must be closed before any of the other switches can be used to light any of the bulbs. Switch 3 controls both bulbs A and B. Switch 2 controls both bulbs C and D

A3

switches closed	bulbs lit in circuit 1	bulbs lit in circuit 2	bulbs lit in circuit 3	bulbs lit in circuit 4
1	none	A	none	none
2	none	B	none	none
3	none	C	C	none
1 and 2	A	A, B	none	C and D
2 and 3	none	B, C	B, C	none
1 and 3	B	A, C	A, C	A, B
1, 2 and 3	A and B	A, B, C	A, B, C	A, B, C, D

Chapter 9

Forces and Motion

What you should already know

- ☐ A force is needed to make an object start moving, to speed it up or to slow it down.
- ☐ When forces act on an object, its shape may change.
- ☐ Some types of material sink in water and others float.

Introduction

There are eight words to do with forces hidden in this word search grid. Can you find them? The words may be written forwards, backwards, up, down or diagonally.

A	B	N	E	W	T	O	N	T	W
E	I	S	T	P	W	U	L	P	Y
C	S	H	W	E	I	G	H	T	F
R	L	I	P	U	S	H	I	A	X
O	N	U	E	W	T	V	T	O	N
F	L	O	A	T	A	F	O	L	W
L	T	G	A	R	R	H	G	I	E
V	I	T	G	W	O	C	O	O	M

The words are: twist, pull, push, float, newton, force, weight, gravity.

What you need to know

When Sanjay drops a ball from his bedroom window, it will fall to the ground. It falls down because it is pulled towards the centre of the Earth by a force. This force is the Earth's pull and is called the pull of gravity or **gravitational force**.

When the ball falls, another force acts on the ball, resisting its fall to the ground. This force is called **air resistance**.

When Sanjay's ball hits the ground it will deform (change shape) for the very short time that it is in contact with the ground.

Because the ball is made from a flexible and elastic material (one which will return to its original shape), it will bounce back from the ground.

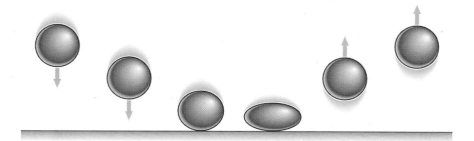

air
resistance

gravity

Parachutists use the fact that air resistance opposes (acts against) the motion of the parachute to control their fall through the air.

If Sanjay had dropped a piece of modelling clay it would have changed shape when it hit the ground but it would not have bounced back. The modelling clay would keep the shape it had become when it hit the ground. This is because modelling clay is flexible but not elastic.

Christine is playing with a beach ball in a swimming pool. When she tries to push the ball down under the water she can feel a force opposing the motion. In order to push the ball down through the water, Christine has to push with a bigger force than the force opposing the motion. The ball will only stay under the water if Christine continues to push downwards on it.

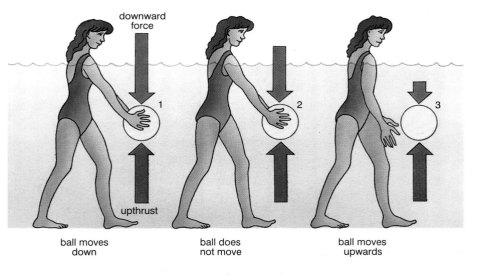

downward
force

upthrust

ball moves
down

ball does
not move

ball moves
upwards

When she pushes down harder on the ball (1), it speeds up as it moves downwards. The forces on the ball are unbalanced because the force downwards is larger than the force upwards.

When she holds the ball so that it is not moving under the water (2), the two forces are balanced, with the forces being the same size and in opposite directions.

When Christine releases the ball (3), the upthrust of the water (the upward force) is larger than the weight of the ball (the downward force). The forces are unbalanced and the ball moves upwards to the surface of the water.

Check yourself

ANSWERS & TUTORIALS

A1 a Earth's pull *or* pull of gravity *or*
gravitational force.
b Air resistance.

T1 Remember air resistance always acts in the
opposite direction to the direction in which the
object is moving.

A2 a The spring will be squashed.
b The spring will return to its original
shape and size.
c The modelling clay will stretch.
d It will remain stretched.

T2 Take care to check the direction of the force.
Remember that some objects have their shape
permanently changed by a force. Other objects,
made from elastic materials, will go back to their
original shape when the force is removed.

A3 a

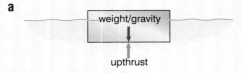

weight/gravity

upthrust

b It will increase.

T3 When the object is floating in water, its weight
(the force due to gravity) is equal to the upthrust
of the water. The two forces are balanced so the
wood remains at the surface of the water.
It becomes more difficult to push the piece of
wood down through the water because the
upthrust acting on the wood increases.

QUESTIONS

Q1 A bird sitting high in a tree loses a feather.
a What is the name of the downward force
that acts on the feather?
b What force opposes the motion of
the feather?

Q2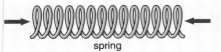

spring

Look at the diagram of a spring.
a What will happen to the spring when
the forces act on it?
b What will happen to the spring when
the forces are removed?

c What will happen to the modelling clay
when the forces act on it?
d What will happen to the modelling clay
when the forces are removed?

Q3

wood

A piece of wood floats in water.
a Draw and label arrows to show two
forces acting on the wood.
b If the piece of wood is pushed under the
water, what will happen to the upward
force acting on it?

1. The animals shown below live in different parts of a river.

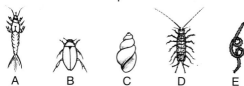

A   B   C   D   E

(a) Use this key to identify animals **A**, **B** and **C**.

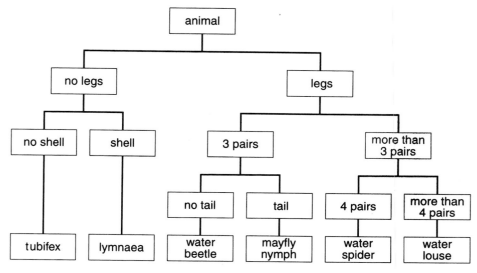

(i) Animal **A** is a _____   *1 mark*

(ii) Animal **B** is a _____   *1 mark*

(iii) Animal **C** is a _____   *1 mark*

2. The drawings show five different lichens which grow on rocks or trees.

A   B   C   D   E

Very pale green lichen   Bright orange lichen   Olive green lichen   Pale grey-green lichen   Pale yellow-green lichen

Identify lichens A, C and D using the key below.   *3 marks*

1. The lichens grow on tree bark .... Go to 2
   The lichens grow on rocks .... Go to 4
2. They grow flat against the surface .... *Parmelia subrudecta*
   They have branches which grow away from the surface .... Go to 3
3. They have long dangling branches .... *Usnea*
   They have short branches .... *Evernia*
4. They are bright orange .... *Xanthoria*
   They are pale grey-green .... *Parmelia saxatilis*

The name of Lichen A is _____

The name of Lichen C is _____

The name of Lichen D is _____

3. The drawing shows part of an organ system.

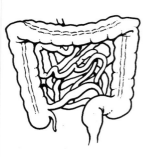

(a) Which organ system is it part of?

Tick the correct box. *1 mark*

circulatory system ☐ reproductive system ☐

digestive system ☐ respiratory system ☐

(b) Where is this part of the organ system found in the body?

Tick **one** box. *1 mark*

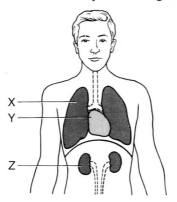

4. The picture shows part of the human body. Three organs are labelled X, Y and Z.

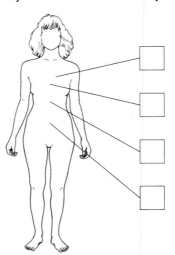

Write the names of the organs X, Y and Z. *3 marks*

X is a _____

Y is the _____

Z is a _____

5. The drawing shows a flower that has been cut in half.

    A, B, C and D are different parts of the flower.

    (a) Put the correct letters in the empty boxes in the table.   *4 marks*

part of flower	letter
ovary	
ovule	
sepal	
stamen	

    (b) What is the function or job of part A?

    _____ *1 mark*

6. (a) During pollination, pollen grains from one flower are carried to other flowers. The pollen sticks to the stigma.

    Put an '**X**' on the drawing to show the stigma.   *1 mark*

    Put a '**P**' on the drawing to show where the pollen is formed in a flower.   *1 mark*

    (b) Put an **S** on the drawing to show where the seeds are formed.   *1 mark*

7. This question is about **three** different fuels, A, B and C.

    Fuel A is stored in tanks. It is not stored under pressure. It flows along a pipe to where it is needed.

    Fuel B is stored under pressure in small cylinders. It is used by campers.

    Fuel C can be stored in sacks or bags.

    (a) (i) Tick the correct box.
            Fuel A is a: *1 mark*

            solid ☐   liquid ☐   gas ☐

            Name a fuel which A could be.   *1 mark*
        (ii) Tick the correct box.
            When fuel B comes out of the cylinder this fuel is a: *1 mark*

            solid ☐   liquid ☐   gas ☐   *1 mark*

            Name a fuel which B could be.

8. Solids, liquids and gases have different properties and different uses.
Some of these are described in the table.
Tick either **one** or **two** boxes in each row to show whether a solid, liquid or gas
matches the description in that row.   *4 marks*

property or use	solid	liquid	gas
it is used to build rigid or stiff structures			
it flows easily through a pipe or tube			
it can be squeezed into a much smaller volume			

9. (a) Vinegar is sometimes put on chips. It has a sharp, sour taste.
    What does the taste tell you about vinegar?   *1 mark*
    Tick the correct box.

    It contains salt. ☐   It is an acid. ☐

    It contains sugar. ☐   It has turned bad. ☐

   (b) Washing soda crystals react with acid to give off carbon dioxide. If you added some
       washing soda crystals to vinegar, what would you **see** happening?   *1 mark*
   (c) Red cabbage can be used to test for acids and alkalis. It is bright red in acids and purple
       in alkalis.
       (i) What colour is it in lemon juice?   *1 mark*
       (ii) Complete the sentence below.
            Substances which change colour when
            you add acid or alkali are called _____   *1 mark*
   (d) The labels have fallen off two bottles.
       The labels say 'Distilled Water' and
       'Sulphuric Acid'.
       (i) Why should you **not** taste the liquids
           to see which is which?_____   *1 mark*
       (ii) You can use some washing soda crystals
            to find out what is in each bottle. Describe what you would do and
            what you would **see** in each case. _____
            _____   *2 marks*

10. (a) Neutral litmus paper is: purple in neutral solutions;
                                          red in acids;
                                          blue in alkalis.
     Use this information to answer the questions.
     (i) A piece of neutral litmus paper turned red in some grapefruit juice. What does this
         show about the grapefruit juice? _____ *1 mark*
     (ii) Gwen added drops of sodium hydroxide solution to the grapefruit juice. The litmus
          paper soon turned blue. What does the blue colour show about the sodium hydroxide
          solution? _____ *1 mark*
     (iii) Gwen then tested some water with a new piece of neutral litmus paper. The pH of the
           water was 7. What colour was the litmus paper in the water? _____ *1 mark*
   (b) What name is given to the reaction between an acid and an alkali?
       Tick the correct box.   *1 mark*

       distillation ☐   neutralisation ☐   precipitation ☐   separation ☐

11. John ground some coffee beans into little pieces. He put them into a coffee filter and poured 800 cm³ of boiling water over them to make a jug of coffee.

   (a) Complete the sentences below. For each sentence, choose **one** of the following words.
   insoluble   soluble   solution   solvent

   Coffee filter

   Jug of coffee

   (i) The liquid in the jug is brown because parts of the coffee beans are
   _____ in water.   *1 mark*

   (ii) Some bits of coffee beans are left on the filter because they are _____
   in water.   *1 mark*

   (iii) The brown liquid which drips through the filter is a _____ of coffee.   *1 mark*

   (b) How could John get dry, solid coffee from the brown liquid in the jug of coffee?_____   *1 mark*

   (c) John tried making coffee in the same way using cold water. He used 800 cm³ of cold water and the same amount of ground up coffee beans.

   (i) The liquid in the jug was a lighter colour. Why was this?

   _____   *1 mark*

   (ii) How much solid coffee could John get back from this liquid?
   Tick the correct box.   *1 mark*

   More than before ☐   less than before ☐

   the same as before ☐   none ☐

12. Shadow puppets are sometimes used in children's shows.

   (a) Where will the shadow of the puppet's foot be on the screen?
   Tick the correct box.   *1 mark*

   screen

   puppet

   bright light

   • A
   • B
   • C
   • D

   A ☐   B ☐   C ☐   D ☐

   (b) How is the shadow of the puppet formed?   *1 mark*

   (c) When the light is turned on, the shadow and the brightly lit part of the screen can be seen immediately. What does this tell you about the speed of light?

   _____   *1 mark*

13. The diagram shows the Earth seen from a satellite above the North Pole. Sunlight is shining on to the Earth.

Five places on the Earth are labelled, **A**, **B**, **C**, **D** and **E**. The North Pole is labelled **N**.

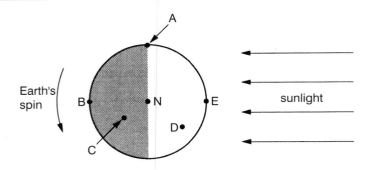

Give the letters of the places described in the table. The first one is done for you. Letters may be used more than once.

5 marks

description		place
	two places in the daytime	**D and E**
(i)	one place at noon (midday)	
(ii)	one place at midnight	
(iii)	one other place at night	
(iv)	one place at sunset	
(v)	two places from which you can see the stars	

14. Pressure pads can be used to set off burglar alarms. The alarm is set off when someone steps on the pad. The alarm works by sounding a buzzer or switching on a lamp **or** both.

The symbols for a pressure pad, a two way switch, a buzzer and a lamp are shown below.

open pressure pad   closed pressure pad

two way switch   buzzer   lamp

Here are five circuit diagrams.

Look carefully at the five circuit diagrams.

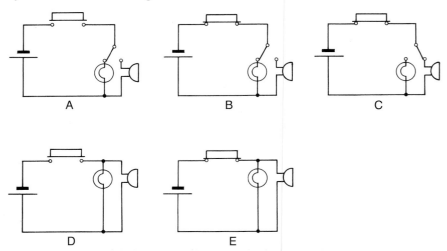

Tick the correct box to show what is happening in each circuit.   *5 marks*

circuit diagram	only the buzzer is on	only the lamp is on	both the buzzer and the lamp are on	neither the buzzer nor the lamp is on
A				
B				
C				
D				
E				

15. The diagrams show circuits using three switches labelled **A**, **B** and **C**, to control a lamp and a motor.

The diagrams show whether the switches are open or closed.

For each circuit, put a **tick** or a **cross** in the correct box to show if:

The lamp is on (✓) or off (✗).

The motor is running (✓) or not (✗).

(a)   (b)

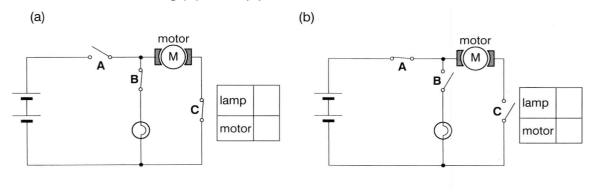

(c)   (d)

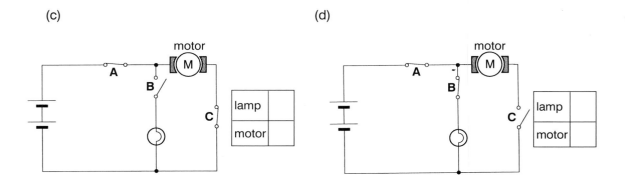

maximum 4 marks

16. (a) Some of the statements in the list describe forces, and some do not.

Tick the boxes by the **three** forces. *3 marks*

the movement of a car travelling along a road ☐

the push of a jet engine on an aeroplane ☐

the flow of electricity through a light bulb ☐

the weight of a book on a table ☐

the pull of a horse pulling a cart ☐

the speed of a hockey ball flying through the air ☐

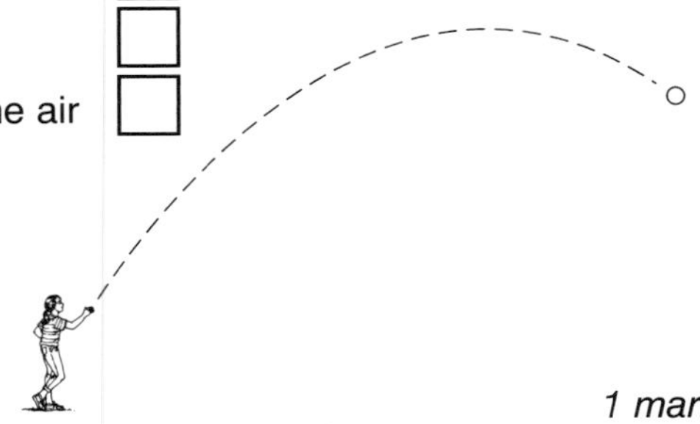

(b) A girl throws a ball. The diagram shows the path of the ball after she has thrown it.
How can you tell from the **path** of the ball that there is a force acting on the ball? *1 mark*

_____

(c)

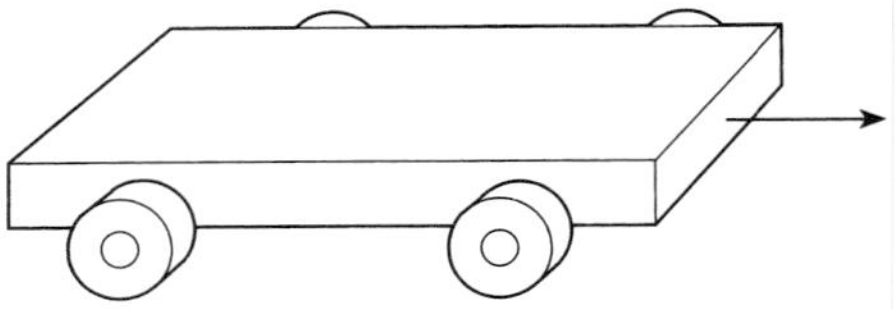

The drawing shows a trolley rolling along a table from **A** to **B**.
Then another force acts on the trolley. This is shown by the arrow on the drawing.
What effect does this force have?
Tick the box. *1 mark*

It makes the trolley go faster. ☐

It makes the trolley go slower. ☐

It makes the trolley change direction. ☐

It has no effect. ☐

17. The diagram shows a firework rocket.

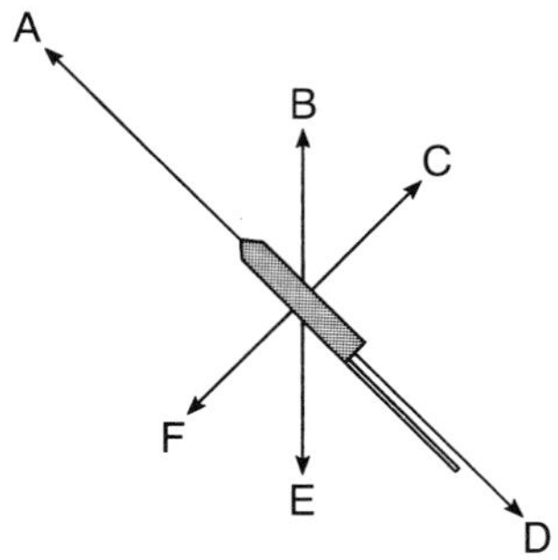

(a) Three forces act as the rocket flies through the air.
Which arrows show the directions of these three forces? _____ _____ _____ *3 marks*

(b) When there is no fuel left, the rocket falls to the ground.
(i) Give the name of the force which pulls it down. _____ *1 mark*
(ii) Give the name of the force which acts against the motion of the rocket. *1 mark*

_____

Chapter 10

Classification

What you should already know

☐ Living things can be put into groups using keys based on observable features.

☐ There are many different types of living things.

Introduction

Try this 'crosstick' puzzle. It contains the names of individual animals or groups of animals that have backbones.

1 Animals that have feathers. Most of them can fly.

2 The group that includes humans, dogs and cats.

3 A flat fish that you can eat with chips.

4 Very dark coloured birds often seen in gardens.

5 The group of animals that live in both water and on land, and includes frogs and toads.

6 A freshwater fish that is caught by fly fishing and is often farmed for eating.

7 A British amphibian that has four legs and a tail (unlike frogs and toads).

8 Lizards, crocodiles and snakes belong to this group.

Answers:
1 BIRDS 2 MAMMALS 3 PLAICE 4 BLACKBIRDS 5 AMPHIBIANS 6 TROUT 7 NEWT 8 REPTILES

What you need to know

Scientists sort living things into **groups**. The members of each group have similar features. The process of sorting things into groups is called **classification**. Classification enables scientists to understand the relationships between living things. Although no two human beings are exactly the same, they all have many features in common. For example, the human form has two legs for walking on, two arms, a skeleton inside their body, and so on. A group of organisms that have many similar features and that can successfully interbreed is called a **species**. For example, cats are one species and dogs are another species.

Different species that are quite similar to each other can be put into larger **groups** of species. For example, although tigers and rats are very different, both species have the following features in common: hair on their skin;
the mothers feed their young with their own milk;
they have backbones;
they give birth to live babies.

They are collected together into a group called **mammals.** Human beings are also mammals.

We can divide up all the living things on Earth into five kingdoms:

- the animal kingdom;

- the plant kingdom;

- Prokaryotes (which include bacteria);

- Protoctista (single-celled organisms);

- fungi.

The branching diagram below shows how the animal kingdom is divided up. The first big division within the animal kingdom is whether or not the animals have a backbone. Animals that have a backbone are called **vertebrates** and animals that do not have backbones are called **invertebrates**.

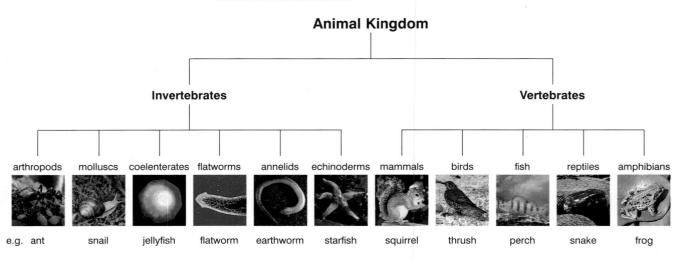

Animal Kingdom

Invertebrates

arthropods · molluscs · coelenterates · flatworms · annelids · echinoderms

e.g. ant · snail · jellyfish · flatworm · earthworm · starfish

Vertebrates

mammals · birds · fish · reptiles · amphibians

squirrel · thrush · perch · snake · frog

Although vertebrates all have a backbone, each group within the vertebrates has special features in common that make it very different from the other groups. Look at the vertebrate fact file below to see why the different vertebrates are grouped in the way they are.

VERTEBRATES

GROUP	FEATURES THEY HAVE IN COMMON
Amphibians	smooth damp skin, live on land and in water, lay soft eggs in water
Birds	feathers, lay hard-shelled eggs on land
Fish	scales, fins and gills
Mammals	hair or fur, young feed on mother's milk
Reptiles	hard dry scales, lay soft-shelled eggs on land

The fact file below shows the main groups of invertebrates and the important features that members of each group has in common.

INVERTEBRATES

GROUP	FEATURES THEY HAVE IN COMMON	EXAMPLES
Coelenterates	jelly-like, gut has only one opening, live in water, radially symmetrical	jelly fish
Echinoderms	hard outer skeleton often with spines, five sections to the body	starfish, sea urchin
Arthropods	jointed legs and an external skeleton	insects, crabs and spiders
Flatworms	flat bodied worms, many without sections, have a mouth but no anus	tapeworms
Annelids	segmented worms	earthworms
Molluscs	soft bodied, no segments, many have a hard shell	snails and slugs

The plant kingdom is organised in a similar way. The first two large groups within the plant kingdom are plants that make seeds and plants that do not make seeds (seedless). The plants that have seeds belong to one of two groups – either flowering plants or conifers. The diagram below shows how the plant kingdom is divided up.

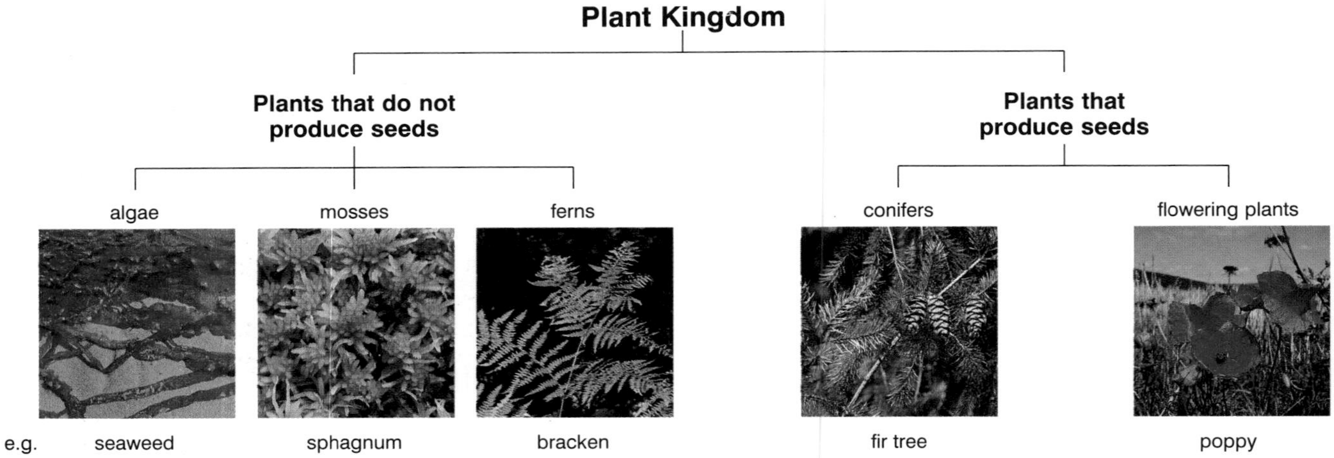

Plant Kingdom

Plants that do not produce seeds

algae — e.g. seaweed

mosses — sphagnum

ferns — bracken

Plants that produce seeds

conifers — fir tree

flowering plants — poppy

Check yourself

ANSWERS & TUTORIALS

A1

Name of invertebrate	Group it belongs to
Spider	arthropod (an arachnid)
Slug	molluscs
Jelly fish	coelenterates
Tapeworm	flatworms
Earthworm	annelids

T1 Remember that 'arthropods' is a group that includes all the animals with a hard external skeleton and jointed legs: the insects, arachnids, myriapods (centipedes and millipedes) and crustaceans.

QUESTIONS

Q1 Complete the table about invertebrates.

Name of invertebrate	Group it belongs to
Spider	arthropod (an arachnid)
Slug	
Jelly fish	
Tapeworm	
Earthworm	

QUESTIONS

Q2 List the five groups of vertebrates and write a sentence or two about each group, describing what the members of that group have in common.

ANSWERS & TUTORIALS

A2
a **Mammals.** They have hair or fur and give birth to live young. The young feed on their mother's milk.
b **Birds.** They have feathers and lay hard-shelled eggs on land.
c **Amphibians.** They have smooth, damp skin, live on both land and water and lay their soft eggs in water.
d **Fish.** Fish have scales, fins and gills and live in water.
e **Reptiles.** Reptiles have hard, dry scales and lay their soft-shelled eggs on land.

T2 The differences between birds, mammals and fish are very straightforward. However, you should be careful not to confuse reptiles and amphibians. Remember that amphibians do not have scales. They have smooth, moist skin. Reptiles have dry scales. Also, amphibians live in both water and on land and always lay their eggs in water. Reptiles always lay their eggs on the land.

It is useful for you to be able to draw classification charts for the different kingdoms. Look back at the charts in this chapter. For the animal kingdom, you start off by splitting the animals into those with backbones and those without backbones. The vertebrates can be split into groups of mammals, birds, fish, amphibians and reptiles. You should try to find a way of remembering these groups and groups within other kingdoms, and eventually you can build up a chart that contains all living things.

ANSWERS & TUTORIALS

A3

Group	Things they have in common	Example
Algae	no roots, stems or leaves	seaweed
Mosses	simple stems and leaves, make spores	moss, sphagnum
Ferns	have roots, stems and leaves, make spores	bracken
Flowering plants	have roots, stems, leaves and flowers, seeds are made inside the ovary	rose
Conifers	have roots, stems and leaves, seeds grow inside cones	Scots pine

T3 Plants are classified largely on the basis of how they reproduce (using seeds or spores). Check back to the chart for the plant kingdom. It shows the seed-producing plants on one side and the spore-producers on the other. Looking at the photographs will help you to remember that they are also classified according to whether they have a body with a clearly developed stem, root and leaf system.

QUESTIONS

Q3 Complete this table showing the features that different plant groups have in common.

Group	Things they have in common	Example
Algae	no roots, stems or leaves	seaweed
Mosses		
Ferns		
Flowering plants		
Conifers		

Chapter 11

Body Organs

What you should already know

☐ The scientific names of some major organs in the human body.
☐ The position of these organs in the human body.
☐ Body systems are made up of several organs.

Introduction

Chapter 2 introduced the major organ systems and looked in particular at the digestive system. Solve the clues below to give the names of organs, parts or functions (jobs) of the digestive system.

1 To break down food.
2 The largest internal organ in the body, it is red/brown.
3 The tube which forms the digestive system.
4 Gland that releases digestive juices into the small intestine.
5 The small intestine does this to digested food.
6 Food is stored here and mixed with digestive juices before moving into the intestine.
7 There is a small one and a large one.
8 Tiny finger-like things that help the small intestine absorb food.
9 Important chemicals in the break down of large food molecules.

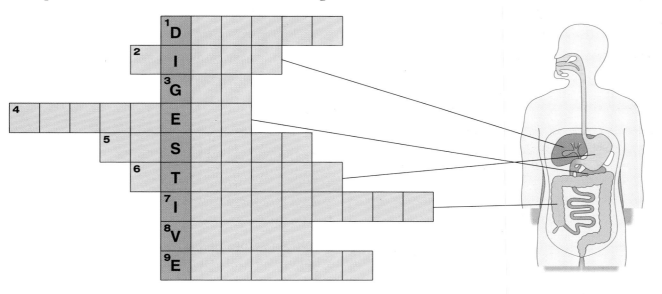

What you need to know

In chapter 2, four of the organ systems were listed: the circulatory system, the reproductive system, the digestive system and the respiratory system. The main organs of the respiratory system are the lungs; these are the organs that allow oxygen to be absorbed into the blood. We will deal with respiration in greater detail in chapter 30. This chapter looks at the function (job) of organs in the three other systems.

The digestive system

The function of the digestive system is to break down insoluble food into small particles of food that can dissolve. Only after they are broken down can the dissolved food be absorbed through the intestine wall and into the bloodstream. The breakdown of food in this way is called digestion.

The organs of the digestive system have different jobs. They may help in:

- breaking down the food;
- carrying food from one place to another;
- absorbing the food.

Each organ in the digestive system (and other systems) is well suited to doing its job. We say that the organs are well **adapted**. The table below lists some organs that are part of the digestive system and their functions.

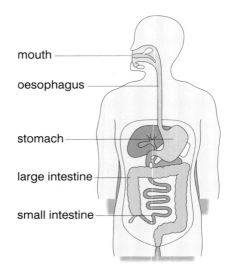

mouth

oesophagus

stomach

large intestine

small intestine

Organs	Main functions in digestion
mouth	teeth break down food into smaller pieces; saliva starts breakdown of starch
oesophagus (food tube)	carries food from the mouth to the stomach
stomach	starts breakdown of protein
small intestine	digests fat; completes digestion of protein and starch; absorbs digested food into blood
large intestine	absorbs water from the indigestible food that is left

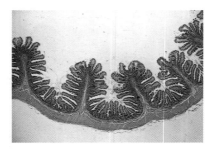

The photograph in the margin shows the lining of the small intestine. It is covered with tiny finger-like **villi**. These make the surface area of the small intestine wall much larger and make it better at absorbing the digested food.

The circulatory system

The circulatory system is made up of a set of organs whose main function is to ensure the circulation of the blood around the body. Just like the digestive system, it is made up of organs that each have a particular function.

The organs of the circulatory system help to:

- protect the body against disease;

- carry oxygen, carbon dioxide, digested food and waste products around the body.

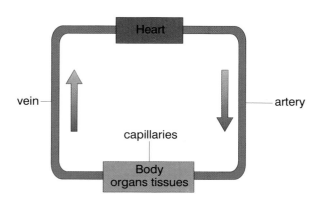

Organ	Main function in circulation
heart	pumps blood around body
capillary	releases useful substances to living cells and absorbs waste materials
artery	carries blood at high pressure away from the heart
vein	carries blood at low pressure back to the heart

The blood is made up of different parts to carry out its functions:

Blood part	Function
red cells	carry oxygen
white cells	kill bacteria and viruses, defend body against disease
plasma	carries carbon dioxide, digested food and many other dissolved substances

The reproductive system

The organs of the reproductive system were shown in chapter 2. In the table below, some of these organs are listed with their main functions.

Organ	Main function in reproduction
uterus	this is where the baby develops
penis	it becomes erect to be pushed into the vagina and deposit sperm inside the female's body
ovaries	these two organs in the female body release an ovum (egg) each month
placenta	the organ which allows food and oxygen to pass from the mother to the baby in the uterus, and allows waste to pass out from the baby to the mother
vagina	the passage into which the erect penis is pushed and through which the baby is born
testes	these two egg-shaped organs are held in a sac of skin outside the male body and make sperm

Check yourself

ANSWERS & TUTORIALS

A1 The functions of the digestive system are:
breaking down food;
absorbing food into the blood stream;
carrying food from one place to another.

A2 The main functions of the circulatory system are:
transport of substances around the body;
defending the body against disease.

A3 a – 5
b – 7
c – 4
d – 3
e – 1
f – 2
g – 6

T3 Arteries and veins are easily confused. Arteries carry blood away from the heart. The arteries have thick walls to withstand high blood pressure. Veins return blood to the heart. Because this blood has been around the body, it is at a low pressure. The veins have valves to stop the blood from flowing backwards.

Perhaps one of the most important things is to be clear about which system an organ belongs to. This will help you to remember its function. The stomach belongs to the digestive system, so it must have something to do with digestion and not pumping blood.

QUESTIONS

Q1 What are the functions of the digestive system?

Q2 What are the functions of the circulatory system?

Q3 Match the beginnings of these sentences about the functions of human body organs with the correct endings:

Beginnings		Endings	
a	The stomach	1	pumps blood around the body.
b	Arteries are blood vessels that	2	carry oxygen.
c	White cells	3	carry blood back to the heart.
d	Veins are blood vessels that	4	kill bacteria and viruses.
e	The heart is a muscular organ that	5	starts the breakdown of protein.
f	Red cells	6	completes the digestion of food and absorbs it into the blood.
g	The small intestine	7	carry blood at high pressure away from the heart.

Chapter 12

Functions of Plant Organs

What you should already know

☐ Plants have organs that enable processes such as
reproduction to take place.
☐ The names and positions of the main organs in plants.

Introduction

These drawings show parts of a flower after they have been dissected
from the plant. What are the names of each part?

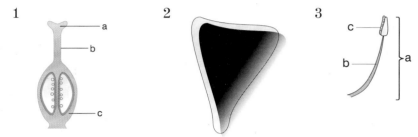

What you need to know

You saw in chapter 11 how different organs and organ systems in
humans have different functions (jobs). This is also true for plants.

The leaf is a plant organ. Its function is to use light to convert carbon
dioxide and water into **biomass** (biological mass) by photosynthesis.
We will look more closely at the leaf and how it is well suited to its job
when we look at photosynthesis in chapter 21.

The root is an organ specialised to take up water and minerals into
the plant and to help anchor the plant into the soil.

The flower is an organ *system* made up of male and female sex
organs. The function of the flower is to enable the plant to reproduce
sexually, i.e. to make seeds so that new young plants will be produced.
The flower is the reproductive system in flowering plants.

The function of the flower

The function of the flower is to bring about reproduction. This ensures
that there are plenty of young plants that may survive when the
parent plant dies. In chapter 3, you learned the names of plant parts.
Now we are going to consider the function of each part of the flower.

Flowering plants reproduce **sexually**. This means that the first cell of
the new plant is made by a male sex cell joining with a female sex cell.
This joining together of sex cells is called **fertilisation**.

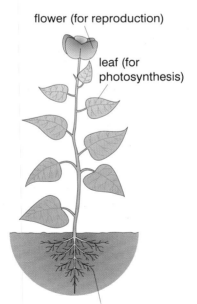

flower (for reproduction)

leaf (for photosynthesis)

roots (for anchoring and absorbing water and minerals)

The male and female parts are specialised for reproduction. It is the job of the male parts to make the male sex cell. The male sex cell is found inside a pollen grain. It is the job of the female parts to make the female sex cell. The female sex cell is found inside the ovule. The male and female sex cells are called **gametes**. Flowers normally use the wind or insects to make sure that these two sex cells are brought together so that fertilisation can take place. The table lists the male and female parts of a flower with their function.

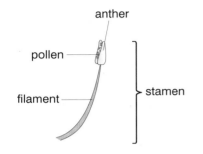

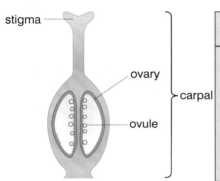

Male part	Function
anther	makes the pollen
filament	supports the anther
pollen	contains information influencing what the seedling will be like, fertilises female sex cell (ovule)

Female part	Function
stigma	receives the pollen (it is sticky to make sure the pollen stays there)
ovary	makes the ovules and provides a place for seeds to develop, grows into a fruit after fertilisation
ovule	contains information influencing what the seedling will be like, is fertilised by the male sex cell

The anther and filament together are called the **stamen**.
The stigma, ovary and ovule together are called the **carpel**.

Pollen must travel from the anther (where it is made) to the stigma. This is called **pollination**. In some types of flower, the wind does this. In others, insects pollinate the flower. If insects are needed to pollinate a flower, the flower usually has brightly coloured petals and a strong scent to attract them. Wind-pollinated flowers usually have smaller, less brightly coloured petals but have their anthers hanging out to allow the pollen to be spread by the wind. Usually, the stigma of a wind-pollinated flower also hangs out from the flower to help catch any pollen being carried by the air. The stigma of some plants looks like a feathery net to make it better for catching pollen.

The function of the root

The root (see left) secures or anchors the plant into the soil. Its other function is to take up water and minerals from the soil. For the root to be as efficient as possible, it has a very large surface area. This is produced by the main roots having smaller roots branching off them. These smaller roots are also branched to make the surface area as large as possible. The finest roots are actually called **root hairs**.

Check yourself

QUESTIONS

Q1 Write down one function of the leaf.

Q2 What is the function of the flower?

Q3 Explain what each of the following parts of a flower does to help bring about successful reproduction:
stigma, petal, ovary, ovule, anther, pollen.

Q4 What are the functions of the root?

ANSWERS & TUTORIALS

A1 **To make biomass from water and carbon dioxide (to carry out photosynthesis) *or* to allow gas exchange of carbon dioxide and oxygen between the inside of the leaf and the atmosphere.**

T1 Leaves contain the green coloured chemical called chlorophyll. This is the important chemical that allows photosynthesis to take place. Leaves have specialised cells that perform other functions and these are described in chapter 21.

A2 **Sexual reproduction is the function of a flower. The flower makes seeds after pollination and fertilisation. The seeds grow into new plants.**

T2 The only function of the flower is sexual reproduction. It is not the job of a flower to look pretty or to smell nice, but to bring about the successful joining of a pollen grain with an ovule.

A3 **The anther is the male part of the flower and it makes pollen grains. Pollen grains contain the male sex cell. Pollen needs to be transferred to the stigma, either by wind or by insects. Brightly coloured petals help to attract insects. The sticky stigma holds the pollen grains. The pollen joins with the female sex cell in the ovule and fertilises it. The fertilised ovules develop into seeds inside the ovary.**

A4 **Three jobs of the root are to:
anchor the plant in the soil;
take up water;
take up minerals.**

T4 It is important to make it clear that roots take up minerals and water – not food. Plants make biomass using light energy from the Sun.

Chapter 13

The Properties of Metals

What you should already know

☐ Different materials have different properties.
☐ Different materials have different uses because of their particular properties.
☐ There are three states of matter: solid, liquid and gas.

Introduction

Solve these six clues to build the stack of words. Identify the letter which all the words have in common.

1 metal container for fizzy drinks
2 a circle of metal or the sound from a bicycle bell
3 metal will do this when it is brightly polished
4 a bouncy coil of metal
5 this happens to iron when it is left out in the rain
6 a compass needle points north because it is ....

(Grid puzzle with letters: 1 A, 2 I, 3 H, 4 R, 5 S, 6 E)

What you need to know

Metals are a very important group of substances and they have many properties in common. All metals are shiny if they are pure (especially if they are polished). Many of them are a silvery colour, but copper and gold are not. Colour and lustre (shine) are probably the first properties you would use to decide if something was metallic.
All metals are solid at 20 °C with one exception. Mercury is a liquid at this temperature.

Why metals are useful

Metals have been used throughout history for making tools and household objects such as pots and pans. This is because metals are generally very strong and can withstand heat (they have high melting points). Another useful property is that it is fairly easy to change their shape. They can be drawn out into wires or tubes, or flattened into sheets and they still keep their strength.

There are some other important properties that you cannot see but you can still test for. The most important one is conductivity. All metals are excellent conductors of both thermal energy and electricity and both of these properties can be put to good use. The property of conducting thermal energy is called **thermal conductivity**. It is useful in cooking pans because it allows thermal energy to pass through the metal in order to heat the food inside.

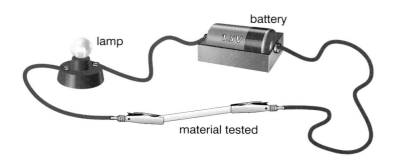

battery

lamp

1.5 V

material tested

All metals allow electricity to pass through them. This property is called **electrical conductivity** and it can be demonstrated using the apparatus shown. The material to be tested is placed between two crocodile clips to form a circuit. If the bulb lights up, the electricity is passing round the circuit and through the material, so it must be a conductor. The table shows the results of this test for four different materials.

Material	Does lamp light?	Conductor
copper	yes	✓
wood	no	✗
steel	yes	✓
rubber	no	✗

A few metals are magnetic. The most important is iron, but nickel and cobalt are also magnetic. Another magnetic substance is steel, which is an **alloy** containing iron. An alloy is a mixture of different metals or a mixture of a metal and non-metals. Brass is a mixture of copper and tin; pewter is a mixture of tin and lead; steel is an alloy of iron which is made by adding small quantities of carbon (a non-metal). All alloys have the properties of metals and they are made to produce a metallic substance which is suitable for a particular purpose.

Properties of non-metals

Metals have many properties in common, but non-metals are much more varied in their properties. The appearance of non-metals tends to be dull (not shiny), their colours are varied and many non-metals exist as liquids or gases at room temperature. Non-metals that are solid at room temperature tend to be brittle rather than flexible. Some of them occur as powders and they are generally not very strong. They do not conduct thermal energy or electricity well, and are therefore thermal and electrical insulators.

One exception to the pattern of properties for non-metals is carbon. Two different forms of carbon are diamond and graphite. Diamond is very hard and graphite fibres, used in sporting equipment, are very strong. Graphite will conduct electricity well. These are not typical properties of non-metals.

You need to be able to classify substances as metals or non-metals. The table gives a summary of the most common properties of most metals and most non-metals. There are some exceptions in each group which have some of these properties but do not have some of the others.

METALS	NON-METALS
good conductor of electricity	poor conductor of electricity
good thermal conductor	poor thermal conductor
shiny	dull
usually silvery	different colours
usually high melting point	usually low melting point
flexible	brittle
usually strong	usually weak

Check yourself

ANSWERS & TUTORIALS

A1

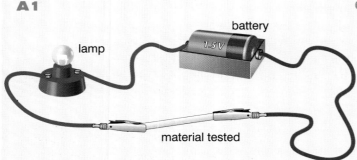

Set this apparatus up and put the material to be tested between the two crocodile clips. If the bulb lights up, the material must be a conductor.

T1 The only way to test whether a material conducts electricity or not is to make it part of an electrical circuit. You must have something there to show that the electricity is flowing. In this case, it is a bulb which lights up. If the electricity flows and the bulb lights, the material conducts electricity.

QUESTIONS

Q1 Describe how you could test if a material conducts electricity. Use a diagram if that is helpful.

QUESTIONS

Q2 Summarise the most common properties of both metals and non-metals.

Q3 **a** For this table of data decide whether the substances are metals or non-metals.

Substance	Conducts electricity	Conducts thermal energy	Colour	Flexibility	Approximate melting point	Strength	Metal?
1	✓	✓	silvery	very flexible	medium	strong	
2	✓	✗	black	brittle	very high	strong	
3	✗	✗	yellow	brittle	low	weak	
4	✓	✓	brown	very flexible	high	strong	
5	✓	✓	grey	flexible	high	strong	
6	✗	✗	brown	brittle	low	weak	

b Which one of the non-metals shows some unusual properties?

ANSWERS & TUTORIALS

A2 METALS – good conductor of electricity, good thermal conductor, shiny, usually silvery, usually high melting point, flexible, usually strong

NON-METALS – poor conductor of electricity, poor thermal conductor, dull, different colours, usually low melting point, brittle, usually weak

T2 You have to be familiar with some of the properties, so have a go at writing them out. Each list has the most useful property first, so start there and learn as many as you can. When you have to learn a list like this, try writing it, then check the ones you missed. Then learn those ones and have another go at writing the whole thing.

A3 **a** 1 Metal
2 Non-metal
3 Non-metal
4 Metal
5 Metal
6 Non-metal
b number 2

T3 The best property to go for is electrical conductivity. That sorts most of them out! But you have to be careful of the exceptions so you cannot rely on just one property.

Substance 2 has a high melting point, is strong and conducts electricity. A property that enables us to decide that it is a non-metal is its poor conduction of thermal energy. All metals conduct thermal energy very well. In addition, metals are not black and they are flexible.

Chapter 14

Evaporation and Condensation

What you should already know

☐ The scientific meanings of the terms 'evaporation' and 'condensation'.

☐ The correct context in which to use each of these words to correctly describe each sort of change.

☐ Different materials change state at different temperatures.

Introduction

The photographs below show examples of evaporation or condensation. For each example, decide which one of these two changes is taking place?

A puddle drying up on a sunny day

Droplets of water forming on a cold bottle

Clothes drying on a windy day

Water droplets forming on a cold window pane

What you need to know

When a liquid boils it changes to a gas. The temperature at which this happens is different for each type of liquid. The boiling temperature of water is 100 °C, but liquid water can change to a gas at lower temperatures by the process of **evaporation**. At any temperature when water is liquid, there are always some water particles that move fast enough to escape from the surface of the liquid. The higher the temperature of the water, the more particles there are that are moving fast enough to escape from the surface of the water. This means that the rate of evaporation is faster at higher temperatures. The other two factors that affect the rate of evaporation from a liquid are:

● the amount of water vapour present in the air immediately above the surface of the liquid;

● the speed at which air is moving past the surface of the liquid.

Answers:
Evaporation taking place in A and C
Condensation taking place in B and D

For any liquid – not just water – the rate of evaporation from its surface is greatest if the liquid is hot and the air immediately above it is dry and moving quickly. This is why wet clothes hanging on a washing line will dry quickly on a windy and sunny day.

The water that evaporates from washing – along with the huge volume of water that evaporates from rivers, lakes and seas – rises into the air. As it rises, it cools and turns back to water as tiny droplets which form clouds. These droplets get larger and larger until they eventually fall as rain. The process by which gases, including water vapour, turn into liquids is called **condensation**. This process is the opposite of evaporation. The diagram below summarises the reversible change from liquid to gas which is happening constantly all around us.

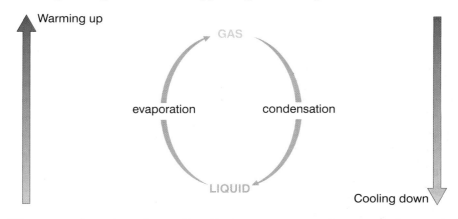

The examples of condensation that we see around us occur because water vapour comes into contact with much cooler air or a cold surface. Once, in contact, the water vapour loses thermal energy and cools to a temperature where it changes from gas to liquid. What we often call 'condensation' appears on a cold mirror in a 'steamy' bathroom. What appears on the mirror is actually water that has been formed by the process of condensation.

Anything left to 'dry' does so by losing liquid by evaporation. Evaporation is used to good effect in applying paint. Paint is a mixture of coloured particles and a liquid. When it is applied to a wall or ceiling, the paint comes into contact with warm air and the liquid evaporates. This leaves a solid coat of paint on the wall.

Inside its sealed container, the paint remains fluid because the liquid is prevented from evaporating by the air-tight lid. However, if the paint tin is left for several days with the lid removed, the paint at the surface will lose its liquid by evaporation and form a thick solid 'skin' on top of the remaining liquid paint.

On a rainy day you and your classmates may have slightly damp clothing when you go into your classroom. Very soon the windows may 'steam up' (become covered with condensed water). Because the room is warm, water can evaporate from your clothing into the air. The water vapour in the air then condenses on the windows which are colder than the rest of the room.

Filtration

You need to know that some substances are soluble and that others are insoluble in water. It is a good idea to learn some of the more common ones. For example, salt, copper sulphate and sugar are soluble in water; sand, mud and chalk are insoluble. Filtration is used to separate insoluble substances from liquids. This works because an insoluble substance such as sand has particles that are too big to pass between the fibres of the filter paper. The liquid part of the mixture passes through the filter. The insoluble part is stopped by the paper.

Distillation

Distillation is used to separate a mixture of liquids. The mixture is heated in a closed container until one liquid boils. You collect the vapour and cool it. It condenses to form the pure liquid. You can also use this method to separate solids from liquids.

Chromatography

Chromatography is used to separate different coloured dyes. The dyes which are more soluble move further up the chromatography paper. The dyes move different distances before they can no longer remain in solution, so they separate from each other.

Choosing a method

When you have to suggest a method of separation for a mixture, you need to think carefully about the states and properties of the substances in the mixture. A useful way to decide which method to use a checklist like this one.

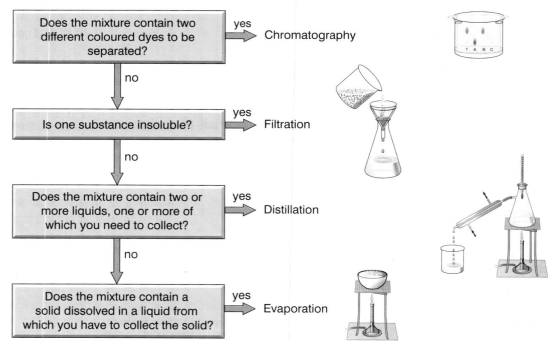

Does the mixture contain two different coloured dyes to be separated? — yes → Chromatography

no

Is one substance insoluble? — yes → Filtration

no

Does the mixture contain two or more liquids, one or more of which you need to collect? — yes → Distillation

no

Does the mixture contain a solid dissolved in a liquid from which you have to collect the solid? — yes → Evaporation

Check yourself

QUESTIONS

Q1 Sand is insoluble in water and copper sulphate is soluble.
  a What will happen if a mixture of these two substances is stirred into water?
  b What happens if you then pour this mixture through a filter paper.
  c How could you recover the copper sulphate from the mixture?

Q2 How can you separate pure water from a solution of salt and water?

Q3 How can you separate a mixture of different oils? They are all liquid and have different boiling points.

Q4 Why is evaporation not suitable for collecting water from sea water?

ANSWERS & TUTORIALS

A1 a The copper sulphate dissolves (giving a blue solution) and the sand does not dissolve.
  b The sand collects in the filter paper and the copper sulphate solution passes straight through.
  c The copper sulphate is best obtained by evaporation.

T1 Remember soluble means it dissolves and insoluble means it does not.
Did you go through your checklist? If the question says soluble/insoluble then filtration is the answer. The insoluble part is trapped by the filter paper because the grains of sand are too big to pass through. Copper sulphate is a blue soluble solid, so it forms a blue solution and can pass through the filter paper.

A2 Using distillation. Heat the sea water in a flask until it boils. The steam passes into the condenser and cools to form water. The salt is left behind in the flask.

T2 Water boils to form a gas and passes into the condenser. This gas condenses to form water.

A3 Fractional distillation.

T3 All oils are liquids, so fractional distillation can be used to separate them.

A4 The water evaporates into the atmosphere without being collected.

T4 If you want to collect the water you must condense it back to a liquid first. Evaporation is only suitable for collecting the solid from a solution, e.g. salt from sea water.

ANSWERS & TUTORIALS

A5

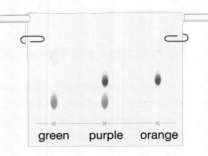

green   purple   orange

T5   When doing chromatography, it is important to realise that:
each type of dye will travel to a particular level;
different dyes travel to different levels.

QUESTIONS

Q5   Shanti has used red, blue and yellow dyes to make three new colours:
blue and yellow were mixed to produce green;
blue and red were mixed to produce purple;
red and yellow were mixed to produce orange.

Now she wants to separate them using chromatography. She has set up the apparatus shown to carry out this experiment. She knows that the yellow dye travels furthest up the paper and that the blue dye travels the least distance. Draw a diagram to show what the filter paper would look like when the experiment is finished.

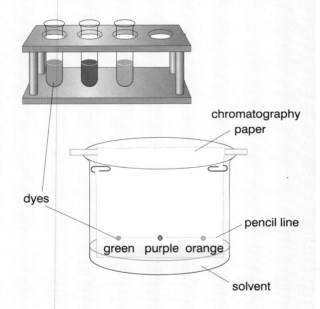

chromatography paper

dyes

pencil line

green   purple   orange

solvent

Chapter 16

Vision and Reflection

What you should already know

- ☐ Light travels from a source.
- ☐ Light cannot pass through some materials, leading to the formation of a shadow.
- ☐ Light is reflected by shiny surfaces.
- ☐ Light travels in straight lines.

Introduction

Try to find seven words to do with reflection in the wordsearch. When you have found the words, use them to fill in the blanks in the sentence below the wordsearch.

R	E	F	L	E	C	T
O	P	R	I	Y	G	L
R	L	E	G	A	M	I
R	A	S	H	I	N	Y
I	N	Y	T	V	I	S
M	E	X	S	P	O	J

A M _ _ _ _ _ has a S _ _ _ _, P _ _ _ _ surface that is able to
R _ _ _ _ _ _ R _ _ _ of L _ _ _ _ to form an I _ _ _ _.

What you need to know

You can read the writing on this page because light from the sun or a lamp is shining onto the page. Because the surface of the paper is uneven, light that hits the paper is scattered (spread out in all directions) and some of this light reaches your eyes. Light has to enter your eyes before you are able to see the paper and other objects. All objects that are not luminous can only be seen because they scatter light that falls onto them. Light is not reflected in a regular way unless the surface it hits is shiny, such as a mirror, polished metal or very calm water.

Very calm sea water can reflect light like a mirror

When a ray of light hits a plane (flat) mirror it is reflected. The diagram shows that the angle at which it hits the mirror is the same as the angle at which it leaves the mirror.

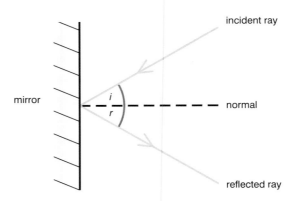

The ray of light hitting the mirror is called the **incident ray** and the ray of light leaving the mirror is called the **reflected ray**. The dotted line is called the **normal**. This is a line drawn at right angles to the surface of the mirror where the ray of light hits it.

Angle i is called the **angle of incidence** and angle r is called the **angle of reflection**. These two angles are always the same size for the reflection of light at a plane mirror. We can write this as:

angle of incidence = angle of reflection

$$i = r$$

When you look at an object in the mirror, its image (what you see) appears to be:

- the same size as the object;

- the same distance behind the mirror as it is in front of the mirror;

- the other way round (**laterally inverted**).

The image is **virtual** – it is not really there, since you cannot catch it on a screen. These are the properties of any image seen in a mirror, including yourself, and you should try to remember them.

Check yourself

QUESTIONS

Q1 When light hits a plane mirror it is reflected. Which two diagrams correctly show how two different rays of light are reflected?

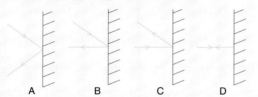

A   B   C   D

Q2

Alex uses a periscope to look over a wall. Copy and complete the diagram to show a ray of light coming from the tree to Alex's eye. Alex can only see one creature in the tree; which one will he see?

ANSWERS & TUTORIALS

A1 **A and D**

T1 If you draw in the normal on each diagram you can see whether:
the angle of incidence = the angle of reflection.
The two angles are equal in A. In D, the angles are both zero. A ray of light travelling along the normal must be reflected back along the same path.

A2

Alex can see the cat.

T2 Always use a ruler to draw rays of light. Do not forget to show that the light is travelling from the tree to Alex's eye, by putting arrows on the ray. To draw the rays, first draw a line from the eye to the lower mirror. Then draw in the normal at this point. You can now draw the ray hitting the upper mirror. Remember that:

the angle of incidence = the angle of reflection.

Now continue the ray to the top mirror and again draw the normal so that you can draw the ray of light from the tree.

ANSWERS & TUTORIALS

A3

a **Ms Wong can see their reflection in the mirrors next to the blackboard.**

b

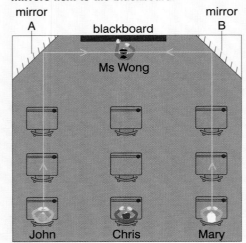

c **In order to see Chris, Ms Wong needs to move one of the mirrors:**

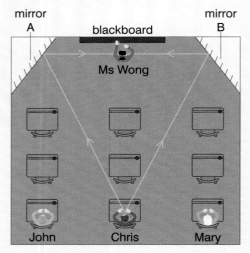

T3 The only way that Ms Wong can see behind her is by looking in a mirror.

Draw the ray of light from Ms Wong to the mirror, then draw in the normal at that point. Next, draw the ray of light from the pupil to the mirror, making sure that the angle of incidence = the angle of reflection.

QUESTIONS

Q3

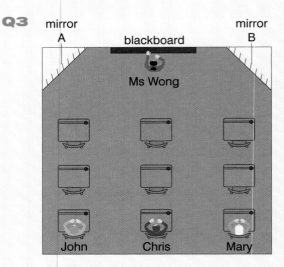

The pupils in Ms Wong's class think that she has 'eyes in the back of her head'. When she is writing on the blackboard she can still see which pupils are not working.

a How can she see the pupils when she is writing on the board?

b Complete the diagram with a ray of light to show how Ms Wong can see:
 i John;
 ii Mary.

c Ms Wong cannot see Chris. What should she do so that she can see him when she is writing on the blackboard?

Chapter 17

Sound

What you should already know

- [ ] Sound is produced when an object vibrates.
- [ ] You cannot always see the object vibrating.
- [ ] Sound can travel through a variety of materials.
- [ ] Sound cannot travel through a vacuum.

Introduction

Object	What vibrates?
Drum	
Guitar	
Saxophone	
Tambourine	
Singer	

Fill in the table to say what is vibrating and causing the sound produced by each of the musicians.

What you need to know

We can hear a wide range of different sounds. These sounds vary in two important ways. They can have a different **loudness** and a different **pitch**. If you are playing a piano, you can vary the loudness of a note by hitting that key harder. You can vary the pitch of the sound by pressing keys that hit different strings.

When we talk about sounds, we discuss sound **waves**. Sound waves are invisible. The only way we can 'see' them is to use an **oscilloscope**. An oscilloscope is similar to a television. It displays electrical signals as lines on its screen.

Answers:
DRUM SKIN   STRINGS   REED   METAL DISCS   VOCAL CHORDS

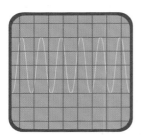

wavelength   amplitude

A microphone can be connected to an oscilloscope so that when a sound is made a trace is seen on the screen. This trace represents the sound wave.

The height of the wave is called the **amplitude**. It tells us how loud the sound is. The larger the amplitude of the vibration, the louder the sound.

The length of a single wave is called the **wavelength**. This is the distance from one point on one wave to the same point on the next wave. A wave with a short wavelength represents a high pitch sound. If the wavelength is long then the pitch of the sound is low.

If an object is vibrating very quickly (very frequently) there are more waves on the screen, so their wavelength is shorter. The pitch of the note will be higher and we say it has a higher **frequency**. If the object is vibrating slowly (not very frequently) then there are few waves on the screen, and the wavelength of the waves is longer. The pitch will be lower because it has a lower frequency.

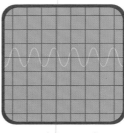

| loud sound | loud sound | quiet sound | quiet sound |
| high frequency | low frequency | high frequency | low frequency |

Changing the loudness of a sound

The loudness of a sound can be increased by increasing the size of the vibrations that are providing the sound. You might pluck a guitar string harder or hit a drum skin harder to increase the loudness of a sound. Reducing the size of the vibrations producing the sound will make the sound quieter.

Changing the pitch of a sound

To alter the pitch of a sound produced by a vibrating object you have to change the size of the vibrating object. Look at the two musical instruments in the margin.

On an organ, the low pitched notes are produced by air vibrating in the long pipes and the high notes are produced by air vibrating in the short pipes.

On a xylophone, the low pitched notes are produced by hitting the long bars and the high pitched notes are produced by the short bars.

Check yourself

QUESTIONS

Q1

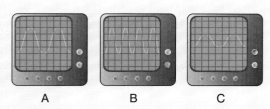

A   B   C

Three different sounds are represented by waves on the oscilloscope screens above.
a   Which wave shows the sound with the highest pitch?
b   Which wave shows the quietest sound?
c   Which two sounds have the same pitch?
d   Which two sounds have the same amplitude?
e   Which sound has the highest frequency?

Q2

Jim whistles into a microphone and the sound is displayed on an oscilloscope screen as shown in the diagram below. Tony then whistles into the microphone. Tony's whistle is twice as loud, and half of the pitch of Jim's.

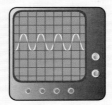

a   Complete the diagram to show what Tony's whistle would look like on the oscilloscope screen.
b   Whose whistle has the greater frequency?

ANSWERS & TUTORIALS

A1
a   **B**
b   **C**
c   **A and C**
d   **A and B**
e   **B**

T1
a   The waves in B are close together; they have a shorter wavelength.
b   The amplitude of the note in C is less than A and B, so C must be the quietest note.
c   The waves in A and C are the same length; there are the same number of waves on the screen.
d   The waves in A and B are the same height; therefore, they have the same amplitude.
e   Part **e** has the same answer as part **a**. This is just checking that you understand a note with a high frequency has a high pitch.

A2
a

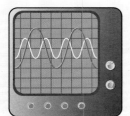

b   **Jim's whistle has the greater frequency.**

T2
The wave representing Tony's whistle must be twice as tall as Jim's if it is twice as loud. The wavelength must be longer than Jim's as the pitch is lower. There will be fewer waves of Tony's whistle displayed on the screen.

Chapter 18

LEVEL 5
PHYSICAL PROCESSES

The Movement of the Earth

What you should already know

☐ The apparent position of the Sun changes over the course of a day.
☐ The Earth revolves once every twenty four hours.
☐ The Earth completes one orbit of the Sun every year.

Introduction

Imagine someone from deepest space wanted to send a letter to you. Write your name and the full address that they would need to use on the envelope below.

name: _____

street: _____

town/city: _____

county: _____

country: _____

planet: _____

nearest star: _____

galaxy: _____

What you need to know

Every day the Sun appears to rise in the east and set in the west. People used to think that the Sun travelled around the Earth, but we now know that this is wrong. The Earth actually orbits the Sun. As it does this, it also spins round. It does one full turn in 24 hours. The Sun appears to move from east to west so the Earth must spin from west to east.

Your address should end with Earth, Sun, Milky Way

The half of the Earth that faces the Sun is in daylight and the half of the Earth that is facing away from the Sun is in darkness. You can see from the diagram that the axis of the Earth (the line around which the Earth rotates) is tilted.

When the Earth is in the position shown, the South Pole will have constant daylight and the North Pole will be in darkness. The northern hemisphere (half of the Earth) is tilting away from the Sun and the southern hemisphere is tilting towards the Sun. This happens in winter and causes our cold winters with short days and long nights.

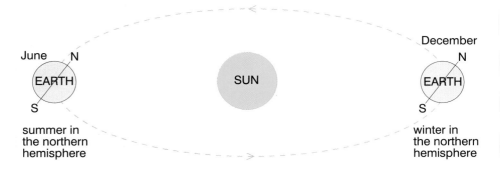

In summer, however, the northern hemisphere is tilting towards the Sun. We have longer periods of daylight and shorter periods of darkness each day and the weather is warmer. It takes about 365 days (one year) for the Earth to make one complete orbit of the Sun.

The Earth revolves on its axis, which makes the Sun appear to move across the sky each day. During the course of a year, the apparent path of the Sun across the sky changes. In this country, the apparent path taken by the Sun across the sky in December is lower than the path it appears to take in March and this is lower than the path the Sun appears to take in June. This change is because the northern hemisphere inclines (leans) towards the Sun in June and away from the Sun in December. During the winter months, the Sun appears to reach its highest point at 12.00 noon. During British Summer Time, when the clocks have gone forward by one hour, its highest point occurs at 1 p.m.

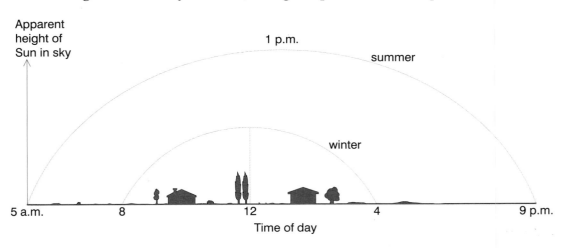

Check yourself

ANSWERS & TUTORIALS

A1

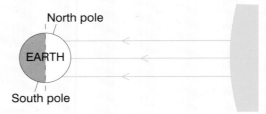

   c day

T1 The Earth spins from west to east (the Sun rises in New York 5 hours after it has risen in Manchester).

When showing which part of the Earth is in darkness, make sure you draw a vertical line, not one along the Earth's axis.

The North Pole is not in the dark area because light from the Sun is reaching it. Therefore, it is in daylight.

A2 **a** **365 days / 1 year**
     b **24 hours / 1 day**
     c **A** **winter**
         B **summer**

T2 The southern hemisphere is tilted away from Sun and receives less sunlight than the northern hemisphere. In winter, it has shorter days and is colder.

In summer, the southern hemisphere receives more sunlight, is warmer and has longer days.

QUESTIONS

Q1

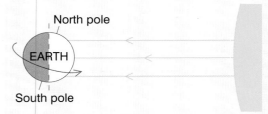

 a **Draw an arrow to show which way the Earth turns.**
 b **Shade in the part of the Earth where it is dark.**
 c **Is it day or night at the North Pole?**

Q2 **The diagram shows the path taken as the Earth orbits the Sun.**

 a **How long does it take for the Earth to complete one orbit of the Sun?**
 b **How long does it take for the Earth to turn once about its axis?**
 c **What season is the southern hemisphere having when the Earth is in positions *A* and *B*?**

1. The human body has organs and organ systems which have different functions.

   (a) (i) In which organ does the foetus develop? _____ *1 mark*
      (ii) In which organ is oxygen absorbed into the blood? _____ *1 mark*
   (b) Complete the table.   *2 marks*

organ system	function in the human body
circulatory system	
_____ system	this system of organs breaks down food and absorbs it into the body

   (c) Give **one** function of the skeleton. _____ *1 mark*

2. The diagram shows a baby developing inside its mother's body.

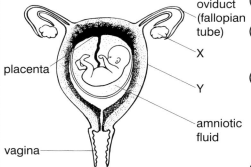

oviduct (fallopian tube)

X

placenta

Y

vagina

amniotic fluid

   (a) Eggs are produced in organ X.
      What is the name of organ X? _____ *1 mark*
   (b) The baby grows in a bag of amniotic fluid which is inside organ Y. What is the name of organ Y?   *1 mark*

   (c) (i) Through which part, labelled in the diagram, is food passed from the mother to the baby?   *1 mark*

      (ii) Name **one** useful substance, other than food, which passes from the mother to the unborn baby.   *1 mark*

   (d) The diagram shows an organ system of the mother's body. What is the name of this organ system? ____ *1 mark*

3.

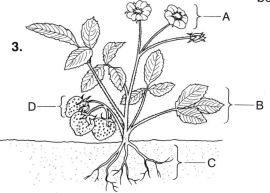

A

D

B

C

The diagram shows a strawberry plant. Four organs of the plant are labelled A to D.
Write the names of organs A to D in the correct spaces in the table. Write the function or job of each organ next to its name.
Only choose functions from the list below.

   to attract insects for pollination
   to attract birds for pollination
   to attract animals for seed dispersal
   to take up water
   to absorb light
   to protect the plant from animals

letter	name of organ	function
A		
B		
C		
D		

4 marks

4. The diagram below shows a bee visiting a flower.

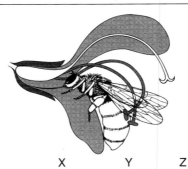

X   Y   Z

(a) (i) Draw a line from the letter **X** to the part of the flower where the seeds are produced.
1 mark

(ii) Draw a line from the letter **Y** to a part of the flower where pollen is produced.   *1 mark*

(iii) Draw a line from the letter **Z** to the stigma.   *1 mark*

(b) Complete the sentences below by choosing words from the list: *3 marks*

anthers	**fertilisation**	**germination**	**ovule**
pollination	**seed production**	**sepal**	**stigma**

When a bee with pollen on it visits a flower, pollen rubs off the bee onto the _____ of the flower. This process is called _____ . A tube grows from each pollen grain until it reaches an ovule. A nucleus of the pollen grain joins with a nucleus in the ovule. This process is called _____ .

5. A scientist investigates the paints used in oil paintings. She takes tiny pieces of yellow, blue and green paint and tries to dissolve them in different solvents. Her results are shown in the table.

solvent	yellow paint	blue paint	green paint	
water	yellow pieces are left	blue pieces are left	green pieces are left	
ethanol	yellow pieces are left	clear blue liquid	clear blue liquid but yellow pieces are left	
propanone	clear yellow liquid	clear blue liquid	clear green liquid	

(a) Which solvent does **not** dissolve the blue paint? _____ *1 mark*

She then uses chromatography to investigate the paints.

(b) Only **one** of the solvents in the table will make all three paints move up the chromatography paper. Which solvent is this? _____ *1 mark*

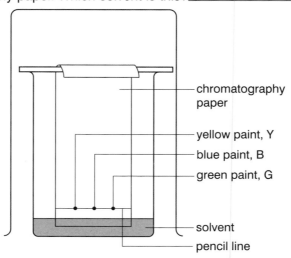

chromatography paper

yellow paint, Y

blue paint, B

green paint, G

solvent

pencil line

(c) The scientist then investigates the paint used in three different oil paintings. She takes tiny pieces of yellow, blue and green paint from each picture and uses chromatography to compare them. Her results are shown opposite:

Which of the paints in the 1993 picture contains only one substance? Tick the correct box.

picture 1
painted in 1993

picture 2
painted in 1625

picture 3
date unknown

Y   B   G   Y   B   G   Y   B   G

yellow, Y ☐   blue, B ☐   green, G ☐   *1 mark*

The scientist decides that picture 3 is probably recent and not from around 1625.

(d) Look at the chromatography results for the three pictures. Explain how the scientist was able to decide this.   *2 marks*

6. The opposite diagrams show two methods of separating substances.

mixture ——— ——— funnel

thermometer

water out

flask ———

cold water in

heat

method 1   method 2

(a) What is the name of each method?
Method 1 is _____ *1 mark*
Method 2 is _____ *1 mark*

(b) (i) Tick **one** box to show which of the mixtures can be separated by method 1.   *1 mark*

sugar and salt ☐   sand and water ☐   dissolved salt and water ☐

sand and iron filings ☐   sugar and salt dissolved in water ☐

(ii) From the list give a mixture which can be separated by method 2 but not by method 1 _____ .   *1 mark*

(c) Chromatography was used to analyse some soluble inks. The results are shown opposite.
(i) A purple ink is a dissolved mixture of the red dye and the blue dye. On the right of the diagram draw the pattern you would expect to see for purple ink.   *1 mark*
(ii) Which **three** inks contain only one dye?   *1 mark*
(iii) What colour is spot X?   *1 mark*

X—

| blue ink | brown ink | green ink | red ink | yellow ink | purple ink |

7. Different elements have a wide variety of properties. The list below gives some of them.

    brittle   **insulator**
    good electrical conductor   **magnetic**
    good thermal conductor   **melting point above room temperature**

    (a) Magnesium is a metal.
        Give **two** properties of magnesium from the list above.   *2 marks*

        1. _____

        2. _____

    (b) (i) What is the name of the compound formed when
             magnesium reacts with sulphur? _____ *1 mark*
        (ii) Give **two** properties from the list above which this solid compound will **not** have.
                                                                                     2 marks

             1. _____

             2. _____

8. Humming-birds make a noise by beating their wings very fast.

    Humming-bird

    microphone

    oscilloscope

    A scientist used an oscilloscope to record the 'hums' from four different humming-birds.
    The controls on the oscilloscope were not altered.
    Four traces are shown, one for each bird.

    A   B   C   D

    (a) Which **one** of the traces **A**, **B**, **C** or **D** shows the hum with the **highest** pitch? _____ *1 mark*
        Explain your answer. _____ *1 mark*
    (b) Which **one** of the traces **A**, **B**, **C** or **D** shows the **loudest** hum? _____ *1 mark*
        Explain your answer. _____ *1 mark*
    (c) Trace **E** was made by a humming-bird
        beating its wings ten times a second.
        Draw on the same diagram the trace from
        another humming-bird which was beating its
        wings with twice the frequency and making a
        quieter noise.   *2 marks*

    trace **E**

9. A pupil is observing the behaviour of a woodpecker. He uses a periscope to look over a wall at a tree, and waits for the bird to land on the trunk.

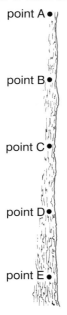

point A •

point B •

point C •

point D •

point E •

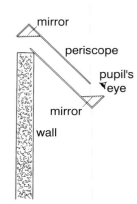

The pupil can only watch one part of the tree trunk at a time.

(a) Tick the box to show the point on the tree trunk which he can see using the periscope in the position shown. *1 mark*

point A ☐   point B ☐   point C ☐   point D ☐   point E ☐

(b) Draw the path of the ray of light to show how the pupil sees this point. Use a ruler. Show the direction of the ray of light. *3 marks*

(c) What should the pupil do to the periscope to watch point C? *1 mark*

10. The Sun appears to move across the sky each day.

○
the sun

East   **West**

The drawing shows the position of the Sun at mid-day on the 21st March.

(a) (i) Draw the path which the Sun appears to take **from sunrise to sunset** on the 21st March. Label the path 'March'. *1 mark*

(ii) Put an arrow on the line you have drawn to show the direction in which the Sun appears to move across the sky. *1 mark*

(b) Draw another line to show the path which the Sun appears to take **from sunrise to sunset** in December. Label the path 'December'. *2 marks*

Chapter 19

Variation

What you should already know

☐ There is great variety in living things.
☐ Living things can be classified into groups.
☐ A species is a group of living things that can interbreed successfully to produce fertile young.

What you need to know

There are great differences between animals or plants of different species. For example, a lion and a common frog both belong to the vertebrate family but they are very different. Even within one species we find many differences between individual members. If we concentrate on our own species – human beings – we can see a great many differences between people. Look at the picture below and try to spot as many differences as you can between the people shown:

The photograph shows that there is a lot of variety of individuals within each species. We say that a species shows **variation**. A survey was carried out looking at the height of all the 14-year-old pupils in a particular school. The results are shown below.

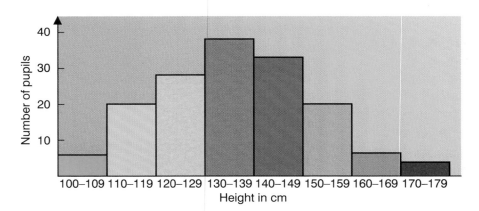

So what causes members of a species to be so different from one another? There are two main causes of variation (differences) within a species: **inherited** causes and **environmental** causes.

Inherited causes

Children look more or less like one or both of their parents. They inherit certain things from their parents, such as eye colour, hair colour, nose and ear shape. The plans for these inherited features are carried inside the nucleus of each cell on tiny thread-like structures called **chromosomes**. Each of us has inherited information from both of our parents. Half of this information comes from the father and half from the mother.

A baby's life starts when a sperm from its father joins an egg from its mother. The nucleus of the sperm cell carries the father's half of the information and the nucleus of the egg cell carries the mother's half of the inherited information. At **fertilisation**, the sperm's nucleus joins with the egg cell's nucleus and the inherited make-up of the new baby is determined by the combination of information from the parents.

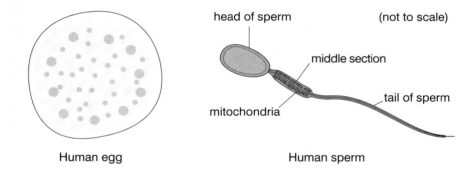

head of sperm   (not to scale)

middle section

tail of sperm

mitochondria

Human egg   Human sperm

Environmental causes

The information that we inherit from our parents is not the only thing that decides our characteristics. Even if a child has two tall parents and inherits information that gives them the potential to be tall, they may still turn out to be quite short if they do not eat a good balanced diet. In a similar way, if they eat too much food they may become fat, despite what their inherited information may say. In other words, the way a child is brought up, what they eat, the education they receive and the amount of exercise they take, amongst many other influences, can all have an affect on the appearance and characteristics of the person. These influences are called environmental causes of variation.

Scientists have studied sets of identical twins to try to find out more about the importance of inherited and environmental causes of variation. Identical twins have exactly the same inherited information, because they both grow from the same fertilised egg. Any differences between identical twins must be due to environmental influences.

Check yourself

ANSWERS & TUTORIALS

A1   All of the following are possible types of
variation between humans:

hair colour, eye colour, height, weight, nose
shape, the accent you speak with, curly hair or
straight hair, intelligence, blood group, the
ability to roller-skate, the language you speak,
skin colour, mouth shape, hand span, freckles
and moles – and so on (there are many more).

T1   Any possible difference between people is
acceptable here.

A2   The missing words are shown in **bold**:

Children **inherit** some features from their
parents. For example, **eye** colour,
hair colour and **nose** shape are all
features that are passed on from parents to their
children. Each child gets **half** their
inherited information from their **mother/father**
and **half** from their **father/mother**. The inherited
information from the father is carried inside the
sperm and the mother's part of the
information is carried in the **egg**. These
two sets of information are brought together
when the sperm **joins** with the egg. This is
called **fertilisation**.

T2   Look carefully at the text if you are not sure of the
word used to complete the passage.

QUESTIONS

Q1   Make a list of ten characteristics that vary
between human beings.

Q2   Complete the sentences below using the words
at the bottom of the page.

Children _____ some features from their
parents. For example, _____ colour,
_____ colour and _____ shape are all
features that are passed on from parents to their
children. Each child gets _____ their
inherited information from their _____ and
_____ from their _____ . The inherited
information from the father is carried inside the
_____ and the mother's part of the
information is carried in the _____ . These
two sets of information are brought together
when the sperm _____ with the egg. This is
called _____ .

egg	eye	fertilisation
father	hair	half
inherit	mother	nose
joins	sperm	half

QUESTIONS

Q3 A list of variations that are found between humans is given below.

natural hair colour, eye colour, height, weight, nose shape, the accent you speak with, naturally curly hair, intelligence, blood group, the ability to roller-skate

Complete the table putting each variation into one column depending on whether you think it has an environmental cause, an inherited cause or if it is caused by both the environment and inherited information.

only the environment causes these:	inherited information causes these:	both the environment and inherited information causes these:

ANSWERS & TUTORIALS

A3 The table should be completed as shown below:

only the environment causes these:	inherited information causes these:	both the environment and inherited information causes these:
the accent you speak with	natural hair colour	height
the ability to roller-skate	eye colour	weight
	nose shape	intelligence
	blood group	
	naturally curly hair	

T3 It is important that you understand the difference between environmental and inherited causes of variation, and also that many types of variation have both environmental and inherited causes. There is an interaction between the inherited information of the person and the environment that they grow up in. The way they are brought up has an effect on the information that they inherited from their parents. Only a few features are controlled solely by the inherited information or by the effects of their environment.

If in this question we talked about 'hair colour' rather than natural hair colour, then we could talk about hair colour sometimes being environmentally controlled, such as when people dye their hair. Even natural hair colour can be influenced by the environment – many people's hair lightens when it is in the sun for a long time. So even some of the more obviously inherited features can in some circumstances be influenced by the environment.

Chapter 20

Cell Structure

What you should already know

☐ The main functions of some organs of the human body and of flowering plants.

☐ How the functions of organs are essential to the organism (plant or animal).

☐ Animals and plants are made up of cells.

What you need to know

You need to be able to list the main features of plant and animal cells and be able to see the differences between them.

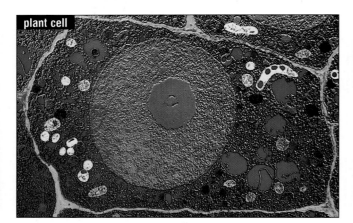

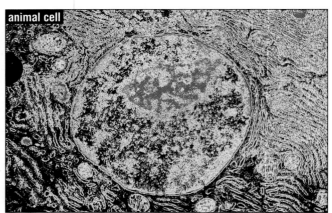

If you look at animal or plant tissue under a microscope, you can see that the tissue is made up of lots of very tiny building blocks. Scientists call these tiny building blocks **cells**. Cells are too small to see without using a microscope to magnify them. All living organisms are made up of cells.

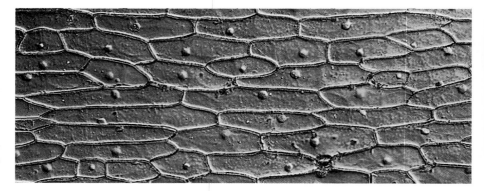

This magnified view of the epidermis of an onion shows the arrangement of its cells. The spot near the centre of each cell is its nucleus.

A closer look at cells

If you turn up the magnification on your microscope, from low power to medium or high power, then you can see that the cells are made up of smaller parts. The top diagram on the next page shows the parts of a human cheek cell as seen through a high-power microscope.

Each part of the cell has a reason for being there – a function that is essential to the working of the cell.

The **nucleus** is the control centre of the cell. It contains information that determines which chemicals will be made and the structure of the cell. The nucleus contains chemical codes that control the development and function of the whole organism.

The **cytoplasm** is a watery jelly-like liquid that fills the cell. Inside it, important chemical reactions take place and we find other cell parts such as the nucleus.

The **cell membrane** is the outer layer of the cell. It allows some substances to pass in and out of the cell, e.g. carbon dioxide and oxygen. Other substances cannot pass through, e.g. protein molecules.

The human cheek cell is a typical animal cell. However, not all animal cells are the same. Most have the parts we have listed, but some animal cells look very different to others. This is because each cell type has a special job to do. We will look more closely at these cell specialisations in chapter 29, *Specialised cells*.

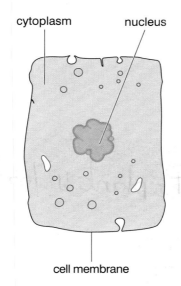

Human cheek cell

Plant cells

Plant cells are different from animal cells in some important ways. Look closely at the diagram on the left, which shows a plant cell from a leaf. Study the parts of the plant cell carefully.

Plant cells contain all of the parts also present in animal cells, but there are some other important structures.

Cell parts found in all plant cells

The **cell wall** is the outermost covering of the plant cell. It is made of a substance called **cellulose**. Fibre in our diet is cellulose from plant cells. The cell wall is relatively strong and tough and gives the cell its shape.

A **large vacuole** contains a solution of sugars and salts that we call **cell sap**. The vacuole is in the middle of the cell and it takes up most of the volume of the cell. This is not true of animal cells, which may have small, temporary vacuoles.

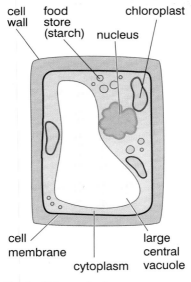

Plant cell from a leaf

Cell parts found in many plant cells

Chloroplasts contain the green pigment called **chlorophyll**. Chlorophyll absorbs light to enable photosynthesis to take place (photosynthesis is explained more fully in chapter 21). Root cells do not contain chloroplasts as they are not exposed to sunlight.

Starch grains are the most common food store of the plant cell. The plant stores glucose made by photosynthesis in the form of starch.

Animal cells have a wide variety of different shapes, but plant cells are more often a box-like shape and generally show less variety of cell shape. We can summarise the differences between animal and plant cells in the table below:

Structures present in both plant and animal cells	Structures present only in plant cells
nucleus	cell wall
cytoplasm	chloroplasts
cell membrane	large vacuole

Check yourself

ANSWERS & TUTORIALS

A1

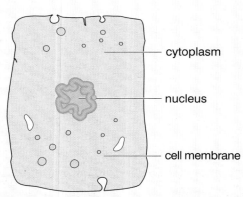

cytoplasm

nucleus

cell membrane

T1 A very common mistake is to label the cell membrane as the cell wall. Remember only plant cells have a cell wall – animal cells never have a cell wall.

A2 Cell membrane, nucleus, cytoplasm.

T2 If you said *vacuoles*, you need to make it clear that plant cells always have a large central vacuole, whereas some animal cells may have a number of small, temporary vacuoles. Both can have food stores in the cell but in plant cells this will often be starch and in animal cells it will never be starch.

QUESTIONS

Q1 Draw and label a typical animal cell.

Q2 Make a list of all the parts that animal and plant cells have in common.

QUESTIONS

Q3 Here is a diagram of a plant cell from a leaf. Complete the diagram by adding the names of each of the labelled parts.

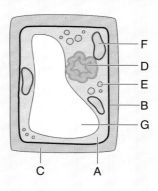

ANSWERS & TUTORIALS

A3 A: cytoplasm, B: cell membrane, C: cell wall, D: nucleus, E: starch grain, F: chloroplast, G: large central vacuole.

T3 Check that you have labelled the cell wall and cell membrane correctly.

Q4 Copy and complete this table of differences between plant and animal cells.

Plant cells have	Animal cells have

A4

Plant cells have	Animal cells have
a cell wall	no cell wall
chloroplasts	no chloroplasts
starch grains	no starch grains, but may store food as fat or glycogen
a regular box like shape	a wide variety of shapes
large central vacuole	no large central vacuole, but may have a number of small vacuoles

T4 Plant cells have several things that animal cells do not have. In a test question asking about differences between cells it is better to stick to very clear differences such as the cell wall, chloroplasts and the fact that plant cells always have a large central vacuole.

Chapter 21

Photosynthesis

What you should already know

- [ ] Plants need light for growth.
- [ ] The importance of the leaf in absorbing light.
- [ ] That plants in food chains are described as producers.
- [ ] The main functions of some organs of plants.
- [ ] How these functions are essential to the plants.

What you need to know

Animals get their food by eating other animals or plants (or both). Plants do not feed in this way. Plants grow by producing biomass (biological mass). This is done by using light energy to turn water and carbon dioxide into **glucose** (a type of sugar). This process is called **photosynthesis**. Oxygen gas is made as a waste product. This might seem a little strange because we usually think of oxygen as being a very useful gas and not as a waste product. The oxygen produced may be used up in respiration (see chapter 30) or it may pass out of the leaf.

Photosynthesis is not quite as simple as this. If we shine light onto carbon dioxide and water, will glucose and oxygen be made? Of course not! There are very complicated structures inside green plant cells that make photosynthesis happen in the way that it does. The leaf is a biomass factory, specially designed to make glucose and starch as efficiently as possible.

The structure and function of the leaf

Photosynthesis takes place in all of the green parts of plants. In most plants, the leaves are the major site of photosynthesis. The leaves are adapted to make them the most effective site for photosynthesis.

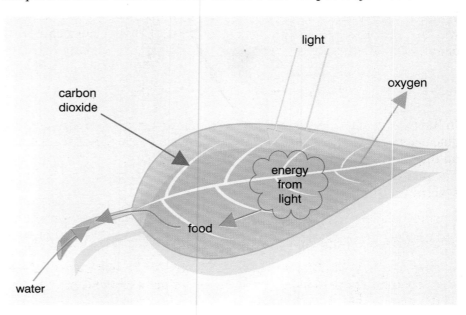

The leaf is a good site for photosynthesis because:

- the leaf contains many specialised cells that are packed with **chloroplasts**. The chloroplasts contain the green colour **chlorophyll**. Chlorophyll absorbs sunlight and makes this energy available for the process of photosynthesis.

- the leaf has a large **surface area**, so it is able to absorb sunlight more efficiently.

- the leaf has many tiny holes in it called **stomata** which allow carbon dioxide to pass in and oxygen to pass out during the day.

- **veins** carry water into the leaf from the roots. The part of the plant's veins that carries water is called the **xylem**.

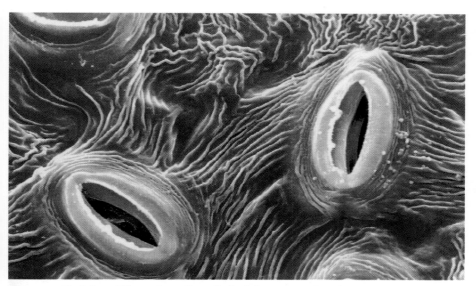

This magnified view of the undersurface of a leaf shows open stomata

Veins carry water through the leaf

We can write down what happens in photosynthesis in a shorthand way as a word equation (this will be dealt with in more detail in chapter 22, *Word equations*).

$$\text{carbon dioxide} + \text{water} \xrightarrow{\text{light energy}} \text{glucose} + \text{oxygen}$$

In the presence of light, carbon dioxide and water react to produce glucose and oxygen. The rate at which glucose is produced depends on the amounts of carbon dioxide, water and light present.
The plant can use the glucose it makes during photosynthesis in several ways:

- glucose is used in respiration (see chapter 30, *Respiration*);

- glucose can be changed into starch, which is stored for use later;

- glucose can be built up into other large molecules such as cellulose or protein. These substances are used for growth and repair of the plant.

ANSWERS & TUTORIALS

A1 **Plants produce biomass by using light energy to produce glucose from carbon dioxide and water. This is called photosynthesis.**

T1 Plants do not build up their biomass from the soil. Plants get water and minerals from the soil. Which are both important in the production of biomass.

A2

Inputs	Outputs
carbon dioxide	glucose
water	oxygen
light energy	

T2 Carbon dioxide and water are the raw materials needed to build up the glucose molecules. The light energy may come from the Sun or artificial lighting. In photosynthesis, light energy becomes chemical energy stored in the glucose molecules. This stored energy is released by the plant in respiration. (See chapter 30, Respiration)

QUESTIONS

Q1 **How do plants produce biomass?**

Q2 **Photosynthesis is a process. It has inputs (raw materials needed by the process) and outputs (things that the process makes). Complete the following table with the inputs and outputs of photosynthesis.**

Inputs	Outputs	

QUESTIONS

Q3 List four reasons why the leaf is a good site for photosynthesis.

Q4 **a** Write a word equation to summarise photosynthesis.

b A market gardener grows tomatoes in a greenhouse. Suggest ways that she can make the tomato plants grow faster so that she can get large, ripe tomatoes to market earlier than the other local tomato growers.

ANSWERS & TUTORIALS

A3 The leaf:
- contains lots of specialised cells that are packed with chloroplasts. The chloroplasts contain the green colour chlorophyll. Chlorophyll absorbs sunlight and makes the energy from the sun available for the process of photosynthesis.
- has a large surface area so that it can absorb sunlight efficiently.
- has many tiny holes called stomata that allow carbon dioxide to pass in and oxygen to pass out during the day.
- has veins that carry water into it from the roots. The part of the plant's veins that carries water is called the xylem.

A4

a
$$\text{carbon dioxide} + \text{water} \xrightarrow{\text{light energy}} \text{glucose} + \text{oxygen}$$

b The gardener could make the plants grow faster by speeding up photosynthesis. She could:
- increase the amount of carbon dioxide in the greenhouse;
- make sure the plants have a good water supply;
- shine lights on the tomato plants over night, so that the plants get light 24 hours a day (this means that they will be photosynthesising all the time);
- make the lights brighter and have them come on if the day becomes too dull and cloudy.

T4 All of these things would make the tomato plants grow faster and make large ripe tomatoes more quickly. This is because they all make photosynthesis happen faster.

Chapter 22

Word Equations

What you should already know

☐ Chemical substances have names and these can often tell you which chemical elements they contain.

☐ In any chemical reaction new and different substances are produced from the reacting substances.

☐ Useful products can be made from chemical reactions.

What you need to know

All matter is made of tiny particles called **atoms**. There are about 100 different types of atom. A substance that is made of just one type of atom is called an **element**. You have probably heard the names of the most common elements, such as oxygen, hydrogen, iron and carbon. Most of the substances around us contain more than one type of atom. Atoms of different elements can join together in a chemical reaction to form a **compound**. Water is a compound of hydrogen atoms and oxygen atoms. Elements are like building blocks which join together in different combinations to form different compounds.

We can use a word equation to give a simple summary of a chemical reaction between two or more substances. It contains only the names of the substances which are involved in the reaction. To write accurate word equations you will have to be familiar with the names of chemical substances. The names of some important elements are written below.

Metals	Symbol	Non-metals	Symbol
sodium	Na	hydrogen	H
potassium	K	nitrogen	N
magnesium	Mg	oxygen	O
calcium	Ca	sulphur	S
aluminium	Al	chlorine	Cl
iron	Fe	neon	Ne
copper	Cu	argon	Ar
zinc	Zn		
silver	Ag		
gold	Au		

The symbol for each element is the shorter version of its name. Symbols are used in chemical equations.

Understanding chemical names

Compounds contain *either* a metal with non-metals, *or* just non-metals. You can get a good idea of what elements are contained in a compound from the way the name is written:

magnesium oxide contains **magnesium** and **oxygen**

magnesium chloride contains **magnesium** and **chlorine**

The names seem to be logical apart from what has happened to the ending of the word. The ending gives some more information.

- The ending '**-ide**' tells you that there are only two elements in the compound. The first example above contains only magnesium and oxygen. In the second example, only magnesium and chlorine are present.

- Some compounds end in '**-ate**', such as copper sulphate. This ending indicates that there are three elements present and one of them will be oxygen.

For example:

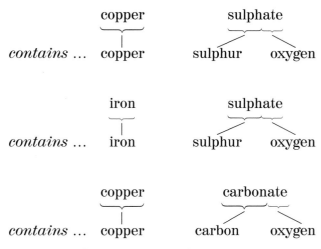

Here are a few more examples.

Compound	Elements
iron ox<u>ide</u>	iron and oxygen
iron sulph<u>ide</u>	iron and sulphur
iron sulph<u>ate</u>	iron and sulphur and oxygen
sodium chlor<u>ide</u>	sodium and chlorine
sodium nit<u>rate</u>	sodium and nitrogen and oxygen

The names of some other substances give different information about the chemical composition of the substance:

carbon dioxide is made up of two ('**di**' = two) lots of oxygen for every one lot of carbon;

carbon monoxide contains only one ('**mono**' = one) lot of oxygen for one lot of carbon.

However, there are some substances with common names that do not give any clues about which elements they contain. For example, the name water gives no clue that it is made up of two lots of hydrogen for every one lot of oxygen. Sugar and marble are other examples of this type of name although they both have chemical names.

Word equations

When you write a word equation, only the names of the substances involved in the reaction and the names of the substances produced are important. Word equations must be written in a very specific and particular way. On the left-hand side, you write the names of the starting substances which take part in the reaction. These are called the **reactants**. On the right-hand side you write the names of all the substance produced as a result of the reaction. These are called the **products**. For example:

methane + oxygen → carbon dioxide + water

When methane (natural gas) burns in oxygen (contained in air) the reaction produces carbon dioxide and water. Methane and oxygen are the reactants, carbon dioxide and water are the products. The arrow points from the reactants to the products with the + sign meaning 'and'. So this word equation reads like this:

methane *and* oxygen *react to produce* carbon dioxide *and* water

A word equation only provides a summary of the names of the substances that take part in the reaction and its products. A word equation does not provide any information about:

- the physical states of the reactants and products (whether they are solid, liquid, gas or a solution);
- the quantities of the substances reacting and of the products;
- the energy changes that take place during the reaction;
- the rate of the reaction;
- any special conditions necessary for the reaction to take place.

Check yourself

QUESTIONS

Q1 When calcium metal is put into water, calcium hydroxide and hydrogen gas are produced. Complete this word equation:

calcium + _____ → calcium hydroxide + _____

Q2 When magnesium burns in oxygen, magnesium oxide is produced. Complete this word equation:

_____ + oxygen → _____

Q3 When magnesium reacts with hydrochloric acid, magnesium chloride and hydrogen are produced. Write a word equation to summarise this reaction.

Q4 During photosynthesis in plants, carbon dioxide and water react to produce sugar and oxygen. Write a word equation for this reaction.

ANSWERS & TUTORIALS

A1

calcium + water → calcium hydroxide + hydrogen

T1 The first sentence tells you that calcium is put into water – calcium and water are the two reactants. You are then given the two products, calcium hydroxide and hydrogen. This word equation is partially complete with both calcium and calcium hydroxide already shown. Remember: reactants on the left and products on the right, with the reaction arrow pointing from left to right.

A2 magnesium + oxygen → magnesium oxide

T2 The only product of this reaction is magnesium oxide. Just read the question. Do not go looking for more detail than is actually required.

A3 magnesium + hydrochloric acid →
                magnesium chloride + hydrogen

T3 Make sure that the reactants – magnesium and hydrochloric acid – are written on the left, with products written on the right.

A4 carbon dioxide + water → sugar + oxygen

T4 You should be familiar with the process of photosynthesis. If you are not sure, then refer to chapter 21 and check your understanding before you look at the equation again. Read the equation carefully to make sure you understand the order of events. Identify what reacts with what (reactants) to form the products. Do not forget the arrow to show the direction of the reaction, and the + signs between both of the reactants and both of the products.

Chapter 23

LEVEL **6**
MATERIALS AND THEIR
PROPERTIES

Particles

What you should already know

- [ ] Materials can exist as solids, liquids or gases.
- [ ] Solids are hard to compress, have a fixed volume and a fixed shape.
- [ ] Liquids are hard to compress, have a fixed volume but do not have a fixed shape.
- [ ] Gases are easy to compress, do not have a fixed volume and do not have a fixed shape.

What you need to know

In order to explain our ideas we often use scientific models. A scientific model helps us to understand a new idea by comparing it with something we already know about. We can then use the scientific model to predict the behaviour of things we haven't seen before. One useful model is the **particle model**.

Scientists think of materials as being made up of very tiny particles, too small to be seen. If we could split up any substance into smaller and smaller pieces, we would eventually find the particles that make it. You might think of particles this way. Imagine you are standing on a beach. If you look closely, you would be able to see the individual grains of sand. If you looked around, you would see the whole beach made of sand. Now imagine you are taking off in a helicopter above the beach – first you would see the sand swirling about, but as you get higher, you would not be able to see the individual grains of sand. All you would see is that it is yellow and it is a sandy beach. It is like that with particles – you cannot see each one, but when there are enough of them close together they make a substance that you can see. We can use this particle model to represent a solid, a liquid and a gas.

In a solid, the particles are very close together. We draw them touching which means that they are fixed together. They make up a **regular** pattern. The particles move slightly – they vibrate in their fixed positions, they do not move about from one place to another.

In a liquid, the particles start to move away from each other. They are not all fixed together – only some of them are still touching. They are not arranged in any particular pattern. The particles are moving about from one place to another.

In a gas, the particles are a long way apart from each other and move very rapidly in all directions. They show **random** movement.

solid

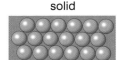

liquid

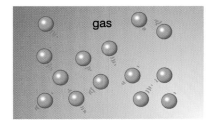

gas

Expansion and contraction

Supplying energy to the particles increases the amount of movement in the particles. The effect is that the particles move further apart, so the whole substance takes up more space – it expands. If energy is removed (by cooling) the particles move closer together and the material contracts.

expanded

contracted

By supplying more energy, a solid will melt and form a liquid. If even more energy is supplied to the particles, the movement will be even greater and the liquid can become a gas. If you remove energy (by cooling), a gas can become a liquid and a liquid can become a solid.

The rock cycle

Expansion, contraction, melting and solidifying are important processes in the rock cycle. There are three groups of rock – **igneous, sedimentary** and **metamorphic**.

- **Igneous rocks** are formed when magma (molten rock from inside the Earth) cools. They are very hard and have a speckled appearance. An example of an igneous rock is granite.

- **Sedimentary rocks** are formed when sediments, such as sand and mud, settle out and are compressed and cemented together by the weight of the sediment above. Sedimentary rocks are layered and often contain fossils. An example of a sedimentary rock is sandstone.

- **Metamorphic rocks** are formed when existing rocks are changed by the considerable heat and pressure under the earth. They have a streaky or layered appearance. An example of a metamorphic rock is slate.

Check yourself

ANSWERS & TUTORIALS

A1

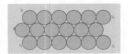

solid

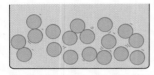

liquid

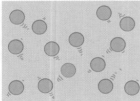

gas

a **In a solid, the particles:**
   - **are close together;**
   - **are in a regular pattern;**
   - **vibrate about fixed points.**
b **In a liquid, the particles:**
   - **are further apart than in solids;**
   - **are not in any pattern;**
   - **move about randomly.**
c **In a gas, the particles:**
   - **are far apart;**
   - **are not in any pattern;**
   - **move about rapidly and randomly.**

T1   A good way to learn the particle model is to be
able to draw the diagrams and remember there are
three things to be mentioned with each diagram:
1   how close the particles are;
2   the pattern of the particles;
3   the type of movement.
The particles become more energetic and more
irregular at each stage from solid to liquid to gas.

Q1   **Draw a diagram and describe the arrangement
of particles in:**
a   **a solid;**
b   **a liquid;**
c   **a gas.**

QUESTIONS

Q2 Describe the movement of particles and the arrangement of particles in the following changes:
a melting;
b the expansion of a solid;
c condensation.

ANSWERS & TUTORIALS

A2 a **Melting**
Particles in a solid gain enough energy to vibrate sufficiently violently to break out of the regular pattern. As the pattern breaks down, the substance melts and becomes a liquid. The particles in a liquid move in a random way.

b **Expansion**
When a solid gains more energy, the particles vibrate more (further and faster) from their central position. This causes particles to move slightly away from each other and the size of the solid increases.

c **Condensation**
When particles of a gas are cooled, they slow down and come closer together until eventually enough particles come together to become a liquid.

T2 Look carefully at the notes on pages 96 and 97 if you find the question difficult to answer. Firstly identify the sort of change that is occurring, e.g. is it a change of state? Then consider whether the particles are gaining or losing energy before you attempt to describe the arrangement and movement of the particles.

Q3 Describe how metamorphic rocks are formed.

A3 Metamorphic rocks are formed when existing rocks are changed by the heat and pressure under the earth.

T3 Remember that igneous rock comes from Inside the earth, so it is very hot and molten. Sedimentary rock is made from sediment and metamorphic is the one that changes due to heat and pressure under the earth.

Chapter 24

Chemical Reactions

What you should already know

☐ Changes of state are reversible changes.
☐ Chemical reactions such as burning and rusting are examples of non-reversible changes.

What you need to know

Changes that take place in chemical reactions are called **chemical changes**. Changes such as evaporation and condensation that do not involve a chemical reaction are called **physical changes**. The differences between chemical changes and physical changes are summarised in the table below.

Physical changes	Chemical changes
do not form a new substance	form a new substance
do not release large amounts of energy	sometimes release large amounts of energy
can be changed back quite easily	cannot be changed back easily

If you study some chemical reactions you can spot **patterns** in the way that some groups of substances react with other groups. A good example is the reaction between acids and indicators. If you put Universal Indicator into an acidic solution, the indicator will turn red. It does not matter which acid you use – all acids turn Universal Indicator red. This pattern is very useful. It means that you can use indicators to test whether or not something is an acid. There are also patterns in the way that acids react with other substances.

Acid and metal

The reactions between metals and acids are all very similar and can be summarised in this word equation:

metal + acid → metal salt + hydrogen

For example:

calcium + hydrochloric acid → calcium chloride + hydrogen

magnesium + sulphuric acid → magnesium sulphate + hydrogen

Hydrogen is produced in all of these reactions but the time it takes for the reaction to happen is different for each type of metal and each type of acid. Some metals react very quickly, some are slower and some react so slowly they can hardly be seen to react at all. This is an example of a **trend** in properties. The reactions are very similar – they all produce hydrogen – but there is a difference in speed of reaction from one metal to another.

Magnesium, calcium and lead in dilute acid

Acid and carbonate

There is also a pattern in the way acids react with compounds called carbonates. Each of these reactions produces carbon dioxide. The reaction between acids and carbonates can be summarised by the word equation:

acid + metal carbonate → metal salt + carbon dioxide + water

Some examples of such reaction are:

hydrochloric acid + calcium carbonate → calcium chloride + carbon dioxide + water

sulphuric acid + sodium carbonate → sodium sulphate + carbon dioxide + water

Metals and oxygen

Metals also have other similarities in how they react with other substances. Nearly all metals react with the oxygen in air. When they do this they lose their shine and go dull (they 'tarnish'). Some metals like sodium will do this in a few seconds. Others take much longer. The time it takes for different metals to tarnish is another trend. When a metal reacts with oxygen it forms a chemical compound called an **oxide**. Iron forms iron oxide which is more commonly known as rust. Magnesium and aluminium also react with oxygen in the air to form an oxide, resulting in a dull looking layer on the surface of the metal.

Aluminium (top) and magnesium scratched to show a shiny surface

Millions of years ago, the metallic elements that were formed in the Earth reacted with oxygen in the atmosphere to form oxides. These oxides are still present and they are the source of metals that are used in industry. The metal compounds in the earth are called ores. A metal can be extracted from its ore by carrying out a chemical reaction. Oxygen is removed in the reaction, leaving the pure metal.

Burning is another example of a reaction with oxygen. Burning releases large quantities of energy which can be used to warm things. A substance that is burned to release energy is called a **fuel**. Some fuels that are extracted from the Earth are called **fossil fuels**. Non-metallic elements such as carbon and hydrogen burn very well and chemical compounds made from these elements, such as methane (natural gas), also burn very well. The most important fossil fuels – coal, gas and oil – are all composed of carbon and hydrogen.

Check yourself

ANSWERS & TUTORIALS

A1
  a **Metals react with acids to give hydrogen.**
  b **Metals react with oxygen in the air to give oxides.**

T1
  a Acids react with metals and in each case the reaction produces hydrogen gas. This saves you learning all the possible combinations of reactions. You should know that if a metal reacts with an acid it gives hydrogen and that if you are told something gives hydrogen from an acid, it is a metal.
  b All metals (with the exception of gold) react with oxygen to give a metal oxide. It is called an oxide because the metal is reacting with oxygen. The name of the oxide depends upon which metal is reacting, e.g. magnesium reacts with oxygen to give magnesium oxide.

A2

Physical changes	Chemical changes
a **melting ice**	b **burning a fuel**
d **condensation on a window**	c **magnesium and acid reacting**

T2
Physical changes are quite easily reversed, and they never cause a new chemical compound to form. The process of ice melting is easily reversed (by putting it in a freezer) and the water remains water whether it is solid or liquid. Condensation is similar. The water droplets formed on a window by cooling water vapour can be changed back to water vapour by warming them.
Burning a fuel is a chemical change. It uses up the fuel and you cannot get any oil or coal back after it has been burnt. It also releases a lot of energy and forms new substances, e.g. the ash formed by burning coal is a new substance. Magnesium and acid reacting is a chemical change because it gives off hydrogen, a new substance.

A3 **Carbon dioxide**

QUESTIONS

Q1 **Write down the ways in which metals show patterns in their chemical reactions with:**
  a **acids;**
  b **air.**

Q2 **Which of the following are physical changes and which are chemical changes:**
  a **melting ice;**
  b **burning a fuel;**
  c **magnesium and acid reacting together;**
  d **condensation forming on a window?**

Q3 **What gas is produced when an acid reacts with a metal carbonate?**

Chapter 25

Refraction

What you should already know

- ☐ Light travels in straight lines.
- ☐ Light cannot pass through opaque materials, but it can pass through transparent materials.

What you need to know

When light passes from one transparent medium (material) to another it almost always changes direction. If you look at a frosted glass window, the objects on the other side of the glass always look distorted. What you see through the glass is different from the real object because the frosted glass affects the light passing through it. Frosted glass has a pattern created by changes in the surface and thickness of the glass sheet. Because of the variation in the surface of the glass, individual rays of light have their direction changed by different amounts. This causes the effect that you can see in the photograph on the right.

The process which causes light to change direction when it passes from one transparent medium to another is called **refraction**. For example, when light travelling in air enters a block of glass it changes direction. Refraction also takes place when light passes from water into air.

Diagram 1 shows a ray of light travelling from air into glass and out into air again. When a ray of light, **A**, passes from air into glass, the ray changes direction getting closer to the **normal**. The normal is a line drawn at right angles (90°) to the surface of the glass at the point the light ray enters or leaves the glass block. When the ray leaves the block it changes direction again getting further away from the normal. The rays of light at **A** and **C** are **parallel** to each other.

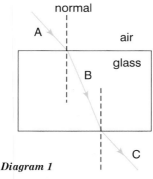

Diagram 1

The ray of light in diagram 2 is not refracted because it enters the glass block at right angles to its surface (in other words, along the normal). This is the only situation in which refraction does not occur when light enters another transparent medium.

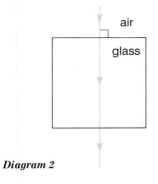

Diagram 2

When a ray of light passes from air into Perspex, it travels from a less-dense medium into a more dense medium. Light slows down as it enters the more dense Perspex. Think about the ray entering the Perspex. Because it is entering the Perspex at an angle of less than 90°, point **A** of this ray reaches the Perspex and is slowed down before point **B**. This means that in the time it takes for the top part of the ray to move from **B** to **D**, the bottom part of the ray only moves from **A** to **C**. The ray has travelled a shorter distance inside the block than outside. We say it has been **refracted**.

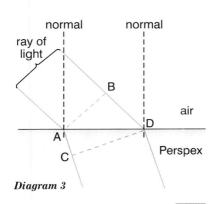

Diagram 3

Energy Resources

What you should already know

☐ There are a variety of energy resources, including coal, oil, gas, biomass, wind, waves and batteries.

☐ Some of the Earth's energy resources are renewable and some are not.

What you need to know

We use huge amounts of energy to run our homes, schools, factories and for transport. Much of the energy comes from coal, oil and gas. These are called **fossil fuels**. Fossil fuels were formed from dead plants and animals that lived many millions of years ago.

There is only a limited supply of fossil fuels in the Earth's crust. If we continue to use them at the present rate, some scientists have predicted that there is only enough coal to last about 300 years and enough oil and gas to last about 50 years. All of the energy contained within these energy resources came originally from the Sun. All of the plants that were turned into coal used energy from the Sun – in the form of light – to produce glucose and oxygen from carbon dioxide and water (see chapter 21, *Photosynthesis*). All of the animals that were turned into oil and gas got their food from plants. This means that the Sun is the source of most of the Earth's energy resources.

Today energy that can be used for domestic or industrial purposes comes from a wide range of sources. Some of these are shown in the diagram below.

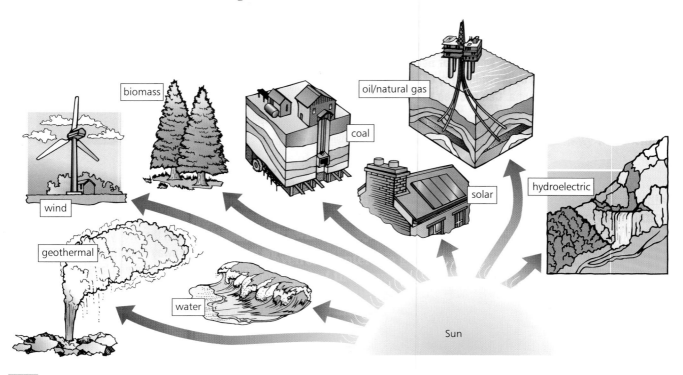

biomass

oil/natural gas

coal

solar

hydroelectric

wind

geothermal

water

Sun

Plants need energy from the Sun to grow. Animals take advantage of this energy directly by eating plants or indirectly by eating animals that have eaten plants. When fossil fuels are burnt, the energy (that originally came from the Sun) is released.

Many power stations generate electricity by burning fossil fuels. The flow chart on the right shows – in a simplified way – what happens inside a thermal power station.

The Earth's supply of fossil fuels is limited. We can extend the time that they will last by developing other ways of producing electricity.

Alternative energy resources

Biomass is any plant or animal material that can be used as a fuel or to produce a fuel. Wood, methane (from decaying animal and plant material) and alcohol (made from sugar) are all biomass. They can all be burnt in the furnace of a power station. Alcohol can also be used to provide fuel for cars.

Wind is caused by the Sun heating air in some areas more than others. The hot air rises and cool air takes its place. The movement of air in the atmosphere is called wind. Wind can be captured by the blades of large windmills. In exposed areas, hundreds of these windmills (called 'aerogenerators') make up a wind farm. The wind provides energy to drive the windmill that turns a generator to produce electricity.

Waves are caused by wind blowing across the sea. The rocking motion of waves can be used to drive generators. One type is the 'nodding duck'. It consists of a line of floats that are fixed on one side, allowing the other side to nod up and down with the waves. A pump is driven by the nodding action, pushing water through a turbine to drive a generator.

Hydroelectric power uses the flow of water down a hill to drive turbines. Rain water that has fallen high in mountains can be trapped in a reservoir and then allowed to flow downhill through pipes. Turbines at the bottom of the pipes are driven by the flow of water and they turn generators to produce electricity.

Solar energy can be collected by using solar cells, solar panels and solar furnaces. Solar cells produce electricity from chemicals when light falls onto them. Solar panels can produce hot water. Solar furnaces use many mirrors to direct heat from the Sun onto a water tank. The water boils, producing steam, which can be used to drive turbines.

The energy resources we have dealt with so far come directly or indirectly from the Sun. There are, however, some energy resources that do not come from the Sun.

Nuclear energy is used to heat water to produce steam, which drives a turbine. Radioactive materials, such as uranium, undergo nuclear reaction. As a result of this, they give out a lot of energy. Nuclear energy is non-renewable – the radioactive materials in the Earth's crust that are used in nuclear reactors will eventually run out.

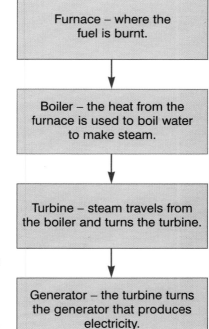

Furnace – where the fuel is burnt.

Boiler – the heat from the furnace is used to boil water to make steam.

Turbine – steam travels from the boiler and turns the turbine.

Generator – the turbine turns the generator that produces electricity.

Geothermal energy is energy from hot rocks deep inside the Earth's crust. Water can be pumped down to the hot rocks where it turns to steam. The steam is used to generate electricity.

Tidal energy uses the tides to generate electricity. Tides are caused by the pull of the Moon on the Earth. At high tide, water flows behind a barrage where it is trapped. As the water flows back to the sea, it can be used to turn turbines and generate electricity.

Check yourself

ANSWERS & TUTORIALS

A1

Energy resource	Renewable	Non-renewable	From the Sun
coal		✓	✓
oil		✓	✓
gas		✓	✓
wave	✓		✓
tidal	✓		
hydroelectric	✓		✓
biomass	✓		✓
nuclear		✓	
solar	✓		✓
wind	✓		✓

T1 You must be clear about which energy resources are renewable and which are non-renewable. Renewable energy resources are always being replaced. Non-renewable resources will eventually run out. Geothermal energy is not included in the table – it is not renewable, but there is so much of it that it will take a very long time to be used up.

Most energy resources come originally from the Sun. Nuclear energy, geothermal energy and tidal energy do not.

QUESTIONS

Q1

Energy resource	Renewable	Non-renewable	From the Sun
coal			
oil			
gas			
wave			
tidal			
hydroelectric			
biomass			
nuclear			
solar			
wind			

Tick in the correct column of the table to show whether the energy resource is renewable or non-renewable. Put a tick in the last column if the energy has originally come from the Sun.

QUESTIONS

Q2 Why can't we depend only on wind energy or solar energy in the UK?

Q3 Explain how electricity is made using:
a a fossil fuel;
b wind.

ANSWERS & TUTORIALS

A2 The weather in the UK is variable and unpredictable. We do not get sufficient sun or wind for us to be able to rely on them as our only energy resource.

T2 The energy supply depends on the weather. On a sunny and windy day there will be a large supply of energy, but on a still night there will be little wind or solar energy. If this type of energy was to be used to produce electricity, an alternative would be needed for when there was little sun or wind.

A3 a Fossil fuels are burnt in a furnace. This heat is used to boil water, to produce steam. The steam turns a turbine. The turbine turns a generator, which produces electricity.
b Wind is used to turn a turbine in a windmill, which turns a generator.

T3 There are four main parts concerned with the production of electricity in a power station where the fuel is burnt (see the flow chart on page 107).

To generate electricity, kinetic energy (movement) is needed to turn a generator. This energy can come directly from wind, wave motion, falling water (hydroelectric) and tides. The energy can also be produced by burning fuels (fossil fuels or biomass), or producing heat (nuclear fuel and geothermal). Thermal energy is used to produce steam, which makes turbines move. These produce kinetic energy (movement), which can then be used to turn the generators.

Chapter 27

LEVEL 6
PHSYICAL PROCESSES

The Solar System

What you should already know

- [ ] The apparent movement of the Sun and other stars is caused by the movement of the Earth.
- [ ] Luminous objects give out light.
- [ ] We are able to see non-luminous objects because light from a source is reflected from them.

What you need to know

A star is a massive 'ball of fire' which may have planets in orbit around it. A planet is a large object which orbits a star. Any object that orbits a planet is called a moon. Some planets have many moons orbiting them, e.g. Jupiter. The Earth has one moon called the Moon! The star at the centre of our solar system is called the Sun. There are nine planets in orbit around the Sun.

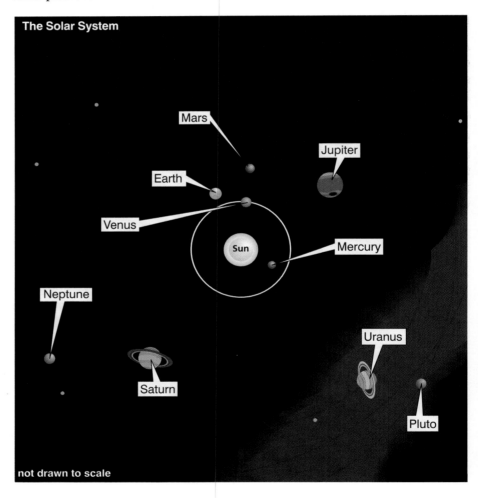

The Solar System

Mars · Jupiter · Earth · Venus · Sun · Mercury · Neptune · Uranus · Saturn · Pluto

not drawn to scale

Starting with the planet nearest the Sun, the order of the planets is: Mercury, Venus, Earth, Mars, Jupiter, Saturn, Uranus, Neptune and Pluto. To help you remember the order of the planets you can make up a funny sentence of words starting with the first letters of the planets (for example, you could try: Most Vegetarians Eat Many Jam Sandwiches Under Nine Planets).

Stars and planets

Stars such as our Sun give out heat and light. There are many other stars much further away from the Earth that also give out heat and light. On a clear night you can see thousands of stars in the sky. The planets do not give out light, they are illuminated by the star that they orbit. Earth is lit by the Sun. We can sometimes see some other planets in our solar system shining brightly in the sky. This is because they reflect the light from the Sun. The further away the planet is from Earth, the less bright it will appear. The closer the planet is to the Earth, the brighter it will appear.

Astronomers have found that different coloured light is produced by different stars. The colour of a star indicates its temperature. Some stars are very hot ($20\,000\,°C$ at the surface) and shine with a blue light. Others are much cooler and look red.

The brightest star in the sky, Sirius, looks white and is very hot (approximately $10\,000\,°C$). The Sun is yellow. It is a medium hot star at approximately $6000\,°C$. Proxima Centauri, the nearest known star to the Sun, is a dim red. Its temperature is about $3000\,°C$. The temperature of the star and its distance from the Earth are factors which affects its relative brightness.

Check yourself

QUESTIONS

Q1 Write down a definition of:
a   a star;
b   a planet;
c   a moon.

ANSWERS & TUTORIALS

A1 a   A star is a massive 'ball of fire' which may have planets in orbit around it.
b   A planet is a large object that orbits around a star.
c   A moon is an object which orbits around a planet.

T1   When you give these definitions, you should not refer to specific stars, planets and moons except to use them as examples.

ANSWERS & TUTORIALS

A2   **a & b**

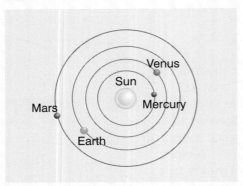

c   **No. Light from the Sun is much brighter than the light reflected from Mercury.**
d   **Yes. Mars will be seen at night because it reflects the Sun's light.**

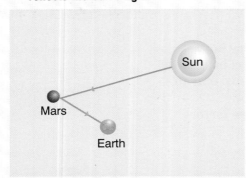

T2   Remember your funny sentence. Mercury is the closest planet to the Sun, next comes Venus and then Earth.

Be careful not to assume that the Sun is in the way. It may not be, because the orbits of planets in the solar system are not all in the same plane.

Remember that planets are not luminous but reflect light from the Sun.

A3   **blue star, white star, Sun, red star, Earth**

T3   Even on a very hot day the Earth's temperature does not get anywhere near that of a cool red star.

QUESTIONS

Q2

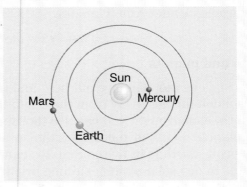

a   **Complete the diagram to show the path taken by Venus as it orbits the Sun.**
b   **Draw Venus on the diagram at its furthest point from Earth.**
When the planets are in the positions shown:
c   **can Mercury be seen from Earth?**
d   **can Mars be seen from Earth?**
Give a reason for your answers in c and d.

Q3   **Put the following in order of temperature starting with the hottest:**
Earth   Sun   a white star
a blue star   a red star

1. The drawing shows a simple animal cell.

(a) Give **one** function of each of these parts.
    (i)   cell membrane _____
    (ii) nucleus _____

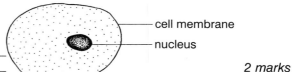

cell membrane

nucleus

2 marks

The drawing below shows a nerve cell.

(b) From the drawings, give **two** ways in which the structure of the nerve cell is different from the structure of the simple animal cell.
Explain how each feature helps the nerve cell carry messages around the body.
    (i)   Difference in structure _____
          Explanation _____ *2 marks*
    (ii) Difference in structure _____
          Explanation _____ *2 marks*

2. The diagram shows a plant cell.

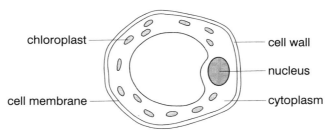

chloroplast

cell membrane

cell wall

nucleus

cytoplasm

(a) (i) The cell is from a leaf. Give the name of the part which is present in this leaf cell but **not** present in root cells. _____ *1 mark*
    (ii) Give **two** parts, labelled on the diagram, which are **not** present in animal cells.
         1. _____   2. _____

(b) The five parts of the cell labelled on the diagram have different functions. In the table below, write the name of the correct part of the cell next to its function. One has been done for you. *4 marks*

function	part of the cell
a place where many chemical reactions take place	cytoplasm
photosynthesis takes place here	
it controls the cell's activities	
it helps to keep the shape of the cell	
it controls substances entering and leaving the cell	

3. Most babies born in Britain 'weigh' about 3 kg at birth.

A few babies 'weigh' more than 5 kg at birth.

Some babies can 'weigh' as little as 1 kg.

One reason for small babies is that they are born early or prematurely.

(a) Suggest **two** more reasons why the birth 'weights' of babies can be so variable.   *2 marks*

(i) _____

(ii) _____

(b) Rakesh and Rinku are twin brother and sister.
At birth, Rakesh 'weighed' 2.7 kg and his sister 'weighed' 2.6 kg.
(i) Suggest **one** reason why the twins were nearly the same 'weight'.

_____ *1 mark*

(ii) Suggest **one** reason why the twins 'weights' were slightly different.

_____ *1 mark*

4. Plant cells use carbon dioxide in photosynthesis. Graph A below shows how the amount of carbon dioxide a tree takes in each day varies over one year.

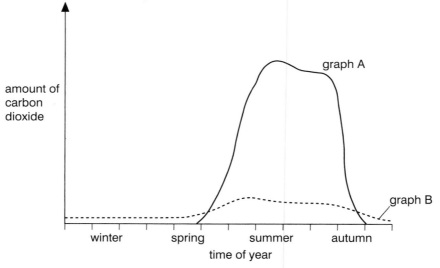

(a) (i) Give **two** reasons why photosynthesis occurs most rapidly in the summer.   *2 marks*

1. _____

2. _____

(ii) Name the **two** substances produced in photosynthesis.   *2 marks*

_____ and _____

(b) Trees which lose all their leaves in the autumn are described as deciduous. How can you tell from graph A that the tree being investigated is deciduous?   *1 mark*

_____

(c) Graph B shows how the amount of carbon dioxide which the tree gives out each day varies over one year. What is the name of the process in the tree which produces carbon dioxide?   *1 mark*

_____

5. The diagram shows a tree growing in a field.
The sun is shining, so photosynthesis is taking place rapidly in the leaves.

(a) Complete each of the boxes with the name of a suitable substance to show what happens during photosynthesis. *3 marks*

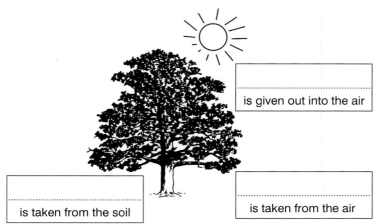

_____
is given out into the air

_____
is taken from the soil

_____
is taken from the air

(b) Complete the following sentence: *1 mark*
Starch is made in the leaves from _____ which is produced during photosynthesis.
The diagrams show both surfaces of a leaf taken from the tree.

upper surface
dark green

lower surface
light green

(c) Name the green pigment present in the leaves. _____ *1 mark*
(d) What is the function of this pigment?_____ *1 mark*
(e) Explain why the upper surface of the leaf is a darker green than the lower surface. *1 mark*
_____

6. The diagrams show two Bunsen burners.
One burner has the air hole closed, and
the other has the air hole open.

(a) Explain why opening the air hole
of a Bunsen burner makes
the flame hotter.

_____
_____
_____ *1 mark*

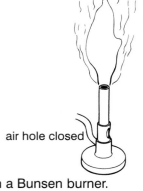 

air hole closed   air hole open

(b) Natural gas is methane, CH_4. It is burned in a Bunsen burner.
Complete the word equation for the chemical reaction in the clear blue flame. *2 marks*
methane + _____ ⟶ _____ + _____

7. The table gives information about the colours of four metals.

metal	colour of metal
copper	brown
iron	dark grey
magnesium	silver grey
zinc	light grey

A reactivity series of the metals is:

most reactive   magnesium
                              zinc
                              iron
least reactive   copper

Use this information to help you answer the questions below.

(a) A piece of zinc was placed in a solution of copper sulphate.
    (i) Complete the following word equation. *1 mark*
       zinc + copper sulphate ⟶ _____ + _____
    (ii) Complete the statement about the appearance of this piece of zinc. *1 mark*
       The light grey colour would change to _____.

(b) Excess magnesium powder was put into a test tube containing a blue solution of copper sulphate and stirred. The solution soon turned colourless. A powder settled on the bottom of the test tube.
    (i) Write a word equation for the reaction. *1 mark*
    _____

    (ii) The powder was filtered off. Two different coloured solids could be seen.
       Give the **two** colours.   1._____ *2 marks*
                        2._____

(c) (i) A piece of iron was placed in a solution of magnesium sulphate.
       What reaction, if any, would occur? _____ *1 mark*
    (ii) Explain your answer. _____ *1 mark*

8. An ice cube was placed in a dish and left in a warm room. The following diagram shows the dish at three different times.

   A   B   C
 10.00 am   10.30 am   6.30 pm

(a) What changes of state took place between:
    (i) 10.00 am and 10.30 am? _____ *1 mark*
    (ii) 10.30 am and 6.30 pm? _____ *1 mark*

(b) (i) Tick **two** boxes in each vertical column to describe how the particles are arranged in a solid, a liquid and a gas.   *3 marks*

arrangement of particles	solid	liquid	gas
close together			
far apart			
in a regular pattern			
random			

    (ii) Tick **one** box in each column to describe the movement of particles, at room temperature, in a solid and a gas.   *1 mark*

movement of particles	solid	gas
move around slowly		
move around quickly		
only vibrate		
do not move		

9. The flow chart shows how zinc sulphate can be obtained.

zinc ore → zinc oxide → zinc → zinc sulphate

   (a) In the reaction **zinc oxide → zinc** an element is removed from zinc oxide to leave zinc.
Give the name of the element. _____ *1 mark*

   (b) (i) Zinc sulphate can be made in a reaction between zinc and acid.
Give the name of the acid. _____ *1 mark*

      (ii) In the reaction between zinc and the acid, hydrogen is formed.
Describe the test for hydrogen and the result if hydrogen is present.   *1 mark*
_____

      (iii) How can crystals of zinc sulphate be formed from a dilute solution of zinc sulphate?
_____ *1 mark*

10. The diagram shows the orbits of the Earth, Venus and Jupiter around the Sun. They are not to scale.

   (a) Where is the orbit of Mars?
Tick the correct box.   *1 mark*

      It is between the Sun and the orbit of Venus. ☐

      It is between the orbit of Venus and the orbit of Earth. ☐

      It is between the orbit of Earth and the orbit of Jupiter. ☐

      It is outside the orbit of Jupiter. ☐

Venus and Jupiter can be seen from the Earth.

   (b) Sometimes Venus appears to be larger than at other times.
      (i) On the diagram, draw the position of Venus where it appears to be largest.
Label it **V**.   *1 mark*
      (ii) Why does the size of Venus appear to change?   *1 mark*
_____

   (c) Even on clear nights, Jupiter sometimes appears to be slightly brighter than at other times.
      (i) On the diagram, draw the position of Jupiter where it appears to be brightest.
Label it **J**.   *1 mark*
      (ii) Why does the brightness of Jupiter appear to change?   *1 mark*
_____

11. Oil is an important energy resource. It provides about 38% of the energy used for transport, heating and generating electricity.

(a) The energy stored in oil came from the Sun.
Describe how energy from the Sun became stored in oil.

_____

_____ *2 marks*

(b) (i) Oil can be described as a non-renewable energy resource.
Explain why. _____ *1 mark*

(ii) Tick the boxes by **two** other non-renewable energy resources.   *2 marks*

coal ☐   wind ☐   solar ☐   tidal ☐   natural gas ☐   wave ☐

12. Energy comes from a variety of sources.
Complete the table below.
The first one has been done for you.   *5 marks*

energy resource	source of energy		
	directly from the Sun	**indirectly from the Sun**	**not from the Sun**
wind		✓	
nuclear			
hydro-electric			
solar			
geothermal			
oil			

13. As a beam of light passes from air to glass, it changes direction. This is known as refraction. Complete the diagram to show what happens to the light waves as they cross the boundary between air and glass.   *2 marks*

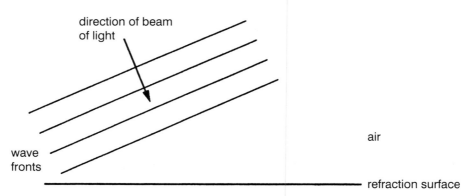

direction of beam of light

wave fronts

air

refraction surface

glass

Chapter 28

What you should already know

☐ Different habitats support different plants and animals.
☐ Food chains describe the feeding relationships that exist between organisms in a habitat.
☐ Different organisms are found in different habitats because of differences in environmental factors.
☐ Environmental factors affect the distribution and abundance of organisms in each habitat.

What you need to know

You should already know that a **habitat** is a place where a plant or an animal lives. **Food chains** show the feeding relationships in a habitat. A simple food chain is shown in the diagram below:

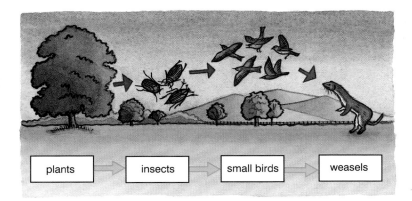

The arrow means 'eaten by' and points towards the organism that does the eating. The arrow shows the direction that food and the energy stored in the food is moving. Food chains do not tell the whole story of what is happening in a habitat because most animals eat a variety of different organisms. A plant or animal usually belongs to several food chains, not just one. So, to get a clear picture of what the feeding relationships are in a habitat, we need to show all of the food chains that there are in that habitat.

Instead of just making a list of all the food chains, scientists put all the food chain information together to make a **food web**. An example of a food web that includes the food chain shown above is at the top of the next page.

Food chains and food webs always start with a plant. The plant at the start of a food chain or food web is called a **producer**. It is called a producer because it makes or produces its own biomass by photosynthesis (see chapter 21, *Photosynthesis*). All organisms that come after the producer in the food web are called **consumers**, because they consume (eat) other things to get their food.

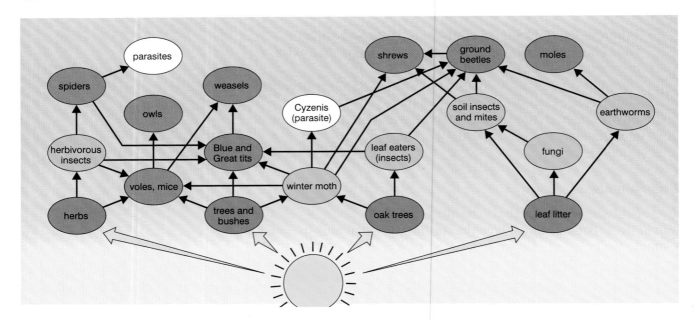

You will notice that even though voles and mice are involved in several food chains, we only write them down once.

Pyramids of numbers

Food webs give us a lot of information about the feeding relationships in any particular habitat. They are much more useful than a simple food chain on its own. But neither food webs or food chains give us any idea about how many spiders there are in a habitat or how many oak trees there are. When scientists study a habitat, they often count how many organisms there are. They don't usually count every single organism in the habitat because it would take far too long. Instead they take a small area of the habitat (called a 'sample area') or a small sample of the population they are interested in from the habitat. From this sample, they work out the total population in the habitat, and how many organisms there are in the habitat.

When we know the numbers of organisms in a habitat, we can 'redraw' our food chain as a pyramid. The number of organisms at each level in the pyramid decides the size of each layer of the pyramid:

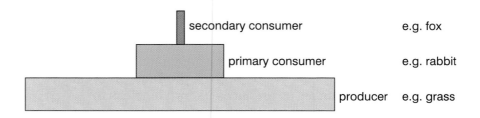

The size of each level in the pyramid shows the number of organisms feeding at that level. Consumers feeding on plants are called **primary consumers** and the consumers at the next level are called **secondary consumers**. Primary consumers only eat producers (plants) so they are completely 'vegetarian'. Scientists call them **herbivores**. Animals that only eat other animals are called **carnivores**. Animals that eat both plants and other animlas are called **omnivores**.

Usually, as you get higher up the pyramid, there are fewer organisms. There are a number of reasons why this is so. As you get higher up in the pyramid, the organisms often get bigger in size. For example, a fox is bigger than a rabbit, so one fox needs to eat more rabbits than if it was eating bigger organisms. Energy is lost at each stage of the pyramid. A rabbit uses up energy when it moves and keeps its body warm. This means that there is less energy available to the fox.

A food chain relies on energy from the sun. A plant uses energy from the Sun to produce its biomass. This energy is stored inside the plant, mainly as starch.

Sometimes a pyramid of numbers can be a very different shape. This occurs when the producer is very large in size and mass. Lots of consumers can feed on it because it has lots of energy stored inside it.

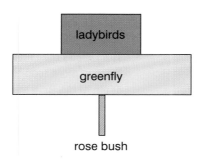

Check yourself

QUESTIONS

Q1 a Draw a food chain with three organisms in it.
    b What does a food chain show?

ANSWERS & TUTORIALS

A1 a The food chain must start with a plant or part of a plant. Each organism must be linked by an arrow and the arrow should point to the animal that is doing the eating.
    b A food chain shows some of the feeding relationships in a habitat. It also shows in which direction food and energy pass in this particular feeding relationship.

T1 You may be tempted to just join the organisms in your food chain with straight lines without any arrows. This is incomplete because it does not show in which direction food and energy are passing. The food chain must have arrows with clear arrowheads pointing towards the organism that is doing the eating. For example:
grass → snowshoe hare → lynx

ANSWERS & TUTORIALS

A2 a Any one of the following producers:
grass, clover, dandelion.

b Any one of the following consumers:
rabbit, field vole, field mouse, fox, barn owl.

c Any one of the following herbivores:
field mouse, field vole, rabbit.

d The dandelions would increase in number.

e The fox population would decrease because
they would have less food.

f The rabbits may increase in number because
there is more food for them as a result of the
death of the field mice. In other words there
is less competition for food.
or
The number of rabbits will go down because
there is now less food for the secondary
consumers (foxes and barn owls). As a
result, the secondary consumers will have to
eat more rabbits.
or
The number of rabbits will stay more or less
the same as a result of the two opposite
effects described above.

g The energy comes from the sun in the first
place.

T2 a Remember that a producer is a plant that
makes its own biomass by photosynthesis.

b Remember a consumer is an organism that
eats something else and that cannot make its
own food.

c A herbivore only eats plants or plant material.
The second organism in a food chain is
always
a herbivore.

f The different possible effects on the rabbit
show that the feeding relationships in a
particular habitat are very complicated.
Remember to describe an effect and support it
with clear reasons.

QUESTIONS

Q2 Study the food web below for a habitat such as
a large field in the countryside. Answer the
following questions.

a Name one producer.

b Name one consumer.

c Name one herbivore.

d If all the field mice suddenly died, what
would happen to the number of dandelions?

e If all the field mice suddenly died, why would
the number of foxes be likely to decrease?

f How do you think a reduction in the number
of field mice would affect the rabbit
population?

g The food chain depends on energy. Where
does all the energy come from in the first
place?

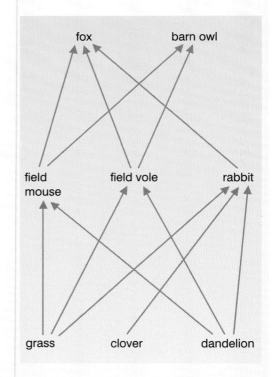

QUESTIONS

Q3 Draw a pyramid of numbers for this food chain:

apple tree → moth caterpillars → thrushes
1   1200   2

Q4 Draw a pyramid of numbers for this food chain:

ladysmock → caterpillars → robin → hawk
10 000   800   10   1

ANSWERS & TUTORIALS

A3 The pyramid should look like this:

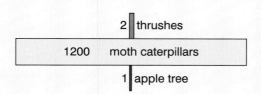

T3 This producer (an apple tree) is very large and has a large mass. One apple tree can feed many moth caterpillars, but these only provide food for a few thrushes.

A4 The pyramid should look like this:

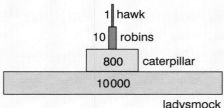

T4 This is a more common pyramid of numbers, where the numbers of the organisms at each successive level gets smaller.

Chapter 29

Specialised Cells

What you should already know

- ☐ The structure of simple animal and plant cells.
- ☐ The differences in structure between simple animal and plant cells.
- ☐ The functions of cell membrane, cytoplasm and the nucleus in plant and animal cells.
- ☐ The functions of chloroplasts and cell walls in plant cells.

What you need to know

All animal cells have several things in common. They all have a nucleus, a cell membrane and cytoplasm. However, animal cells never have a cell wall or chloroplasts.

Not all animal cells are the same. Animal cells come in a variety of shapes and sizes.

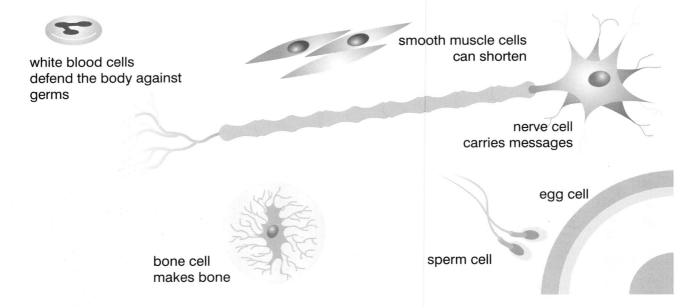

white blood cells defend the body against germs

smooth muscle cells can shorten

nerve cell carries messages

egg cell

bone cell makes bone

sperm cell

The shape of the cells and their structure depends on their particular function. This is a very important idea in science. Each type of cell is specialised or **adapted** to carry out its function.

This chapter looks at four different types of cell, each of which is specialised to carry out a particular function and shows how their structure allows them to do it.

FACT FILE 1

The sperm cell (animal)

Function

To carry the male genetic information to the ovum (egg cell) and bring about fertilisation. The sperm must swim from the vagina after sexual intercourse, up into the Fallopian tube to join with the ovum (egg cell).

Cell structure and adaptations

The sperm cell is a very highly specialised cell with a number of adaptations that make it very good at carrying out its function:

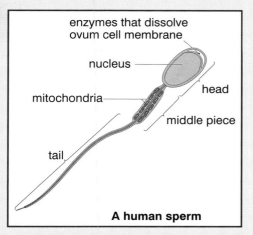

A human sperm

Adaptation	How this makes the cell better at its job
tail	allows it to swim from the vagina to the Fallopian tube
nucleus contains only half the genetic information	when it joins the ovum's half nucleus, a full nucleus will be made
enzymes on the head of the sperm	dissolves quickly through the ovum membrane
lots of mitochondria	provide energy for swimming

FACT FILE 2

Ciliated epithelial cell (animal)

Function

To move liquids or small particles.

Cell structure and adaptations

Cilia are tiny hair-like structures (on the surface of the cell) that the cell can move. We call a cell that has cilia attached to it a ciliated cell. Ciliated epithelial cells are found in the tubes of the respiratory system, e.g. trachea, and bronchi. Ciliated epithelial cells move mucus upwards and away from the lungs.

Adaptation	How this makes the cell better at its job
many cilia	the cilia beat together to move the liquid or particles.
many mitochondria in the cell	mitochondria release energy from food and this energy is used to make the cilia move

125

FACT FILE 3

Root cell hair (plant)

Function

To *absorb water and minerals from the soil water.*

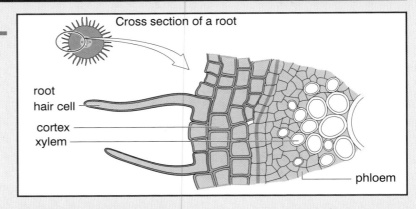

Adaptation

long hair-like structure that comes out from the cell body

no waxy layer outside the cell

no chloroplasts

How this makes the cell better at its job

increases the surface area and allows the uptake of water and minerals to take place quicker

allows for quicker uptake of water

not needed because there is no light for photosynthesis

FACT FILE 4

Palisade cell (plant)

Function

To enable photosynthesis to be carried out efficiently.

Cell structure and adaptations

The palisade cell is found in the upper part of the leaf, as shown in the diagram opposite.

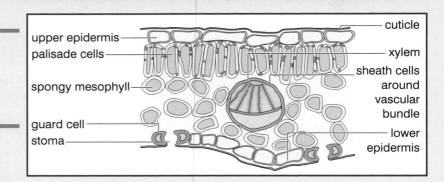

Adaptation

lots of chloroplasts

chloroplasts are arranged in the cell so that they are nearer to the leaf surface

How this makes the cell better at its job

allows more photosynthesis to take place

chloroplasts are exposed to a high light intensity

Check yourself

QUESTIONS

Q1 Why are there many different types of cell?

Q2 Complete the labels on the diagram of a sperm cell below. Explain how a sperm cell is well adapted to its function.

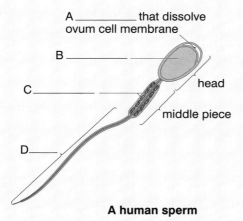

A _____ that dissolve
ovum cell membrane

B _____

C _____

head

middle piece

D _____

A human sperm

Q3 Describe two ways in which root hair cells and palisade cells are adapted to fulfil their particular functions.

ANSWERS & TUTORIALS

A1 There are many different types of cell because each cell type has a different job to do.

A2 A enzymes
B nucleus
C mitochondria
D tail

- the **tail** allows the sperm to swim from the vagina to the Fallopian tube;
- the **nucleus** contains half the genetic information that joins with the ovum's half nucleus to form a full nucleus;
- **enzymes** on the head of the sperm dissolve the ovum membrane;
- **mitochondria** provide energy for swimming.

T2 Check the diagram on page 125 if you are not sure about the parts of this specialised cell.

A3

Cell	Adaptations
root hair cell	no waxy cuticle layer
	long hair-like projections from the body of the cell
palisade cell	many chloroplasts
	chloroplasts near to the upper surface of the leaf

T3 Make sure you are clear which sort of cell you are considering. If you are given a diagram of a cell, look at it carefully, its shape and structure will give you clues about its function and how its structure best enables it to perform that function.

Chapter 30

Respiration

What you should already know

☐ The appropriate scientific terminology to use when describing life processes such as respiration.

☐ How to use word equations to summarise chemical reactions.

What you need to know

Living organisms and energy

All living organisms need energy. Animals need energy for the following reasons:

- so that they can move about;
- for growth;
- to make specialised cells for reproduction;
- in some cases, to keep their body at a constant temperature.

Plants need energy for the following reasons:

- to make their (slow) movements;
- for growth;
- to make specialised reproductive cells;
- to take minerals up from the soil.

Living organisms get their energy from food. Getting energy from food is called **respiration**. All living things do this, and we say that they **respire**. Animals eat other animals or plants to get their food. Plants produce the carbohydrate needed for respiration during the process of photosynthesis (see chapter 21).

Food is a store of chemical energy. Different types of food have different amounts of energy stored inside them.

1 g fat gives about	38 kJ of energy
1 g carbohydrate (sugars and starch) gives about	17 kJ of energy
1 g protein gives about	17 kJ of energy

fat　　　　*carbohydrate*　　　　*protein*

Proteins are not usually used to provide energy. Living organisms normally use carbohydrates to provide energy because it is easier to release energy from carbohydrates than proteins. Living things also use fat, which contains more energy per gram than either of the other two types of food.

Getting energy from food

Respiration takes place inside living cells. It happens inside tiny specialised parts of the cell called **mitochondria** (see chapter 29, *Specialised cells*). The food is usually made to react with oxygen, releasing energy and some waste substances. The waste materials are carbon dioxide and water.

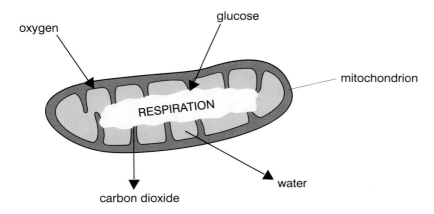

Mitochondria carry out respiration most efficiently when food is in the form of glucose, so foods are normally changed into glucose before the cell uses them in respiration. This type of respiration is called **aerobic respiration**, because it uses oxygen from the air. We can write a word equation to summarise aerobic respiration:

$$\text{glucose} + \text{oxygen} \xrightarrow{\text{energy is released}} \text{carbon dioxide} + \text{water}$$

The full chemical symbol equation is:

$$C_6H_{12}O_6 + 6O_2 \xrightarrow{\text{energy is released}} 6CO_2 + 6H_2O$$

Aerobic respiration is an example of an **oxidation reaction** (you will deal with this in more depth in chapter 42). The cell oxidises glucose producing carbon dioxide and water whilst releasing energy.

To get oxygen to their cells, many animals breathe air into their lungs. The blood then carries oxygen from the lungs to the living cells.

The digestive system breaks down food and the intestines absorb the digested food into the blood. The blood then carries digested food to the cells. It is the blood that brings the oxygen and glucose to the cells so that respiration can take place.

Check yourself

ANSWERS & TUTORIALS

A1 **Respiration is the release of energy from food (getting energy from food).**

T1 Respiration is not breathing – it is getting energy from food. Some people call breathing 'external respiration'. It is less confusing if we call breathing 'breathing' and just use the word respiration to mean releasing energy from food.

A2 **Animals need energy to move, for growth, and reproduction. Some animals use energy to keep their body at a constant temperature. Plants need energy for growth, reproduction and for taking up some minerals from the soil.**

T2 Plants also need energy for movement, although some plant movement is a kind of fast growth. Animals and plants do not need energy for respiration. Respiration is the way that living things get their energy.

A3 **Aerobic respiration**

energy is released

glucose + oxygen $\longrightarrow$ carbon dioxide + water

T3 Remember that aerobic respiration always uses oxygen and makes carbon dioxide and water as waste products.

QUESTIONS

Q1 **What is respiration?**

Q2 **Copy and complete this paragraph:**

Animals need energy to m_____ , for g_____ and for r_____ . Some animals use energy to keep their body at a constant t_____ . Plants need energy for g_____ , r_____ and for taking up some m_____ from the soil.

Q3 **Write down the word equations for aerobic respiration.**

Chapter 31

Symbols and Formulae

What you should already know

- ☐ Matter is made up of particles.
- ☐ Elements consist of atoms.
- ☐ Some elements combine through chemical reactions to form compounds.

What you need to know

Chemical elements can be represented by symbols and chemical compounds can be represented by formulae. There are 92 naturally occurring elements and more than a dozen other elements that have been made by people in laboratories. Each element has its own symbol which is a shorter way of writing its name. The periodic table shows all of the elements that exist, using the symbol to represent each one. The periodic table is organised so that the elements belonging to 'chemical families' are shown close to each other. Elements in families have some properties in common.

Groups: 1, 2, 3, 4, 5, 6, 7, 0

Period																		
1	1 H hydrogen																	2 He helium
2	3 Li lithium	4 Be beryllium											5 B boron	6 C carbon	7 N nitrogen	8 O oxygen	9 F fluorine	10 Ne neon
3	11 Na sodium	12 Mg magnesium											13 Al aluminium	14 Si silicon	15 P phosphorus	16 S sulphur	17 Cl chlorine	18 Ar argon
4	19 K potassium	20 Ca calcium	21 Sc scandium	22 Ti titanium	23 V vanadium	24 Cr chromium	25 Mn manganese	26 Fe iron	27 Co cobalt	28 Ni nickel	29 Cu copper	30 Zn zinc	31 Ga gallium	32 Ge germanium	33 As arsenic	34 Se selenium	35 Br bromine	36 Kr krypton
5	37 Rb rubidium	38 Sr strontium	39 Y yttrium	40 Zr zirconium	41 Nb niobium	42 Mo molybdenum	43 Tc technetium	44 Ru ruthenium	45 Rh rhodium	46 Pd palladium	47 Ag silver	48 Cd cadmium	49 In indium	50 Sn tin	51 Sb antimony	52 Te tellurium	53 I iodine	54 Xe xenon
6	55 Cs caesium	56 Ba barium	57 La lanthanum	72 Hf hafnium	73 Ta tantalum	74 W tungsten	75 Re rhenium	76 Os osmium	77 Ir iridium	78 Pt platinum	79 Au gold	80 Hg mercury	81 Tl thallium	82 Pb lead	83 Bi bismuth	84 Po polonium	85 At astatine	86 Rn radon
7	87 Fr francium	88 Ra radium	89 Ac actinium	104 Db dubnium	105 Jl joliotium	106 Rf rutherfordium	107 Bh bohrium	108 Hn hahnium	109 Mt meitnerium									

Lanthanides:

58 Ce cerium	59 Pr praseodymium	60 Nd neodymium	61 Pm promethium	62 Sm samarium	63 Eu europium	64 Gd gadolinium	65 Tb terbium	66 Dy dysprosium	67 Ho holmium	68 Er erbium	69 Tm thulium	70 Yb ytterbium	71 Lu lutetium
90 Th thorium	91 Pa protactinium	92 U uranium	93 Np neptunium	94 Pu plutonium	95 Am americium	96 Cm curium	97 Bk berkelium	98 Cf californium	99 Es einsteinium	100 Fm fermium	101 Md mendelevium	102 No nobelium	103 Lr lawrencium

Key: metal | non metal | atomic no. / symbol / name

You do not need to know the symbols of all of the elements in the periodic table but you need to be familiar with the symbols of the most common elements. The table at the top of the next page gives the names and symbols for the elements that you are likely to come across in Key Stage 3.

Symbols and Formulae

Metals		Non-metals	
Name	**Symbol**	**Name**	**Symbol**
sodium	Na	hydrogen	H
magnesium	Mg	helium	He
aluminium	Al	carbon	C
potassium	K	nitrogen	N
calcium	Ca	oxygen	O
iron	Fe	neon	Ne
copper	Cu	silicon	Si
zinc	Zn	sulphur	S
silver	Ag	chlorine	Cl
gold	Au	argon	Ar
lead	Pb		

Writing chemical formulae

When two or more atoms are joined together by chemical bonds they form a **molecule**. A molecule can be formed by a combination of different elements or by a combination of the same type of atom. A **formula** states what elements are present in the molecule and how many of each there are.

The formula that most people learn first is that of water, H_2O. This tells you it contains the elements hydrogen H and oxygen O and that there are two hydrogen atoms for every one oxygen atom. The number of atoms of each type is given by the small number that follows it, so H for hydrogen followed by a 2 tells us that there are two hydrogen atoms. The oxygen does not have a number after it so there is only one atom present. No other element is written in the formula, so the molecule only contains these two elements.

The formula for sodium chloride is NaCl. This means that for every sodium atom present, there is one chlorine atom present.

The table below gives some more examples. If there is a metal atom in the compound, it is usually the first symbol to be written.

Formula	Elements	Name
$MgCl_2$	Mg × 1 ; Cl × 2	magnesium chloride
Na_2O	Na × 2 ; O × 1	sodium oxide
Al_2O_3	Al × 2 ; O × 3	aluminium oxide
$CuSO_4$	Cu × 1 ; S × 1 ; O × 4	copper sulphate
Cl_2	Cl × 2	chlorine (molecule)

Sometimes a bracket is used in a formula. This means that everything inside the bracket is multiplied by the number to the right of the bracket. This is shown by the formula for calcium hydroxide, $Ca(OH)_2$. It shows that for every calcium atom, two oxygen atoms and two hydrogen atoms are present. Another example is aluminium hydroxide, $Al(OH)_3$. For every aluminium atom, there are three oxygen atoms and three hydrogen atoms.

If there are numbers inside and outside the bracket you just follow both rules – you must multiply the number of each type of atom inside the brackets by the number outside the brackets to get the total number of each atom. For example, $Ca(NO_3)_2$ contains one calcium atom for every two nitrogen atoms and six oxygen atoms.

Acids are important chemical compounds and they all contain hydrogen. The three most common laboratory acids are:

hydrochloric acid	HCl
sulphuric acid	H_2SO_4
nitric acid	HNO_3

Acids react with bases, which are oxides or hydroxides. Two examples are:

copper oxide	CuO
sodium hydroxide	NaOH

Acids will also react with carbonates. All carbonates contain the CO_3 group. Two examples are:

potassium carbonate	K_2CO_3
calcium carbonate	$CaCO_3$

A formula for a molecule shows that it has a fixed number of each atom that makes up the compound. The formula never changes even if you make the compound in different ways. You can make copper oxide by heating copper carbonate, or you can make it by heating copper in oxygen. It has the formula CuO no matter which method is used to produce it.

Check yourself

ANSWERS & TUTORIALS

A1

Elements	Compounds
Na	NaCl
O_2	$Ca(OH)_2$
Al	Al_2O_3
N_2	H_2O
Ne	H_2SO_4
	HCl

T1 In an element, all the atoms are identical. NaCl, $Ca(OH)_2$, Al_2O_3, H_2O, H_2SO_4 and HCl are compounds because they contain different atoms joined together.

Na, Al and Ne are just symbols. A symbol only represents **one** atom. A formula contains more than one atom. It does not matter whether they are the same or not. O_2, NaCl, $Ca(OH)_2$, Al_2O_3, H_2O, N_2, H_2SO_4 and HCl all have more than one atom in them. In O_2, there are 2 oxygen atoms (the same type) so it is a formula for an element. In NaCl, there is a sodium atom and a chlorine atom (different types) so it is a formula for a compound.

A2 a H_2O
       b H_2SO_4

T2 a To show two hydrogen atoms in the molecule, write a small 2 after the H. To represent the oxygen atom, just write O.
      b Write a small 2 after the hydrogen to show that there are two hydrogen atoms. To represent one sulphur atom, just write S. A 4 after the O shows that there are four oxygen atoms.

QUESTIONS

Q1 Construct a table and sort these substances into either elements or compounds:
Na O_2 NaCl $Ca(OH)_2$ Al Al_2O_3
H_2O N_2 H_2SO_4 HCl   Ne

Q2 Write the correct chemical formulae for the following:
a water, a molecule that contains 2 hydrogen atoms for every 1 oxygen atom;
b sulphuric acid, which contains 2 hydrogen atoms for every 1 sulphur atom and 4 oxygen atoms;

QUESTIONS

Q2 Write the correct chemical formulae for the following:

c   sodium carbonate, which contains 2 sodium atoms for every 1 carbon atom and 3 oxygen atoms;

d   calcium hydroxide, which contains 1 calcium atom for every 2 pairs of 1 oxygen and 1 hydrogen;

e   ethane, a molecule that contains 2 carbon atoms and 6 hydrogen atoms.

Q3 How many atoms of each element are there in the formulae of the following compounds?

a SO_2
b Fe_2O_3
c CH_4
d $Zn(NO_3)_2$
e $(NH_4)_2SO_4$

ANSWERS & TUTORIALS

A2 c Na_2CO_3
d $Ca(OH)_2$
e C_2H_6

T2 d   This example has a hydroxide group, which we write as OH. Because there are two hydroxide groups put brackets around the OH and write the number 2 after the brackets $(OH)_2$. Calcium is a metal, so write Ca before $(OH)_2$.

A3 a   1 sulphur atom and 2 oxygen atoms;
b   2 iron atoms and 3 oxygen atoms;
c   1 carbon atom and 4 hydrogen atoms;
d   1 zinc atom, 2 nitrogen atoms and 6 oxygen atoms;
e   2 nitrogen atoms, 8 hydrogen atoms, 1 sulphur atom and 4 oxygen atoms.

T3 a   The number that tells you how many atoms there are in the compound is written after the atom, so SO_2 means 2 oxygen atoms. If no number is given then there is one atom present, so in this formula there is 1 sulphur atom.

b   In this example, there is a 2 after the Fe and a 3 after the O. This means that there are 2 iron atoms in the compound for every 3 oxygen atoms.

d   When a bracket is used, everything in the bracket is multiplied by the number after it. For $Zn(NO_3)_2$, there are two groups of NO_3, so for every zinc atom there are two nitrogen atoms and six oxygen atoms.

e   This is similar to part d except that the bracket is around the first group of atoms. $(NH_4)_2SO_4$ can be written out as $NH_4 + NH_4 + SO_4$. This gives 2 nitrogen atoms and 8 hydrogen atoms (from the two NH_4 groups) for every 1 sulphur atom and 4 oxygen atoms.

Chapter 32

LEVEL 7
PHYSICAL PROCESSES

Weathering

What you should already know

- ☐ There are similarities between some chemical reactions.
- ☐ Changes of state are related to energy transfers.
- ☐ Materials expand and contract with changes in temperature.

What you need to know

Weathering is the process by which rocks on the surface of the Earth are broken down by the action of 'atmospheric agents'. Some of the agents are **physical**, such as the effect of frost damage. Other agents are **chemical**, such as the effect of a weak acid on some kinds of rocks.

Physical weathering of rocks

Physical weathering is the process that breaks down larger pieces of rock into smaller ones, eventually leading to the formation of sediment. Expansion and contraction play an important part in the physical weathering of rocks. Rocks in very hot places such as deserts can be weathered by the repeated expansion and contraction of the rock. This happens because of the extreme changes in temperature between day and night. Rocks that have expanded during the day because of the high temperatures experience a large and sudden drop in temperature when the Sun goes down. The resulting rapid contraction creates forces in the rock which lead to it fracturing and breaking up. This happens every day, causing the rocks to break down into smaller and smaller pieces.

Most materials contract when they change from a liquid to a solid. Water is an exception. The expansion of water causes weathering of rocks. Just around its freezing point, as it forms ice, water expands. If water seeps into a crack in a rock and then freezes, the force of it expanding is so great that it can make the crack in the rock wider. If this keeps happening, part of the rock will break away.

a)
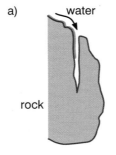
Water runs into the crack

b)
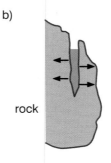
Water freezes in the crack

c)
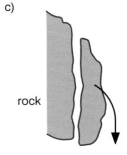
The forces produced crack the rock and the piece breaks away

Chemical weathering of rocks

Chemical weathering is the process where chemicals in the air react with a mineral in a rock. The process happens with acidic solutions and is usually associated with rainwater. All rain is slightly acidic because it dissolves carbon dioxide from the atmosphere (forming carbonic acid). This slightly acidic solution reacts with the calcium carbonate (the main component of limestone, chalk or marble) and produces calcium hydrogencarbonate:

limestone + water + carbon dioxide → calcium hydrogencarbonate
$$CaCO_3 + H_2O + CO_2 \rightarrow Ca(HCO_3)_2$$

Calcium hydrogencarbonate is soluble in water, so the rock is gradually dissolved away.

When rain falls on areas of limestone rock the reaction leads to the formation of underground caverns. Stalagmites and stalactites, like those shown below, are formed when calcium hydrogencarbonate decomposes into insoluble calcium carbonate, carbon dioxide and water.

Burning fossil fuels such as coal increases the amount of carbon dioxide in the atmosphere. In addition, impurities in the fuel lead to the production of compounds in the air such as sulphur dioxide gas. When this gas dissolves in rainwater, it forms a much stronger acid (sulphuric acid) and this is what is called 'acid rain'. The reactions of 'acid rain' with all types of rocks are much more vigorous than the effect of slightly acidic rainwater on limestone. Rocks such as limestone, chalk and marble dissolve much faster, causing serious problems to buildings in areas where there is a high level of atmospheric pollution. Acid rain can also lead to the corrosion of metals.

Check yourself

ANSWER & TUTORIALS

QUESTIONS

A1
- **Rocks can be weathered by expansion and contraction of the rock – the forces are very strong and the rock cracks and breaks apart.**
- **Water can seep into the cracks in the rocks. When it freezes to form ice, it expands. The force of expansion is so great, it can widen the crack in the rock. If this keeps happening, part of the rock will break away.**

T1 Water is unusual because when it freezes it expands. If water seeps into cracks in a rock and the temperature drops below its freezing point, the water will form ice. As it does this, it expands, causing the crack to widen. The force can be large enough to cause the rock to split completely.

A2 **Acidic rainwater attacks limestone because the rock is mainly calcium carbonate. Great amounts of fossil fuels are burned in cities for heating buildings and for transport. Sulphur dioxide, formed from the impurities, makes the rain much more acidic and more reactive. In the country, this is less of a problem because there is less pollution.**

T2 Acids are quite reactive substances and the stronger the acid, the more reactive it is. Carbon dioxide only forms a very weak acid in water, so there is very little reaction. Sulphur dioxide is an impurity from burning fossil fuels – it pollutes the atmosphere and forms a much stronger acid. It is also present in much greater amounts in a city, so the damage to limestone buildings is greater. In many cities this is a major problem, attacking the stonework of old buildings such as cathedrals.

Q1 **Describe two ways in which rock can be weathered by physical processes.**

Q2 **Limestone is a useful source of building stone, but it is affected by chemical weathering. Explain why this is a more serious problem in a city than in the countryside.**

Chapter 33

Reactivity Series

What you should already know

☐ Metals react with oxygen to form oxides.
☐ Metals react with acids and produce hydrogen.
☐ Different metals react at different rates with the same reactants.

What you need to know

Some metals are very reactive and will tarnish (lose their shine) in a few seconds when exposed to the air. The metal sodium does this. Some metals, however, such as copper and silver take a long time to tarnish when left in the same conditions. The tarnishing process occurs when the metal reacts with oxygen and forms a layer of metal oxide on the surface. It is possible to carry out a series of experiments by cleaning the surfaces of several common metals and exposing them to air. By measuring the time taken for each one to tarnish, the metals can be ranked in order of how quickly they react with oxygen in air. This gives a simple comparison of how reactive each metal is in relation to the others. This is known as a **trend in reactivity**.

Results from a wide range of chemical experiments have shown that all metals can be put into a list in the order of their reactivity. This list is called the **reactivity series**.

Sodium (top) reacts very quickly with oxygen in the air; copper reacts very slowly. Sodium is more reactive than copper.

Most reactive	potassium	K	
	sodium	Na	
	calcium	Ca	
	magnesium	Mg	
	aluminium	Al	
	carbon	C	
	zinc	Zn	increasing
	iron	Fe	reactivity
	tin	Sn	
	lead	Pb	
	hydrogen	H	
	copper	Cu	
	silver	Ag	
Least reactive	gold	Au	

This list shows the order of reactivity for the most common metals. It also includes the non-metals hydrogen and carbon because they both take part in reactions with some metals and not with others. With sufficient information, all other metals could be added to this list in the appropriate position.

We can use the reactivity series to predict what will happen in particular chemical reactions. The most reactive metal in the series is potassium. Potassium reacts violently with cold water to produce hydrogen so rapidly that it bursts into flames.

$$2K + 2H_2O \rightarrow 2KOH + H_2$$

Calcium is lower down the series, so it reacts less violently than potassium with cold water. Calcium reacts with cold water, producing a steady stream of hydrogen gas. Because of their relative positions in the reactivity series, it is possible to predict that the reaction of sodium with cold water will be quite vigorous and that the reaction of magnesium with cold water will be slower than that of calcium. This is actually the case. To get magnesium to react quickly with water it has to be heated in the presence of steam instead of cold water. The pattern in these reactions is that all the metals that do react produce hydrogen gas.

The trend in the reactions is that the higher a metal is in the reactivity series, the more vigorous its reaction is with cold water. Knowing this makes it reasonable to predict that copper will not react with cold water because of its position in the reactivity series. None of the metals lower than hydrogen will produce hydrogen in any reaction. Copper will not react with water under any conditions and that is one good reason why we can use copper for water pipes in our homes.

Predicting the reactions of metals

The metals follow the same order of reactivity for all their reactions, so now we can make predictions for the reactions of metals with other substances. We said in chapter 24, *Chemical Reactions*, that metals react with acids and produce hydrogen. For example:

$$Mg + H_2SO_4 \rightarrow MgSO_4 + H_2$$

We cannot try potassium and sodium because their reactions with acids would be too dangerous. Even calcium is very reactive with very dilute acids, but metals like zinc and iron both react steadily. The metals at the lower end of the reactivity series do not react with diluted acids at all. Using the reactivity series, we can predict that magnesium will react with an acid faster than zinc, but more slowly than calcium. Again, this is what happens.

Displacement reactions

The reaction of a metal with an acid is an example from a range of reactions called **displacement reactions**. All acids contain hydrogen and in a metal–acid reaction, the metal displaces the hydrogen from the acid. If a metal is high in the reactivity series, it will displace any element which is lower in the series. For example, magnesium displaces hydrogen from acid – hydrogen is released because it has been displaced. Copper is lower than hydrogen so it cannot displace it and copper will never react to produce hydrogen.

A metal can displace another metal from one of its compounds in solution. For example, if a piece of iron (or steel) is dipped into a solution of copper sulphate for about a minute and is then removed, it emerges from the solution coated with a thin layer of pure copper metal. This happens because iron is higher in the reactivity series than copper. Iron is more reactive so it forms compounds more readily than copper. Because some of the iron forms a compound, some of the copper must be removed from the compound – it is displaced. The copper becomes a metal and the iron forms a compound.

A metal that is higher in the reactivity series than another metal will displace the metal that is below it in the series.

We can use the difference in reactivity to make predictions about what might happen in some chemical reactions. It is reasonable to predict that:

- iron will displace lead from lead nitrate solution;
- copper will not displace magnesium from magnesium sulphate solution;
- calcium will displace zinc from zinc sulphate solution.

However, these are only predictions based on a knowledge of the reactivity series and they do not tell you anything about the reaction itself.

Check yourself

ANSWERS & TUTORIALS

A1 sodium and magnesium

T1 These are the two metals either side of calcium in the reactivity series.

A2 zinc and tin

T2 These are the two metals either side of iron in the reactivity series.

A3 silver and gold

T3 These two metals are so unreactive that they have not reacted with other elements in the environment and are therefore found almost pure in the ground.

A4
a	yes	copper
b	no	
c	no	
d	yes	silver
e	yes	iron

T4 The way to make the correct predictions is to pick out the metal which is higher in the reactivity series. A more reactive metal can displace a less reactive metal from a compound or solution of a compound. The metal that is lower in the reactivity series is the one that can be displaced, so for a displacement reaction to take place, it must be in solution to start with. If magnesium is added then all the metals below it (aluminium, zinc, iron, lead, copper, silver and gold) can be displaced from their compounds.

QUESTIONS

Use the reactivity series on page 139 to answer these questions.

Q1 Name two metals that are about as reactive as calcium.

Q2 Name two metals that are about as reactive as iron.

Q3 Which two metals are likely to be found in the ground in their pure form uncombined with any other elements?

Q4 In which of the following cases can a displacement reaction take place? Name the metals that are displaced.
a $Mg + CuSO_4$
b $Fe + MgSO_4$
c $Cu + Pb(NO_3)_2$
d $Zn + Ag(NO_3)_2$
e $Mg + FeSO_4$

Chapter 34

The Colour of Objects

What you should already know

- [ ] When white light passes through a coloured filter, the colour of light leaving the filter is the same as the colour of the filter.
- [ ] A glass prism can be used to split up (disperse) white light into a spectrum.
- [ ] The three primary colours of light are red, green and blue.
- [ ] Objects appear black because no light is reflected from them.

What you need to know

If three spotlights, each producing one of the primary colours of light, are shone onto a screen so that the areas of light overlap, then the screen will be lit with the colours shown on the right.

When two or more primary colours of light are added together they produce what is called a **secondary colour**. Cyan, magenta, yellow and white are all secondary colours of light. We can represent these combinations of colours in the following way:

Mixing light

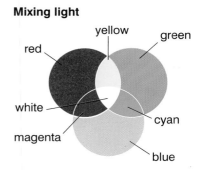

red + green = yellow

green + blue = cyan

red + blue = magenta

red + blue + green = white

When white light shines onto a blue object it looks blue. A blue object will reflect blue light. All of the other colours are absorbed.

If red light shines onto a white object, the object will look red. A white object reflects all of the light shining onto it.

A black object does not reflect any light, so no matter what colour light shines onto it, it will always look black. Black **absorbs** all colours.

When red light shines onto a blue object, it looks black. There is no blue light for the object to reflect, and the red light is absorbed.

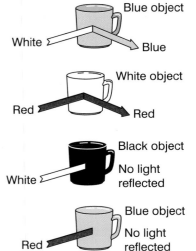

The Colour of Objects

But what happens if we shine coloured lights onto secondary colours? Look again at the chart showing what secondary colours are made up of and then look at the following combinations of coloured objects being illuminated by different colours of light.

If cyan light (made from blue and green light) shines onto a blue object, the blue light is reflected and the green light is absorbed, so the object will look blue.

A yellow object will reflect red and green light. It will look yellow when white light shines on it.

If red light shines onto a yellow object, red light is reflected, so the object looks red.

If blue light shines onto a yellow object it will look black because no light is reflected.

If green light shines onto a yellow object, green light is reflected.

Many objects are coloured using dyes that are not pure colours so if you shine different colours of light onto them they may not reflect light the way you might expect.

Check yourself

QUESTIONS

Q1 A sheet of white paper has red crosses on it. What will be seen when the paper is illuminated by:
a red light;
b magenta light?

Q2 Misha's costume for a school play consists of a red hat, a green jacket, a white scarf and magenta trousers. White, blue, yellow and red spotlights are used on the stage. Complete the table to show what colours Misha's costume will appear under the different coloured spotlights.

	White light	Blue light	Yellow light	Red light
Red hat				
Green jacket	green	black	green	black
White scarf				
Magenta trousers				

ANSWERS & TUTORIALS

A1 a Red paper with no crosses on it.
b Magenta paper with red crosses.

T1 a

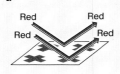

Both the white paper and the red crosses will reflect the red light. It will all look red, so the crosses will not be seen.

b

The white paper will reflect the magenta light. The crosses will reflect the red light from the magenta and absorb the blue light, so they will look red.

A2

	White light	Blue light	Yellow light	Red light
Red hat	red	black	red	red
Green jacket	green	black	green	black
White scarf	white	blue	yellow	red
Magenta trousers	magenta	blue	black	red

T2 When white light shines onto an object, the object reflects all its colours, so the colour that the object appears is its actual colour. A white object will reflect the colour of the light shining on it and so appear to be the colour of the light.
A red object will only reflect red light. If no red light shines on it, it will appear black, because no light is reflected. For the same reason, blue objects will only reflect blue light.
Magenta reflects red and blue light. If neither red or blue light shines on the trousers, they appear black.

Chapter 35

Pressure

What you should already know

☐ Surface area is measured in square metres (m^2) or square centimetres (cm^2).
☐ Objects have weight caused by gravitational attraction.
☐ Weight is a force and is measured in newtons (N).

What you need to know

It is easier to cut an onion with a sharp knife than with a blunt knife. When the knife's blade is sharp, the surface area of blade that is in contact with the onion is smaller. Even though the force you apply with each knife blade may be the same, the smaller surface area of the sharp blade means you can apply greater **pressure**.

The pressure applied to a surface will increase if:

● the applied force increases;

● the area over which the force is applied decreases.

If a person tries to walk on deep snow wearing shoes, they will sink further into the snow than someone wearing skis. When a person wears skis, their weight is spread over a larger area than for someone wearing shoes. Therefore, the pressure is low and they can move easily over the top of the snow. When a person wears shoes, their weight is spread over a much smaller area. The pressure is higher and their feet drop down through the snow as they walk.

Pressure is the force acting **normally** (at right angles) on each unit area of a particular surface. It is calculated by using the expression:

$$\text{pressure} = \frac{\text{force}}{\text{area}}$$

If the force is measured in newtons (N) and the area is in square metres (m^2) then the pressure is measured in N/m^2. This unit (newton per square metre) is also called the pascal (Pa). If the area is measured in square centimetres (cm^2), the pressure is measured in N/cm^2.

The triangle shown below can be used to help answer problems about pressure. First, cover up the part you need to find. Then read off the equation you need to use.

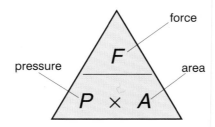

For example, to find force, cover the letter *F* with your finger. The letters that remain show you how to calculate the force.

force = pressure × area

Cover *F* to find *F* = *P* x *A*

To find area, cover the letter *A* with your finger. Now, read off what remains:

area = $\dfrac{\text{force}}{\text{pressure}}$

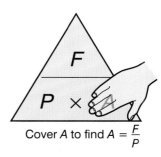

Cover *A* to find *A* = $\dfrac{F}{P}$

To find pressure, cover the letter *P* with your finger and what is left shows you how to calculate pressure:

pressure = $\dfrac{\text{force}}{\text{area}}$

Cover *P* to find *P* = $\dfrac{F}{A}$

Examples of calculating pressure

Consider a paving slab that is 40 cm long, 50 cm wide, 5 cm deep and weighs 200 N.

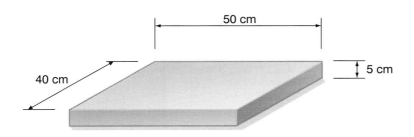

There are three different ways of storing this size of slab, each with a different surface in contact with the ground:

a flat on a 40 cm × 50 cm face   (surface area = 40 cm × 50 cm = 2000 cm^2)

b on its longer side, 50 cm × 5 cm   (surface area = 50 cm × 5 cm = 250 cm^2)

c on its shorter side, 40 cm × 5 cm   (surface area = 40 cm × 5 cm = 200 cm^2)

The pressure applied to the ground in each of these situations is different:

In **a**, $\text{pressure} = \dfrac{\text{force}}{\text{area}} = \dfrac{200\,\text{N}}{2000\,\text{cm}^2} = 0.1\,\text{N/cm}^2$

In **b**, $\text{pressure} = \dfrac{\text{force}}{\text{area}} = \dfrac{200\,\text{N}}{250\,\text{cm}^2} = 0.8\,\text{N/cm}^2$

In **c**, $\text{pressure} = \dfrac{\text{force}}{\text{area}} = \dfrac{200\,\text{N}}{200\,\text{cm}^2} = 1\,\text{N/cm}^2$

The smaller the area of slab in contact with the ground, the higher the pressure it exerts.

Check yourself

ANSWERS & TUTORIALS

A1 $\text{pressure} = \dfrac{\text{force}}{\text{area}} = \dfrac{300\,\text{N}}{6\,\text{m}^2} = 50\,\text{N/m}^2 \text{ (or Pa)}$

T1 Remember that the weight of an object is its force due to gravity.

Always write down the equation you are using and show all your working – even if you end up with the wrong answer you will get some marks if your working is correct.

Do not forget to give the units – you will lose marks if you miss them out.

A2 **Wide tyres will stop the tractor from sinking into the mud. The area in contact with the ground is large, so the pressure on the ground is lower than if it had thin tyres.**

T2 Always comment on what effect the area has on the pressure.

QUESTIONS

Q1 What pressure is applied to the ground when a box which has a weight of 300 N stands on an end that has an area of 6 m²?

Q2 Why does a tractor have very wide tyres?

QUESTIONS

Q3

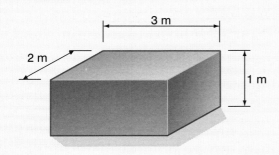

The above box weighs 30 N and is to be placed onto some sand.

a What is the largest pressure it could exert on the sand?

b What is the smallest pressure it could exert on the sand?

c Will the box sink further into the sand when it is placed as in (a) or as in (b)?

Q4

Chris and his snow board weigh a total of 600 N. The snow board has an area of 3000 cm^2.

a What is the total force exerted on the snow by Chris and his snow board?

b Calculate the pressure exerted by the snow board on the snow when the snowboard is flat. Give the unit.

c When Chris carries his snow board, his pressure on the snow is six times greater than when he is snow boarding. Explain why.

ANSWERS & TUTORIALS

A3

a The largest pressure is exerted when the surface area in contact with the sand is smallest (1 m × 2 m = 2 m^2):

$$\text{pressure} = \frac{\text{force}}{\text{area}} = \frac{30\,\text{N}}{2\,\text{m}^2} = 15\,\text{Pa}$$

b The smallest pressure is exerted when the surface area in contact with the sand is largest (2 m × 3 m = 6 m^2):

$$\text{pressure} = \frac{\text{force}}{\text{area}} = \frac{30\,\text{N}}{6\,\text{m}^2} = 5\,\text{Pa}$$

c (a)

T3 Remember to show working and give units.

When the box is placed on its smallest side, the pressure will be greatest. The box will sink further into the sand when the pressure is 15 Pa, as in part (a).

A4

a 600 N

b $\text{pressure} = \dfrac{\text{force}}{\text{area}} = \dfrac{600}{3000} = 0.2\,\text{N/cm}^2$

c Chris' feet have a much smaller area in contact with the snow than when he is on the snow board.

T4

a This is the force due to the weight of Chris and his snow board.

b The area is given in cm^2 so make sure that the pressure is in N/cm^2.

c The weight of Chris and his snow board does not change, but the pressure exerted by his feet is six times the pressure of when he is on the snow board. Therefore, the area of the snow board must be six times bigger than the combined area of Chris' feet. The area of his feet is one sixth of 3000 cm^2 (500 cm^2 total or 250 cm^2 each).

Chapter 36

LEVEL 7
PHYSICAL PROCESSES

Electromagnets

What you should already know

- ☐ Magnetic fields are regions of space where magnetic materials experience forces of magnetic attraction.
- ☐ The shape of the magnetic field pattern produced by a bar magnet.
- ☐ An electric current is a flow of charge around an electrical circuit.

What you need to know

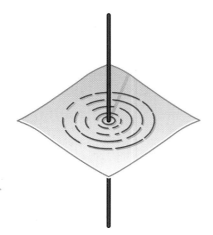

When an electrical current flows through a wire, a magnetic field is produced around the wire. This can be demonstrated by passing a single wire, at right angles, through a horizontal piece of card. With the current switched on, iron filings are spread across the card. By tapping the card gently, the shape of the magnetic field produced becomes visible (as shown in the margin).

When an electric current flows through a coil of wire, the weak magnetic field can be concentrated so that the coil behaves like a bar magnet. The magnetic field around the coil can be represented by the pattern shown in the diagram below.

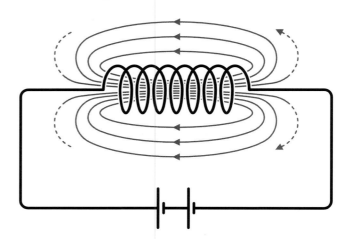

If the current flowing in the coil is reversed, the direction of the magnetic field is also reversed.

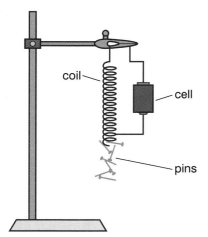

When this current is switched on, the coil can be used to pick up small objects such as pins. The number of pins the coil picks up depends on its strength. The magnetic effect of the coil can be increased by:

- making more turns in the coil;
- increasing the size of the current flowing through the coil;
- placing an iron core inside the coil.

Increasing the number of turns in the coil increases the number of sections of wire. The field around each of the turns contributes to the total magnetic effect of the coil.

Increasing the size of the current through the coil increases the strength of the magnetic field around each length of the coil wire. Placing an iron core inside the coil concentrates the magnetic field into this magnetic material, increasing the overall magnetic effect of the coil.

All commercial electromagnets have a soft iron core. Soft iron is magnetic but, unlike steel, does not become permanently magnetised when surrounded by the coil of the electromagnet. Using soft iron makes it possible to switch the electromagnet off.

Electromagnets have many different uses. The current can be adjusted to change the strength (or attractive force) of the magnet. They can be used in electric bells and relays. A relay is a switch that uses a small change in current to control another circuit. Doctors can use electromagnets to remove steel splinters from a person's eye. Another use is in circuit breakers.

A circuit breaker using an electromagnet

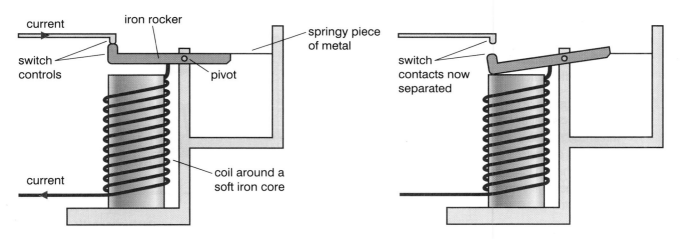

A circuit breaker is a safety switch that opens when the current in a circuit becomes too large. Look at the diagram.

1 The springy piece of metal holds the iron rocker in place so that the switch contacts are together.

2 The coil becomes an electromagnet when a current passes through it.

3 If the current becomes too large, the electromagnet becomes strong enough to overcome the force of the springy piece of metal, and the left-hand side of the iron rocker moves down towards the coil.

4 The switch contacts open and the current can no longer flow, so the components in the circuit are protected.

3. Hydrogencarbonate indicator solution changes colour when the amount of carbon dioxide dissolved in it changes. This is shown in the table.

colour of indicator solution	amount of dissolved carbon dioxide
reddish orange	same amount of carbon dioxide as in the air
yellow	more carbon dioxide than in the air
purple	less carbon dioxide than in the air

Five test tubes were set up as shown below. Air was bubbled through hydrogencarbonate indicator solution, which was then poured into each test tube.

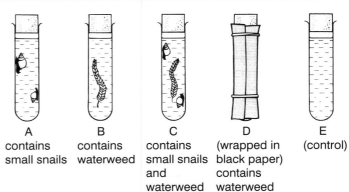

A	B	C	D	E
contains small snails	contains waterweed	contains small snails and waterweed	(wrapped in black paper) contains waterweed	(control)

The test tubes were left in sunlight for two hours.

(a) (i) What would be the colour of the indicator solution in tube A? _____ *1 mark*

    (ii) Name the process taking place in the cells of the snails which causes this colour change. _____ *1 mark*

(b) (i) What would be the colour of the indicator solution in tube B? _____ *1 mark*

    (ii) Name the process taking place in the cells of the waterweed which causes this colour change. _____ *1 mark*

(c) The colour of the indicator solution in tube C did not change.
Explain why. _____ *1 mark*
Tube D is wrapped to keep the light out. It contains waterweed but no snails.

(d) After twenty four hours in the dark what would be the colour of the indicator solution in tube D? Tick the correct box. *1 mark*

    reddish orange ☐   yellow ☐   purple ☐

4. The drawings show five types of plant and animal cell.

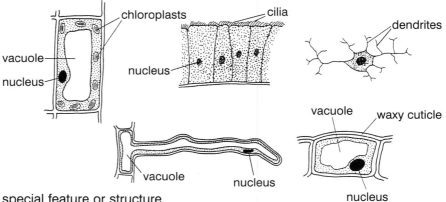

Each cell has a special feature or structure.

Draw a line to join each feature or structure to its function.
One has been done for you.

4 marks

feature or structure	function
large surface area	to remove particles from windpipe
chloroplasts	to carry nerve pulses
waxy cuticle	to absorb water from soil
cilia	to make food by photosynthesis
dendrites	to reduce water loss

5. Air is a gas at room temperature. The chemical formulae below show some of the substances in the air.

Ar CO_2 H_2O N_2 Ne O_2

table A

element	compound

table B

atom	molecule

(a) Put these formulae in the correct columns in table A to show which substances are elements and which are compounds. *1 mark*

(b) Put the formulae in the correct columns in table B to show whether the formula of each substance represents an atom or a molecule. *1 mark*

(c) The coldest possible temperature is 'absolute zero', which is –273°C. As air is cooled towards absolute zero it liquefies. Table C gives the boiling points of the substances in air.
A sample of air at a temperature close to absolute zero is allowed to warm up. Which substance boils first? *1 mark*

_____

(d) Each particle of neon can be represented by a circle.
Carefully complete the diagrams below to show the arrangement of particles in neon gas and liquid neon. Use circles about ◯ in size. *4 marks*

table C

formula	boiling point in °C
Ar	–186
CO_2	–78
H_2O	100
N_2	–196
Ne	–246
O_2	–183

neon gas, Ne

liquid neon, Ne

6. Sandstone can be 'weathered' by doing the following each day for one week.
1. Soak the sandstone in water.
2. Place it in a freezer overnight.
3. Take it out of the freezer each morning.
(a) Explain how this freezing and thawing 'weathers' the sandstone.   *2 marks*
_____
_____

(b) Weathering of rock may be caused by **physical** processes or **chemical** processes.
  (i) The process in part (a) is a physical process which weathers rock.
  Describe **another** physical process which occurs naturally and explain how it
  weathers rock. _____ *2 marks*
  _____

  (ii) Name a chemical process which occurs outdoors and explain how it weathers rocks
  and buildings. _____   *1 mark*
  _____ *2 marks*

7. Aluminium and tin-plated steel are used to make cans for food and soft drinks.
The table below shows the pH values of some soft drinks and cooked foods.

drinks and foods	pH value
cola	2.0
lemonade	3.0
rhubarb	3.0
beef	7.0

(a) Cans were first used about 150 years ago to store food for soldiers. The cans were made
from unplated steel. The soldiers found that beef kept in steel cans was still good to eat
after many months. However they found that steel cans of rhubarb bulged, and when the
cans of rhubarb were opened a gas escaped.
  (i) Why were the steel cans **not** suitable for storing rhubarb? _____ *1 mark*
  _____

  (ii) Name the gas that formed in the cans of rhubarb.   *1 mark*
  Part of the reactivity series is given below.

> magnesium
> aluminium
> zinc
> iron (steel)
> tin
> copper
> silver

(b) In modern 'tin cans' the steel is covered with a thin layer of tin.
  (i) Use the reactivity series to explain why 'tin cans' are better than steel cans for storing
  food. _____ *1 mark*
  (ii) When 'tin cans' are dented, the layer of tin often cracks. What reaction might happen
  when the layer of tin is cracked? _____ *1 mark*
(c) Many drink cans are now made of aluminium. Given the information in the reactivity
series, why is this surprising? _____ *1 mark*

8. The drawings show a skier in **two** different situations.

The girl and her skis weigh a total of 600 N.

The area of contact between the skis and the snow is 2000 cm².

(a) Calculate the pressure exerted by the skis on the snow. Give the correct unit.   *2 marks*

_____

(b) When the girl carries her skis, her feet exert a pressure on the snow.
This pressure is **five** times as great as when she is skiing. Explain why.   *1 mark*

_____

9 A white box of photographic paper has written on it, in large red letters:

WARNING: OPEN ONLY BY THE LIGHT OF A RED SAFELIGHT

(a) The box of paper is in a photographic darkroom where the only light is from a **red** lamp.
  (i) What colour does the white box appear? _____ *1 mark*
  (ii) What colour does the red writing appear?_____ *1 mark*
(b) The red lamp is now switched off and a green lamp is switched on.
  (i) What colour does the red writing appear in green light?_____ *1 mark*
  (ii) Explain why the writing appears to be this colour.

_____ *1 mark*

10. A pupil fixes a small electromagnet close to a thin springy steel sheet. The device acts like a small speaker. She connects a battery and switch to the electromagnet as shown.

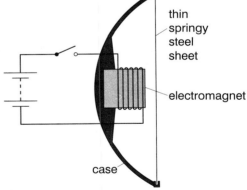

thin
springy
steel
sheet

electromagnet

case

(a) (i) When the pupil closes the switch, what will happen to the steel sheet?   *1 mark*

_____

  (ii) The pupil opens the switch again. What will happen to the steel sheet now?   *1 mark*

_____

  (iii) If the pupil had connected the battery the other way round, what difference would this have made to your answer to part (i)?   *1 mark*

_____

(b) The pupil removes the battery and switch. She connects the electromagnet to a power supply which switches the current on and off 1000 times each second. The steel sheet vibrates and makes a sound.
  (i) She then adjusts the power supply so that the current is switched on and off 3000 times each second. What difference does this make to the pitch of the sound? Give a reason for your answer. _____

_____ *2 marks*

  (ii) The pupil now adjusts the power supply so that the current is larger. Explain why this makes the sound louder.

_____ *1 mark*

Chapter 37

LEVEL 8
LIFE PROCESSES AND
LIVING THINGS

Inheritance

What you should already know

☐ There are variations of characteristics between individuals.
☐ Some features of individuals are inherited and other features can be affected by environmental factors.

What you need to know

Children look like one of their parents or a mixture of both. They inherit features, such as eye colour and nose shape, from their parents.

Chromosomes and genes

The instructions for inherited features are carried by a chemical called **deoxyribonucleic acid** (DNA), found inside the nucleus of every cell. The DNA is arranged into coils called **chromosomes**. All human cells, except sex cells, contain 46 chromosomes. The chromosomes pair up in the nucleus, so that we see 23 pairs of chromosomes. Sex cells carry only one chromosome from each pair, so they have 23 chromosomes.

Along each chromosome are sets of information called **genes**. Each gene contains the information needed to make one tiny part of a human.

When an egg cell is **fertilised** by a sperm, the chromosomes from the sperm nucleus pair up with the chromosomes in the egg nucleus. Half of the chromosomes in a fetus' cells are inherited from its father and half from its mother.

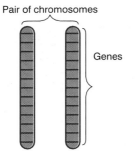

Pair of chromosomes

Genes

Inheritance

A gene carries the information for one tiny body part, but we actually have two copies of each gene – one copy on each of a pair of chromosomes. Both genes contain the information needed to make the body part. The instructions in each gene can be identical or they can be slightly different because one version comes from the father and one from the mother. For example, there are several versions of the eye colour gene – one version makes brown eyes, another version may make blue eyes.

A fetus could inherit a gene for brown eyes from its father and a gene for blue eyes from its mother. But what colour eyes will the baby have? The answer is brown eyes. This is because some versions of genes, such as the gene for brown eyes, are more 'powerful' than others. We say that the gene for brown eyes is **dominant**. You can't see the effect of the gene for blue eyes, so we say that it is **recessive**.

Genes carried by parents   father **BB**   **bb** mother

Genes in sex cells   **B**   **B**   b   b

Possible combinations of genes in the fetus   **Bb**   **Bb**   **Bb**   **Bb**

This diagram shows the combinations of genes that are possible at fertilisation. It is called a **genetic cross diagram**. We show the gene for brown eyes as B (capital letters are used to show dominant genes) and the gene for blue eyes is shown as b (lower case letters are used to show recessive genes). All the possible combinations have a gene for brown eyes and a gene for blue eyes so they would all produce brown-eyed babies. The combination of genes in an individual is called the **genotype**.

Selective breeding

A few thousand years ago all apples were similar to today's wild crab apples. Also, the sheep of the world looked more like the semi-wild Soay sheep than today's Merino, which produces a thick fleece of wool. A few thousand years is not long enough for new varieties – such as the cox apple and Merino sheep – to have developed naturally. So, how has it happened?

More than 2000 years ago, in the area around Turkey and its neighbouring countries, the local semi-wild sheep were being changed by farmers. They were being changed from a sheep similar to the Soay, that had a fleece of both hair and wool, to a sheep that had a lot more fine wool and less hair. The farmers did this by looking at their sheep and choosing the ram (male) and ewe (female) with the best wool and getting them to breed. Their lambs then had more fine wool than the wild sheep. From these **offspring**, the ram and the ewe that had the best quality wool would be chosen to breed from. This happened with each new generation, so over many years the breed was changed to produce a sheep with an enormous fleece of high quality wool.

Selective breeding has been used to produce apples such as the Cox (left), which are tastier and larger than crab apples (right)

This is called **selective breeding**. Selective breeding is also how wild apples like the crab apple were changed over hundreds of years into varieties of apple like the ones we buy today. Apple growers decided what features they wanted in their apples and then chose the plants with those features to breed from.

The same is true of all farm animals and crops that farmers produce today. Features such as high milk production in cows and disease resistance in tomatoes are also often selected.

Check yourself

ANSWER & TUTORIALS

A1 a 46
     b 23
     c genes

T1 a Every human body cell except the sex cells contains 46 chromosomes.
     b The sex cells are the sperm and egg cells that are specialised for reproduction. They contain only 23 chromosomes (half the usual number), the full 46 being made up when the sperm joins the egg at fertilisation.
     c Chromosomes are made up of hundreds of genes. It is the genes that control the passing on or inheritance of features such as hair or eye colour, blood group, nose shape and so on.

QUESTIONS

Q1 a How many chromosomes are there in a normal human body cell?
     b How many chromosomes are there in a human sex cell?
     c What do we call the regions on the chromosomes that control inherited features such as hair colour?

QUESTIONS

Q2 a What is meant by selective breeding?
 b What features might dairy farmers select to improve their herd of dairy cattle?

Q3 a Draw a genetic cross diagram to show the result of a cross between a blonde-haired woman and a black-haired man. H is the dominant gene for black hair and h is the recessive gene for blonde hair. The man's genotype is Hh.
 b What is the chance of these parents having a baby with blonde hair?

ANSWER & TUTORIALS

A2 a Selective breeding is the deliberate selection of certain parent plants or animals for breeding to produce offspring that are better suited for specific human needs.
 b Dairy farmers might select for their cows to:
  ● produce a larger volume of milk;
  ● produce less fatty milk;
  ● produce more creamy (fatty) milk;
  ● have a mild temperament;
  ● be able to resist diseases;
  ● not have horns;
  ● produce more milk on restricted diets.

T2 What the breeder chooses to select for depends on what the customer really wants.

People used to pay more for creamy milk with a high fat content, so dairy farmers bred their cows to produce milk with a higher fat content. Now, with increased thinking on health, supermarkets sell much more skimmed and semi-skimmed milk with a low fat content. The challenge for farmers now is to get their dairy herd to produce milk with a lower fat content.

A3 parents genes

genes in the sex cells

possible combinations of the genes carried in sex cells

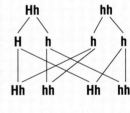

 b There is a 50% (1 in 2) chance of these parents having a blonde haired baby. Of the four possible combinations of genes, two are hh, which means that these babies will have blonde hair.

T3 As can be seen in the diagram, half of the babies would have the genotype Hh (black haired) and half would have the genotype hh (blonde haired).

Chapter 38

Cell Structure and Life Processes

What you should already know

☐ Cells are adapted to their functions.
☐ An explanation of how cell structure relates to these adaptations.
☐ The main underlying chemical changes in the process of respiration.
☐ The particle theory of matter can be used to explain the process of diffusion.

What you need to know

The structure of the cell membrane provides a good example of how the cellular structure of a particular organ is related to its associated life process.

Cell membrane structure

The cell membrane is the outer 'skin' of the cell, which allows some things to pass in and out of the cell but not others. At its simplest level, the cell membrane is drawn as a thin line that indicates the outside limit of a cell (see chapter 20, *Cell structure*). This is how it appears under an optical microscope. However, there must be something about the cell membrane that allows it to have some level of control over what passes into and out of the cell – the cell membrane cannot just be a solid wall.

The cell membrane is actually composed of a complicated arrangement of fat and protein. You do not need to know the precise structure of the membrane, but you do need to understand its physical properties.

At this point it is useful to look at a model of a cell. The diagram below shows a common model used to simulate the action of the cell membrane. Visking tube has similar physical properties to a cell membrane – it allows some molecules through, but not others. A section of Visking tube has been filled with concentrated glucose solution and then sealed. Consider what happens when the tube is put into a beaker of water.

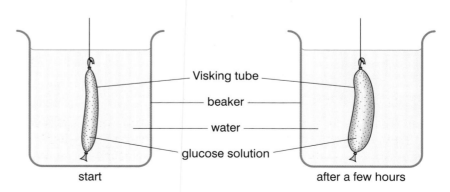

start   after a few hours

Cell Structure and Life Processes

After a few hours, we find that the Visking tube has swollen up. In other words, there is more water in it than there was previously. What has happened? Some water molecules that were surrounding the tube have moved to inside the Visking tube. This can happen because the Visking tube has tiny holes in it. These holes are big enough to let small molecules such as water through, but not big enough to let larger molecules such as glucose through. The Visking tube is a **semi-permeable** (or partly-permeable) **membrane**.

Water molecules **diffuse** through the tiny holes in the Visking tube from where they are in a high concentration (outside the tube) to where they are in a low concentration (inside the tube). This causes the Visking tube to swell up. The process continues until either the concentration of the solution on both sides of the membrane is equal, or no more water can enter because the cell walls restrict further expansion of the cell. The glucose molecules cannot diffuse in the other direction because the holes in the membrane are too small to allow them through. The movement of water thorough a semi-permeable membrane is a special case of diffusion. It is called **osmosis.**

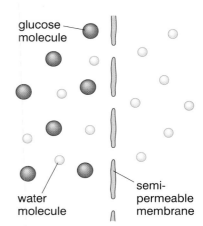

All cell membranes have the property demonstrated by the Visking tube. The semi-permeable nature of the cell membrane allows it to act as a 'molecular sieve'. It allows small molecules such as water to pass through, but prevents larger molecules such as sucrose or starch from passing through.

Three examples of this membrane structure 'in action' are considered in the following paragraphs.

Passive uptake of water by root hair cells

We looked at the way that root hair cells are adapted to their function in chapter 29. The cell sap inside the root hair cell is a solution with a higher concentration than the surrounding soil water. The cell wall is fully permeable and the cell membrane is semi-permeable. Water passes by osmosis from the soil solution (where there is a higher concentration of water molecules), through the permeable cell wall and semi-permeable cell membrane, and into the cell sap (passing through another cell membrane surrounding the vacuole on the way). This is how roots absorb water from the soil. Notice that this takes place solely as a result of the difference in concentration between the cell sap and the soil water. It is sometimes called the passive uptake of water because the plant does not need to use any energy to make it happen.

Active uptake of minerals by root hair cells

As well as taking in water by 'passive' osmosis, root hair cells also take in mineral salts, such as ammonium nitrate and potassium chloride. Mineral salts are dissolved in the soil solution surrounding the root hair cell. When they are dissolved, mineral salts are charged

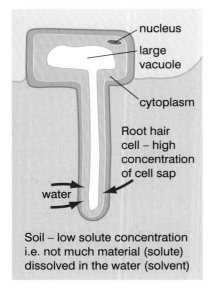

nucleus

large vacuole

cytoplasm

Root hair cell – high concentration of cell sap

water

Soil – low solute concentration i.e. not much material (solute) dissolved in the water (solvent)

particles called ions, so we find potassium ions, ammonium ions and chloride ions dissolved in the soil solution. These ions cannot be taken into the root hair cell by diffusion, because they are found in a higher concentration inside the cell sap than they are in the soil solution. Passive diffusion would take place in the opposite direction – the ions that the plant needs would pass by diffusion out of the cell and into the soil water. The solution to this problem is that the cell has to use energy from respiration to move mineral ions into the cell (against this difference in concentration). It is the cell membrane that does this.

There are special 'carrier' molecules in the cell membrane that carry the mineral ion across the cell membrane and into the cell, against the concentration gradient (difference in concentration). Using energy to move substances across a cell membrane in this way is called **active transport**.

Alveoli wall cells

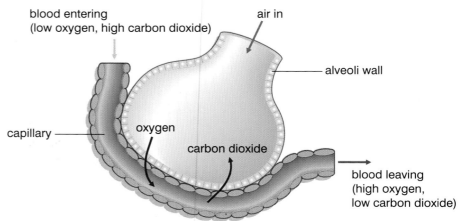

blood entering (low oxygen, high carbon dioxide)

air in

alveoli wall

capillary

oxygen

carbon dioxide

blood leaving (high oxygen, low carbon dioxide)

Alveoli are small air sacs in the lungs. Oxygen that is breathed in passes through the alveoli into the blood. Carbon dioxide passes from the blood into the air sacs and is then breathed out.

Oxygen in the inhaled air dissolves in a thin film of water which lines the inside of the alveoli. The dissolved oxygen molecules are very small and easily pass through the semi-permeable cell membranes of the alveoli wall cells. The oxygen molecules diffuse from the alveoli (where they are in a relatively high concentration), through the alveoli wall cell membranes and into the blood stream where they are in a relatively low concentration.

Oxygen is used in respiration and carbon dioxide is produced as a waste product. The carbon dioxide is taken to the lungs in the bloodstream. The concentration of carbon dioxide in the blood is higher than the concentration in the alveoli, so carbon dioxide moves by diffusion from the blood into the alveoli and then on into the air contained in the lungs.

Check yourself

QUESTIONS

Q1 The diagram below shows a model cell. The cell membrane is made of Visking tube. Inside the model cell is a weak sugar solution. Outside the cell is a strong sugar solution.

If the model cell was left for a few hours, what would you expect to happen?

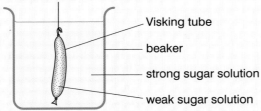

- Visking tube
- beaker
- strong sugar solution
- weak sugar solution

Q2 Draw a labelled diagram that shows what is meant by a semi-permeable membrane.

Q3 Explain the difference between the terms *active transport* and *passive transport*.

ANSWERS & TUTORIALS

A1 The cell would shrink and shrivel.

T1 This would happen by osmosis through the semi-permeable membrane. Water would move from inside the cell (where there is a weaker solution) to the outside of the cell (where there is a stronger solution).

A2

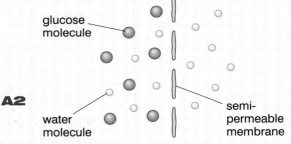

- glucose molecule
- water molecule
- semi-permeable membrane

T2 Check the text and diagram at the start of the chapter if you made any mistakes.

A3 Passive transport is movement of molecules across a membrane as a result of a difference in concentration either side of the cell membrane. No energy is needed to make passive transport happen – it happens because of the difference in concentration.

Active transport is the movement of substances across a membrane requiring the use of energy from respiration. This is because energy is needed to move molecules against the concentration gradient.

T3 These processes can take place at the same time in the same cell. Root hair cells can be passively transporting water into the cell from the soil while also actively absorbing some minerals.

Chapter 39

Biological Systems

What you should already know

- [ ] The chemical changes during respiration.
- [ ] The characteristics of cell membranes.

What you need to know

Biological **systems** are groups of organs that work together to carry out a particular function. Many of the organs are shown in the diagram. For example:

- the kidneys and bladder work together as the excretory system;

- the heart, blood and blood vessels work together as the circulatory system;

- the brain, spinal cord and nerves make up the nervous system;

- the oesophagus, stomach, intestines and pancreas are all parts of the digestive system.

In this chapter we shall look more closely at the digestive system as an example of a typical biological system. We will look closely at what the digestive system does and how it works.

The function of the digestive system

The function of the digestive system is to take in and absorb food into the bloodstream. Absorption of food into the bloodstream happens in the small intestine, which is specially adapted to make it good at absorbing food. Food that is absorbed in the small intestine must pass through the cell membranes of cells in the small intestine wall. In chapter 38, *Cell Structure and Life Processes*, you saw that these cell membranes are only partly permeable. They act like a molecular sieve, allowing small molecules and not large molecules to pass through them.

Food molecules such as water, glucose, vitamins and mineral salts are absorbed into the blood when they reach the small intestine. Unfortunately, not all food molecules are small enough to pass through the semi-permeable cell membranes of the small intestine. Starch, protein, fibre (cellulose) and fat molecules are all very large insoluble molecules, and so cannot be absorbed. They must be broken down into a size that is small enough to pass through the cell membranes before they can be absorbed and made use of inside cells. This breaking down of large, insoluble food molecules into small, soluble food molecules that can be absorbed into the blood is called digestion and is a major function of the digestive system.

Chemicals called **enzymes** are very important in the process of molecular breakdown. An enzyme is a biological catalyst that enables the chemical breakdown of food to take place quickly so that their products can be used by the body.

Mechanical and chemical digestion

When food is first put into the mouth we chew it. Chewing breaks large lumps of food down into smaller lumps. This has two effects:

- it makes the food easier to swallow;
- it increases the surface area of the food available for enzymes to act on, helping to speed up digestion.

This way of breaking food down into smaller bits is sometimes called **mechanical digestion**.

As mechanical digestion (chewing) takes place, salivary glands release saliva into the mouth. Saliva contains an enzyme called amylase. Amylase helps to break down large, insoluble starch molecules into small, soluble glucose molecules. The breakdown of large molecules into smaller molecules by an enzyme is called **chemical digestion**.

You may find it helpful to think of enzymes as 'chemical scissors' which are able to break down large molecules into smaller molecules

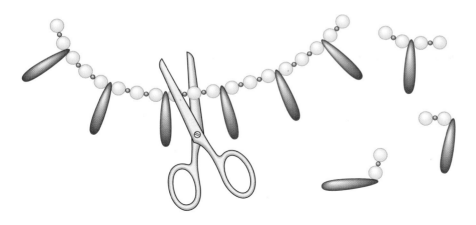

The different enzymes needed to enable different types of large food molecule to be broken down are shown in the table below.

Large food molecule	Enzyme	Enzymes from	Small molecules made
starch	amylase	mouth, pancreas, small intestine	glucose (sugars)
protein	protease	stomach, pancreas, small intestine	amino acids
fats	lipase	pancreas, small intestine	glycerol, fatty acids
fibre	no enzyme in humans		no digestion takes place

In the human digestive system there is no enzyme that enables the digestion of fibre. Fibre cannot be broken down into small molecules and therefore it cannot be absorbed into the bloodstream.

Absorption

Absorption of digested food takes place mainly in the small intestine. The small intestine is adapted for absorbing food in the following ways:

- it is very long, giving a large surface area for absorption;

- its inner lining is covered with tiny villi (finger-like projections) which make the surface area even bigger;

- it has a very thin lining (just one cell thick) allowing faster absorption;

- it has an excellent supply of blood capillaries to absorb the digested food.

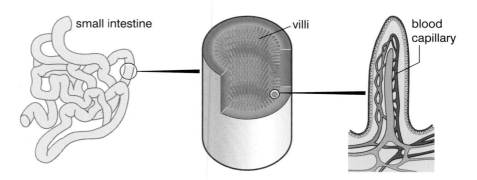

Absorbing small molecules from the small intestine into the blood, through the cell membranes of the villi cells, takes place by both passive transport (diffusion) and active transport which uses up energy produced during respiration.

Egestion

Some foods, such as vitamins, water and sugars can be absorbed with no need for any digestive processing, and others such as starch, protein and fats are processed (broken down) to make them small enough to be absorbed. Fibre is too big a molecule to be absorbed without being digested, but we do not have the enzymes to enable us to digest it. As a result, fibre passes straight through the whole digestive system without being digested.

The large intestine absorbs water from the undigested food. The resulting faeces (undigested remains) pass on to the rectum, where they are stored before being passed out of the body through the anus. Getting rid of undigested food like this is called egestion. Egestion is not the same as excretion. Excretion is getting rid of waste products that have been made inside living cells as a result of their normal chemical activities.

Check yourself

QUESTIONS

Q 1 A bacon sandwich contains protein, starch, fat and some fibre. Imagine that you eat a bacon sandwich and then wash it down with some coke that contains glucose. Explain what happens to this meal as it makes its way through the digestive system. Make your notes in point form and use the diagram below to help you.

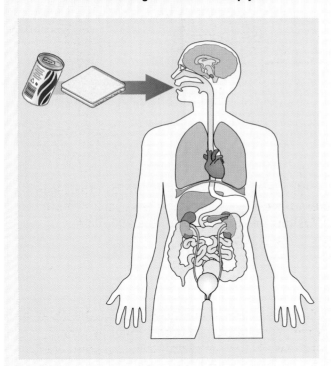

ANSWERS & TUTORIALS

A 1 a The sandwich is chewed in the mouth. This is mechanical breakdown and increases the surface area of the food.

b Saliva is mixed with the food. This contains the enzyme amylase which starts to break down chemically the starch molecules in the bread.

c The food is swallowed and moves down the oesophagus to the stomach.

d Stomach juices including protease enzymes are added to the food. These enzymes start to break down the protein in the bacon to amino acids.

e The food moves on and into the small intestine. The pancreas and small intestine release a range of enzymes (including amylase, protease and lipase) that complete the breakdown of large, insoluble molecules into small, soluble molecules.

f The small intestine absorbs amino acids from the breakdown of the meat, glucose from the breakdown of the bread and glucose from the coke. It also absorbs some of the fatty acids and glycerol from the breakdown of the fat on the meat and any spread on the bread. Both active and passive absorption takes place.

g The fibre in the bread cannot be broken down as there are no enzymes to do it. It passes on through the small intestine and into the large intestine where water is absorbed from the undigested food, making faeces.

h The faeces are stored in the rectum before being passed out through the anus.

ANSWERS & TUTORIALS

A2 The main functions of the digestive system are:
● to break down large insoluble molecules into small soluble molecules;
● to absorb small soluble food molecules into the bloodstream.

A3 Excretion is the process of removing waste products that have been made inside cells from the body. Egestion is the removal of undigested food from the body. In other words, egestion removes substances that have simply passed through the body unchanged.

T3 Many chemical reactions take place inside living cells. Biologists call these chemical reactions the 'metabolism' of the cell. Excretion is often called the removal of the products of metabolism. Examples of excretory products are carbon dioxide (made by respiration) and urea (made by deamination). The point to remember is that excretory products are new substances that have been made within the living cells, whereas egestion is simply the removal of substances which have passed unchanged through the digestive system.

QUESTIONS

Q2 What are the main functions of the digestive system?

Q3 Explain the difference between excretion and egestion.

Chapter 40

Symbol Equations

What you should already know

- ☐ Chemical reactions can be represented by word equations.
- ☐ Elements contain identical atoms and compounds contain different atoms.
- ☐ Atoms can be represented by symbols and molecules can be represented by formulae.

What you need to know

In chapter 22, *Word Equations* we looked at naming compounds and how chemical reactions can be represented by using word equations. This section takes these ideas a little further and we will use symbols to represent the reactants and the products. Symbol equations are more useful than word equations for making predictions about what new substances will be formed in a chemical reaction. The name of a compound gives you some idea of what the compound is made from. In chapter 31, *Symbols and Formulae*, you saw that the formula for a compound tells you **exactly** how many atoms there are of each type. Some examples are given below.

Compound	Elements present	Formula	Number of atoms of each element in each molecule
magnesium oxide	magnesium and oxygen	MgO	1 Mg, 1 O
aluminium oxide	aluminium and oxygen	Al_2O_3	2 Al, 3 O
sulphuric acid	hydrogen, sulphur and oxygen	H_2SO_4	2 H, 1 S, 4 O
calcium hydroxide	calcium, hydrogen and oxygen	$Ca(OH)_2$	1 Ca, 2 O, 2 H

Writing and balancing equations

The word equation for the reaction of iron with sulphur is:

reactants   product
iron + sulphur → iron sulphide

We can use symbols and formulae to represent the reactants and products:

$Fe + S \rightarrow FeS$

This is called a **symbol equation**. When we write a symbol equation we must make sure it is **balanced** – it must have the same number of atoms of each element on each side of the equation. Atoms cannot be created or destroyed in a chemical reaction – they are just arranged differently. The example above has one Fe atom on the left-hand side and one Fe on the right-hand side. There is one S atom both on the left and on the right, so the equation is balanced.

Symbol Equations

The reaction of sodium and sulphur below shows a further aspect of balancing equations. The word equation is:

sodium + sulphur → sodium sulphide

Using symbols and formulae, we have:

$Na + S → Na_2S$

This equation does *not* balance. There is one sodium atom on the left and there are two on the right.

There are rules to follow very carefully if you are going to balance equations. You *cannot change the formula of any compound* because it is fixed. Sodium sulphide always has the formula Na_2S. Written below is one way of balancing equations.

Step 1   Write the equation out

$Na + S → Na_2S$

Step 2   Find the element which is not balanced (Na) and copy this out again underneath

$Na + S → Na_2S$
Na

Now there are two sodium atoms on each side and it balances.

Step 3   To write out the final equation, draw a line underneath and add them all up: 2Na + 1 S on the left and 1 Na_2S on the right.

$Na + S → Na_2S$
Na
$\overline{2Na + S → Na_2S}$

These ideas can be used to consider some of the groups of reactions covered in chapter 33, *Reactivity Series*.

Metals and oxygen

magnesium + oxygen → magnesium oxide

The symbol equation involves an oxygen *molecule*, O_2, so if you look at the equation there are more oxygen atoms on the left than on the right.

$Mg + O_2 → MgO$

This unbalanced equation will take two stages to balance it.
First find the element which is not balanced. In this case, it is oxygen. Because there are two oxygen atoms on the left-hand side, we need an extra oxygen atom on the right-hand side. The formula of magnesium oxide is *always* MgO, so the only way of getting an extra oxygen atom to the right of the arrow is to add another MgO. Copy the formula MgO under the original one.

$Mg + O_2 → MgO$
MgO

Now we have two oxygen atoms on each side, but that means there are two magnesium atoms on the right and only one on the left. This can be balanced by copying out an Mg under the first one.

Draw a line underneath and add up the total for each one.

$$Mg + O_2 \rightarrow MgO$$
$$\underline{Mg \qquad\qquad MgO}$$
$$2Mg + O_2 \rightarrow 2MgO$$

Now there are two magnesium atoms on each side and two oxygen atoms on each side, so it balances.

Thermal decomposition

An example of this type of reaction is heating copper carbonate:

copper carbonate $\rightarrow$ copper oxide + carbon dioxide

This can be written in symbols as:

$$CuCO_3 \rightarrow CuO + CO_2$$

If you check this equation you should see that it balances.

On the left we have: 1 Cu, 1 C and 3 O.

On the right we have: 1 Cu, 1 C and 3 O.

Symbol equations can give clues as to what will be produced in a reaction, because they tell you what atoms are present. The products can only contain atoms that are present in the reactants. In this example above, the products can only be made up of Cu, C and O. CO_2 is a compound that is often a product in reactions. All carbonates decompose in a similar way, so you can use symbol equations to work out what is produced in other examples.

$$CaCO_3 \rightarrow CaO + CO_2$$

Metals and acids

All metal and acid reactions produce a salt and hydrogen and you can predict the name of the salt from the two reactants. Look at this example:

zinc + hydrochloric acid $\rightarrow$ zinc chloride + hydrogen

The symbols and formulae are:

$$Zn + HCl \rightarrow ZnCl_2 + H_2$$

Hydrogen and chlorine do not balance, so copy out HCl again:

$$Zn + HCl \rightarrow ZnCl_2 + H_2$$
$$\underline{\qquad HCl \qquad\qquad\qquad}$$
$$Zn + 2HCl \rightarrow ZnCl_2 + H_2$$

Now this balances.
The salt in this example is zinc chloride.

Acid and base

All acid–base reactions give a salt and water as the products. The balanced equation for the reaction between calcium hydroxide (a base) and nitric acid is constructed in the following way. Add the atoms on each side, find the ones that do not balance, then copy out those underneath until they do balance.

calcium hydroxide + nitric acid $\rightarrow$ calcium nitrate + water

$$Ca(OH)_2 + \quad HNO_3 \rightarrow Ca(NO_3)_2 + \quad H_2O$$
$$\underline{\qquad\qquad HNO_3 \qquad\qquad\qquad H_2O \qquad}$$
$$Ca(OH)_2 + 2HNO_3 \rightarrow Ca(NO_3)_2 + 2H_2O$$

Reduction reactions

This reaction is used to extract iron from iron ore:

$$Fe_2O_3 + CO \rightarrow Fe + CO_2$$

There are 2 Fe, 1 C and 4 O on the left. On the right, there are 1 Fe, 1 C and 2 O. Adding more CO, more Fe and more CO_2, we can make this equation balance.

$$Fe_2O_3 + \quad CO \rightarrow Fe + \quad CO_2$$
$$\qquad\quad CO \qquad Fe \qquad CO_2$$
$$\underline{\qquad\quad CO \qquad\qquad\qquad CO_2 \qquad}$$
$$Fe_2O_3 + 3CO \rightarrow 2Fe + 3CO_2$$

Check yourself

ANSWERS & TUTORIALS

A1 a $2Cu + O_2 \rightarrow 2CuO$
  b $Mg + Cl_2 \rightarrow MgCl_2$
  c $CuO + H_2 \rightarrow Cu + H_2O$

T1 When balancing equations, first add up the number of atoms of each type. Look for the small numbers after each atom that tell you how many there are. Decide whether the elements are single atoms (as in metallic elements) or molecules (as in the gases O_2, N_2 and Cl_2). The first example has copper on the left and copper oxide on the right, so you need some oxygen on the left-hand side. The oxygen occurs as O_2 molecules, so put one in the gap to give $2Cu + O_2 \rightarrow 2CuO$. This equation is now balanced.

QUESTIONS

Q1 Fill the gaps to complete the following three balanced symbol equations.
  a copper reacting with oxygen:
  $2Cu + \ldots \rightarrow 2CuO$
  b magnesium forming magnesium chloride:
  $Mg + Cl_2 \rightarrow \ldots$
  c reducing copper oxide to copper:
  $CuO + H_2 \rightarrow Cu + \ldots$

QUESTIONS

Q2 Some of the equations below are balanced and some are not. If the equation is balanced, write <u>balanced</u>. If the equation is not balanced, complete the balancing.
a $Ca + O_2 \rightarrow CaO$
b $MgCO_3 \rightarrow MgO + CO_2$
c $NaOH + H_2SO_4 \rightarrow Na_2SO_4 + H_2O$

ANSWERS & TUTORIALS

A2 a $2Ca + O_2 \rightarrow 2CaO$
b   balanced
c $2NaOH + H_2SO_4 \rightarrow Na_2SO_4 + 2H_2O$

T2 a   This has 2 oxygen atoms on the left (in the O_2 molecule) and only one on the right, so you need to copy out the CaO again. Remember that you cannot change the formula of a compound.

This gives $Ca + O_2 \rightarrow CaO$
                                       CaO

Now the Ca does not balance, so add a Ca to the left.
$Ca + O_2 \rightarrow CaO$
Ca   CaO

Now it balances. There are 2 Ca and 2 O (as O_2) on the left, and the same number on the right in CaO + CaO. Adding the elements and compounds give:
$2Ca + O_2 \rightarrow 2CaO$.

b   On the left there is 1 Mg, 1 C and 3 O (from O_3). Remember that the number only refers to the atom that it is after (not the carbon). On the right, there is 1 Mg and 1 O in the MgO and then 1 C and 2 O in the CO_2. Adding these up shows that the equation balances.

c   Neither the Na nor the H balances, so you can start by balancing either of them. If you choose to balance Na first, copy out another NaOH under the original one. Then copy out another H_2O.

$NaOH + H_2SO_4 \rightarrow Na_2SO_4 + H_2O$
NaOH H_2O
$\overline{2NaOH + H_2SO_4 \rightarrow Na_2SO_4 + 2H_2O}$

ANSWERS & TUTORIALS

A3 a $Zn + CuSO_4 \rightarrow ZnSO_4 + Cu$
  b $K_2CO_3 + H_2SO_4 \rightarrow K_2SO_4 + H_2O + CO_2$
  c $CuO + H_2SO_4 \rightarrow CuSO_4 + H_2O$

T3 When making predictions about compounds that will be produced, there are two things to remember:

- you can only make compounds from the atoms you start off with (you cannot create any new atoms);
- it is only a prediction – the only way to be sure is to carry out some experiments to prove it.

One way to start is to cross out the atoms that are on both sides and then see what you have left. Remember also that there are types of reactions that always give similar results.

a   On the left there is 1 Zn, 1 Cu, 1 S and 4 O. On the right, there is a Cu missing. By adding a Cu atom, the equation will balance:
$Zn + CuSO_4 \rightarrow ZnSO_4 + Cu$.

b   This is an acid–carbonate reaction. Acid–carbonate reactions always give a salt, water and carbon dioxide. The acid will determine the salt that is formed. HCl gives chlorides, H_2SO_4 gives sulphates and HNO_3 gives nitrates. This reaction uses sulphuric acid, so the salt will be a sulphate. Sulphates contain an SO_4 group. The metal part of the carbonate (K) combines with the SO_4 group to give K_2SO_4.

c   This reaction is an acid–base reaction, which always gives a salt and water as products. Because the acid is sulphuric acid, and the metal present is copper, the salt will be copper sulphate ($CuSO_4$). The Cu comes from the CuO and the SO_4 comes from the acid.

QUESTIONS

Q3 **Predict what might be produced in the following reactions by filling in the gaps.**
  a $Zn + CuSO_4 \rightarrow ZnSO_4 + ...$
  b $K_2CO_3 + H_2SO_4 \rightarrow ... + H_2O + CO_2$
  c $CuO + H_2SO_4 \rightarrow ... + H_2O$

Chapter 41

The Particle Model

What you should already know

☐ The nature and behaviour of materials are linked to the particles of which they are composed.
☐ The particle model of matter can be used to explain phenomena such as changes of state.

What you need to know

The particle model of matter can be used to explain a wide range of properties and processes. In chapter 23, *Particles*, we used it to explain changes of state, where the particles gain energy and separate from each other. It can be used to explain contraction and expansion where the particles move a small distance nearer to or further apart from each other.

The model can also be used to explain dissolving. Whether or not a certain solid dissolves when placed in a liquid depends on the forces that exist between particles of each substance. There are two types of forces to consider:

● forces that hold the solid particles together;

● forces between the solid particles and the water.

If the forces holding the solid particles together are stronger than the forces between the solid and the water, the solid stays undissolved – it is insoluble. If the forces of attraction between the water and the solid are greater than those holding the solid particles together, then the solid will dissolve.

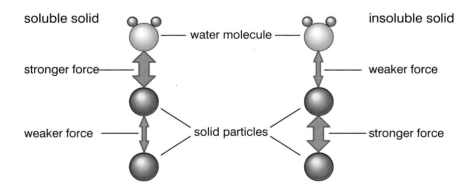

Diffusion

When a solid dissolves, its particles spread through the liquid. This happens because water particles move freely and the particles that have broken away from the solid are also free to move. The solute particles move in the spaces between the particles of water. This can be seen when you put coloured dye in some water. The dye gradually spreads through the liquid, colouring it all. This process is called **diffusion**.

The same process occurs when one gas passes through another. Diffusion means that it is possible to smell some chemicals a great distance from their source. The gas particles that have the smelly property can move in between the spaces of the moving air molecules. The movement is much quicker than in liquids because the space between gas particles is much greater than the spaces between liquid particles.

A party balloon that is inflated and sealed gradually deflates because the rapidly moving gas particles escape through tiny holes in the material of the balloon. This is another example of diffusion.

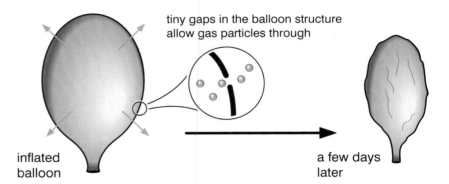

tiny gaps in the balloon structure allow gas particles through

inflated balloon

a few days later

Gas pressure

Consider a gas inside a closed, impermeable container. The particles of gas are continually colliding with each other and with the inside wall of the container. Each of the collisions with the container's wall exert a force on its inside surface. The total force applied to a given area of surface is the **gas pressure** (see chapter 35 for a reminder of how to calculate pressure). If the number of gas particles is kept constant, we could reduce the gas pressure by either:

- increasing the size of the container;
- reducing the temperature of the gas.

The Particle Model

The differences between solids, liquids and gases

The behaviour of solids when they are stretched or compressed can be explained using the particle model. In a solid, there are strong forces holding the particles together. If the material is stretched, the stretching force is trying to pull the particles apart. At the same time, the particles exert a force in the opposite direction, working against the stretching force. This is often called **tension**.

The opposite of tension is **compression**. When a force is applied which squashes the particles closer together, the particles exert a force in the opposite direction, working against compression. The greater the compressing force, the greater will be the force working against it.

If a tension or compression force becomes too great, however, the internal structure of particles in the solid breaks down and the material will fracture.

The more material is stretched
the more it pulls back

The particles are held together rather like springs in a mattress. If the material is stretched, the springs oppose the force. The harder you pull the stronger the force they exert.

The more the material is compressed
the more it pushes back

If the material is compressed, the springs oppose the force. The harder you push, the stronger the force they exert.

Check yourself

QUESTIONS

Q1 Use the particle model to explain when substances will be soluble and when they will not.

ANSWERS & TUTORIALS

A1 If the forces holding the solid particles together are stronger than the forces between the solid and the water particles, then the substance will be insoluble.

If the forces between the solid and the water are stronger than the forces within the solid, the substance will be soluble.

T1 You need to decide which forces are stronger. The stronger forces always win. If the solid–solid forces are stronger, then it stays as solid and is insoluble. If the solid–water forces are stronger, it dissolves.

ANSWERS & TUTORIALS

A2 **a** **The particles that are diffusing pass through the spaces between the particles of the other substance.**
b **Diffusion in gases is quicker than in liquids.**

T2 If a substance diffuses through another substance it can only pass through the spaces. A gas can diffuse much quicker because the spaces between the particles are much greater, so it is easier to pass through.

A3 **The gas pressure inside a closed impermeable container can be increased by:**
● **decreasing the size of container;**
● **raising the temperature of the gas.**

T3 By decreasing the size of the container, the surface area is decreased. Therefore the total force divided by this smaller area results in a higher pressure.

By raising the temperature of the gas, the kinetic energy of the particles is increased. The particles strike the walls of the container more often and with more force. As a consequence, the gas pressure is increased.

A4 **Concrete has very strong forces holding its particles together. When the weight of the building presses down, the forces between the particles push back and stop the building collapsing.**

T4 The concrete particles behave as if they were joined by springs. When the weight of the building presses down on the 'springs', they push back. The harder they are pushed, the harder they push back. Concrete is very good for the foundations of buildings because it is very strong under compression. However, if the concrete is not thick enough and the building is too heavy, the building will collapse.

QUESTIONS

Q2 **a** **How does diffusion take place?**
b **Which is quicker: diffusion in gases or in liquids?**

Q3 **Describe two ways of increasing the gas pressure inside a closed impermeable container.**

Q4 **Explain how concrete foundations can support the weight of a building.**

Chapter 42

Classes of Reaction

What you should already know

☐ Patterns of reactivity can be used to make predictions about chemical reactions.

☐ Your knowledge of physical and chemical processes can be used to explain the behaviour of materials in a variety of contexts.

☐ Elements and compounds can be represented by symbols and formulae.

What you need to know

In chapter 24, we discussed the similarities that can be seen in the reactions of acids with indicators. All acids turn universal indicator red. This is because they all contain hydrogen. The hydrogen gives acids their special properties. In chapter 24, we also saw that any acid that reacts with a metal gives off hydrogen gas. This similarity of reactions means that we can put reactions into groups – we can **classify** them.

Neutralisation reactions

When an acid reacts with an alkali it is known as a **neutralisation** reaction. For example, hydrochloric acid and sodium hydroxide **neutralise** each other and form sodium chloride and water:

$HCl + NaOH \rightarrow NaCl + H_2O$

In sufficient quantities, any acid will neutralise any alkali and water is always produced. This is the one thing that all **neutralisation** reactions have in common.

An alkali is a hydroxide that dissolves in water. Acids will also react with oxides and hydroxides that are not soluble in water. These compounds are called **bases** and their reaction with acids are called **acid–base** reactions. Acid–base reactions are also neutralisation reactions which produce a salt and water. Copper oxide and sulphuric acid will react together to give copper sulphate and water:

$CuO + H_2SO_4 \rightarrow CuSO_4 + H_2O$

When an acid reacts with a carbonate, the reaction is called an **acid-carbonate** reaction. These reactions produce a salt, water and carbon dioxide, so they too are neutralisation reactions. Nitric acid will react with sodium carbonate to give sodium nitrate, water and carbon dioxide:

$2HNO_3 + Na_2CO_3 \rightarrow 2NaNO_3 + H_2O + CO_2$

To summarise, there are three different types of **neutralisation** reaction. They all involve <u>acids</u> and they all produce <u>water</u>.

<u>acid</u> and alkali	gives	salt and <u>water</u>
<u>acid</u> and base	gives	salt and <u>water</u>
<u>acid</u> and carbonate	gives	salt and <u>water</u> and carbon dioxide

Classes of Reaction

Oxidation and reduction

Two other classes of reaction involve oxygen.

If you **add oxygen** to a substance during a reaction, **oxidation** has taken place.

When **oxygen** is removed from a substance during a reaction, **reduction** has taken place.

If copper metal is heated in air it will react with oxygen. The black layer that forms on the surface is copper oxide. The copper has gained oxygen from the air, so it is an **oxidation** reaction. You can reverse this reaction by removing the oxygen with another substance.

When copper is heated in air a black layer of copper oxide forms.

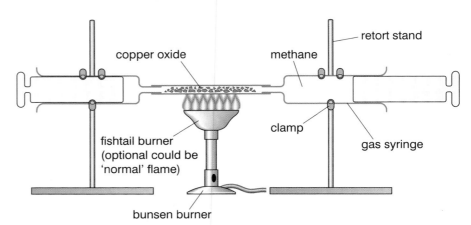

In the diagram, the oxygen is removed from copper oxide, so copper is left behind. Removing oxygen is **reduction**. Reduction reactions are very useful because they allow metals to be obtained from metal ores. Many metal ores, such as iron ore, are oxides. If the ore is not an oxide, it is usually treated to make it into an oxide. The oxide is then **reduced** to the metal, which is then refined to make it pure.

Oxygen will combine with most metals just by leaving them exposed to the air. This usually happens very slowly and in the case of iron we call it **rusting**.

Examples of iron or steel objects rusting can be seen around us every day. Not only does it look unsightly, but can also be very dangerous because it weakens the metal. In a car or a building this could be a very serious problem.

Oxygen does not only react with metals – it can react with non-metallic elements such as carbon or sulphur. These reactions are known as **burning** and they release large quantities of energy. Burning carbon is an example of **oxidation** because carbon combines with oxygen.

Compounds can be **oxidised** as well. Some foods spoil because of oxidisation. The flesh of apples goes brown when exposed to oxygen in the air because of a reaction between the oxygen and an enzyme in the apple.

Another group of chemicals that can be oxidised are fuels, such as gas, coal and oil. Burning fuels is a very important reaction because that is how we get most of our energy. Fossil fuels like coal, oil and gas are mostly compounds of carbon and hydrogen. The carbon is oxidised to carbon dioxide and hydrogen is oxidised to water. Fossil fuels also contain small amounts of sulphur and this is oxidised when the fuel burns to form sulphur dioxide. Sulphur dioxide is one of the gases that produces acid rain.

Thermal decomposition

Some reactions take place just by heating. They do not need any acid or oxygen or other chemical substances – the heat causes the compound to break apart into simpler compounds. These reactions are classified as **thermal decomposition**. They are called this because *thermal* energy is needed to make the reaction happen and because the compound *decomposes* (breaks up) into simpler compounds.

An example of a thermal decomposition reaction is heating calcium carbonate. When heated, calcium carbonate breaks down into calcium oxide and carbon dioxide.

Check yourself

QUESTIONS

Q1 **a** What are the possible neutralisation reactions of acids
   b Explain why they are classified as neutralisation reactions

ANSWERS & TUTORIALS

A1 **a** Acid with alkali; acid with base; acid with carbonate.
   b They all involve acids and they all produce water.

T1 All neutralisation reactions involve an acid, so if you want to classify a reaction, look first of all to see if it uses an acid. Then check to see if water is produced. If it starts with an acid and finishes with water it is neutralisation.

ANSWERS & TUTORIALS

A2 a oxidation
    b oxidation
    c reduction
    d oxidation
    e oxidation

T2 You can get a clue from the name of the reaction –
ox-idation comes from the element ox-ygen, so it
is adding oxygen.

    a Magnesium is burning in air (which contains
oxygen). It has changed from magnesium to
magnesium **ox**ide – its name tells you that it
has gained some **ox**ygen.

    b Iron combines with oxygen and forms iron
oxide (rust).

    c In this reaction the starting material – zinc
oxide – already has some oxygen. When the
hydrogen reacts, the zinc oxide loses this
oxygen and becomes zinc metal. Losing
oxygen is reduction.

    d When an apple is cut open and left open to the
air, it goes brown because the air contains
oxygen. The reaction is oxidation.

    e All things that burn need oxygen. They stop
burning if you do not allow them any oxygen.
This suggests that they gain the oxygen, and
you can confirm this from the names of the
compounds produced. Wax is a type of fuel. It
contains mainly carbon and hydrogen. When
the carbon reacts with oxygen it forms carbon
dioxide. The carbon has gained oxygen, so it
has been oxidised. Hydrogen reacts with
oxygen to form water.

A3 a **Thermal decomposition means breaking
down into simpler compounds by using heat.**
    b **Magnesium carbonate will decompose to
form magnesium oxide and carbon dioxide.**

T3 A single substance is heated and as a result of the
reaction two or more substances will be produced.
One of the products will probably be a gas.

QUESTIONS

Q2 Classify each of these reactions as oxidation or
reduction:
    a magnesium forming magnesium oxide by
heating the metal in air;
    b rust forming on steel;
    c zinc oxide reacting with hydrogen to form zinc;
    d apples going brown;
    e a candle burning in air to form carbon
dioxide and water.

Q3 a What does thermal decomposition mean?
    b Magnesium carbonate can be thermally
decomposed. What are the products of the
reaction?

Chapter 43

Speed-Time Graphs

What you should already know

- [ ] For a moving object, its speed (m/s) = $\dfrac{\text{distance travelled (m)}}{\text{time taken (s)}}$
- [ ] If the speed of a moving object is increasing, the object is accelerating.
- [ ] If the speed of a moving object is decreasing, the object is decelerating (slowing down).

What you need to know

A speed–time graph is used to show how the speed of a moving object changes over a period of time.

Steady speed

Graph 1 is the speed–time graph for a bicycle travelling at a steady or constant speed. The line is horizontal. This tells us that the bike is not accelerating or decelerating (slowing down).

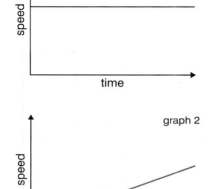

Gentle acceleration

If the bicycle started from rest (not moving) and slowly, but steadily, increased its speed, the speed–time graph would be like graph 2. The slope is not very steep. This tells us that the bike is accelerating slowly.

The graph is a straight line. This tells us that the acceleration of the bicycle is uniform (it is increasing its speed at a steady rate).

Rapid acceleration

The slope in graph 3 is much steeper than the slope in graph 2. The bicycle has started from rest. This time, it has rapidly increased its speed – in other words, it has a bigger acceleration than in graph 2. Again the graph is a straight line, which means that the bike's acceleration is constant.

Non-uniform acceleration

Graph 4 shows that the bicycle started from rest and rapidly increased its speed. The rate of acceleration then slowed down until the bicycle was moving with a constant speed. Before reaching its final constant speed, the acceleration of the bicycle had been non-uniform. It had changed from rapid acceleration to no acceleration, i.e. steady speed.

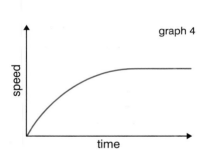

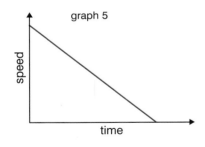

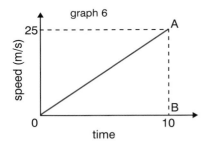

Slowing down

Graph 5 shows the bicycle starting at a high speed and slowing down (decelerating) until it stops (speed is zero).

A speed–time graph can tell us a lot about the movement of an object. We can also use it to find the distance travelled by that object. The distance travelled by the moving object is equal to the area under the graph.

Graph 6 shows a car which speeds up from rest to 25 m/s in 10 seconds. To find out how far the car has travelled in 10 s we need to work out the area under the graph.

$$\begin{aligned}
\text{distance travelled} &= \text{area under the graph} \\
&= \text{area of triangle OAB} \\
&= \tfrac{1}{2} \times \text{base} \times \text{height} \\
&= \tfrac{1}{2} \times 10\text{ s} \times 25\text{ m/s} \\
&= 125\text{ m}
\end{aligned}$$

The car has travelled 125 m in 10 seconds.

The motion of a train travelling between two stations can be represented by the speed–time graph below. We can use this to write a description of the motion of the train.

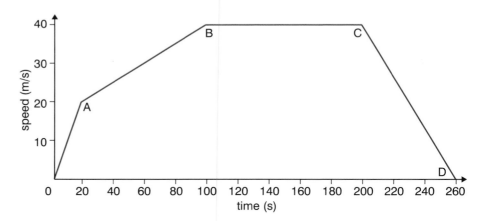

At 0   The train starts from rest (its speed is 0 m/s).

0 to A   The train rapidly accelerates, with uniform acceleration, for 20 seconds, until its speed is 20 m/s.

A to B   The train accelerates steadily but less rapidly until its speed is 40 m/s.

B to C   The train travels at a steady speed of 40 m/s for 100 seconds.

C to D   The train decelerates uniformly until it comes to rest.

It is possible to calculate the acceleration of the train from O to A and from C to D using this relationship:

$$\text{acceleration} = \frac{\text{change in speed}}{\text{time taken}} = \frac{\text{speed (end)} - \text{speed (start)}}{\text{time (end)} - \text{time (start)}}$$

(start) and (end) refer to the time period during which the acceleration or deceleration is taking place. The unit of acceleration is the metre per second per second (m/s/s).

The acceleration of the train from O to A is:

$$\text{acceleration} = \frac{20 - 0}{20 - 0} = 1 \text{ m/s/s}$$

The acceleration of the train from C to D is:

$$\text{acceleration} = \frac{0 - 40}{250 - 200} = \frac{-40}{50} = -0.8 \text{ m/s/s}$$

The value is negative because deceleration (slowing down) is the opposite of acceleration (speeding up).

Check yourself

QUESTIONS

Q1 Here is a speed–time graph for a 20 minute journey of a car.

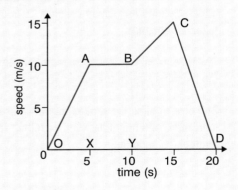

When is the car:
a accelerating most rapidly?
b slowing down?
c travelling at a steady speed?
d stationary?

ANSWERS & TUTORIALS

A1 a O to A
b C to D
c A to B
d O and D

T1 a A rapid acceleration is shown by the steepest part of the graph, from O to A.
b The graph goes from a high speed to a low speed when the car is slowing down.
c When the line is horizontal, the speed is not changing.
d The speed is zero at both O and D; the car is stationary at these points.

ANSWERS & TUTORIALS

A1 e   75 m

f   **Acceleration from B to C = 1 m/s/s.**
Acceleration from C to D = –3 m/s/s.

T1   The distance travelled during the first 10 seconds is equal to the area under the graph for the first 10 seconds:

= area of the triangle OAX + area of the
rectangle ABYX

$$= (\tfrac{1}{2} \times 5 \times 10) + (5 \times 10)$$

$$= 25 + 50$$

$$= 75\,m$$

B to C
$$\frac{\text{change in speed}}{\text{time taken}} = \frac{15 - 10}{15 - 10} = 1\,m/s/s$$

C to D
$$\frac{\text{change in speed}}{\text{time taken}} = \frac{0 - 15}{20 - 15} = \frac{-15}{5} = -3\,m/s/s$$
The value is negative because the car is decelerating (slowing down).

A2

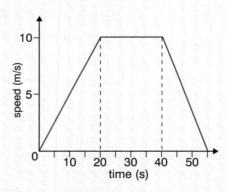

T2   The graph is made up of three straight lines. During the first 20 s, there is a constant acceleration, so draw a straight line from 0 to 10 m/s.
During the next 20 s, the constant speed is represented by a horizontal line.
Finally the speed decreases to 0 m/s over 15 s.
Do not forget to label the axes and give the units of speed (m/s) and time (s).

QUESTIONS

Q1 e   How far did the car travel during the first 10 seconds?

f   Calculate the acceleration of the car from B to C and from C to D.

Q2   Draw a speed–time graph for a cyclist taking part in a race using the description below.

When the race starts, she sets off, accelerating uniformly until her speed reaches 10 m/s. This takes 20 seconds.

She then rides at a steady speed until she crosses the finishing line after another 20 seconds.

She now applies the brakes and decelerates uniformly until stopping after travelling for another 15 seconds.

Chapter 44

Moments

What you should already know

☐ Forces can cause objects to turn about a pivot.
☐ How to use some quantitative definitions and perform
calculations involving physical quantities, using correct units.

What you need to know

If you hold a stick with a weight on it, the weight has a turning effect
which acts around your hand. Your hand acts as the **pivot**. The weight
will pull the stick down and try to make it turn. If you move the weight
further away from your hand, the turning effect is bigger. If you use a
heavier weight, the turning effect is also bigger. This turning effect is
called the **moment**. The size of the moment depends on:

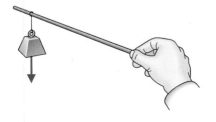

- the size of the force;
- the distance of the force from the pivot.

moment = force × distance from the pivot

Force is measured in newtons (N) and distance is measured in metres
(m), so the unit of moment is the newton metre (N m). Any system
involving forces applied on either side of a pivot is balanced when:

total anticlockwise moment = total clockwise moment

This is called the **principle of moments**. We can use the principle of
moments to work out if the seesaw in the diagram is balanced.

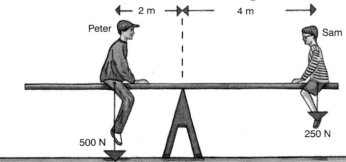

Peter weighs 500 N and is sitting 2 m
from the pivot.
Sam weighs 250 N and is sitting 4 m
from the pivot.

For the seesaw in the diagram to balance, the moment due to Peter
(who is turning the seesaw anticlockwise) must be the same as the
moment due to Sam (who is turning the seesaw clockwise).

anticlockwise moment = Peter's weight × his distance from the pivot
$$= 500\,\text{N} \times 2\,\text{m}$$
$$= 1000\,\text{N m}$$

clockwise moment = Sam's weight × his distance from the pivot
$$= 250\,\text{N} \times 4\,\text{m}$$
$$= 1000\,\text{N m}$$

The anticlockwise moment is equal to the clockwise moment, so the
seesaw is balanced.

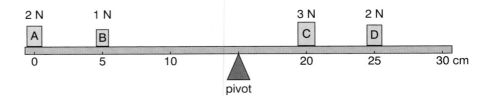

Consider a 30 cm metal ruler resting on a pivot with two weights on each side of the pivot. We can determine if the ruler will balance by calculating the moment due to each weight and then adding up the moments on each side to produce the total anticlockwise moment and the total clockwise moment. To calculate the anticlockwise moment, add up the moments due to both the 2 N weight (A) and the 1 N weight (B) on the left-hand side of the ruler:

Moment due to A = $2\,N \times 0.15\,m = 0.3\,Nm$
Moment due to B = $1\,N \times 0.1\,m = 0.1\,Nm$
Total anticlockwise moment = $0.3\,Nm + 0.1\,Nm = 0.4\,Nm$

The clockwise moment is the total of the moments due to the 3 N weight (C) and 2 N weight (D) on the right-hand side of the ruler:

Moment due to C = $3\,N \times 0.05\,m = 0.15\,Nm$
Moment due to D = $2\,N \times 0.10 = 0.20\,Nm$
Total clockwise moment = $0.15\,Nm + 0.20\,Nm = 0.35\,Nm$

The distances from the pivot in this calculation are stated in metres. The anticlockwise moment is 0.4 N m and the clockwise moment is 0.35 N m. The ruler is not balanced and it will begin to turn anticlockwise.

Check yourself

ANSWERS & TUTORIALS

A1 **a** moment = force × distance
moment = $1\,N \times 0.3\,m = 0.3\,Nm$
b moment = $1\,N \times 0.6\,m = 0.6\,Nm$
c moment = $2\,N \times 0.3\,m = 0.6\,Nm$

T1 Remember to change the mass into force (weight) and the distance into metres:

a 100 g mass produces a force of 1 N;

30 cm = 0.3 m.

Write out the equation and show all your working.

QUESTIONS

Q1

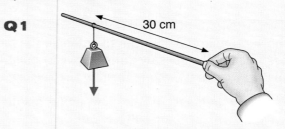

a What is the moment of the 100 g mass?
b If the 100 g mass is moved so that it is 60 cm from the hand, what is its moment?
c If the 100 g mass is replaced with a 200 g mass placed 30 cm from the hand, what is its moment?

QUESTIONS

Q2

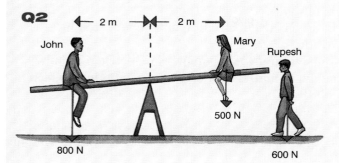

← 2 m → | ← 2 m →

John   Mary   Rupesh
500 N
800 N   600 N

John and Mary sit on opposite sides of a seesaw, each 2 m from the pivot. John weighs 800 N and Mary weighs 500 N. Rupesh weighs 600 N and is about to sit on the right-hand side of the seesaw.

a   Write down the equation of the principle of moments.

b   Where must Rupesh sit to make the seesaw balance?

c   Rupesh decides to go home. If Mary does not move where must John sit so that the seesaw balances?

ANSWERS & TUTORIALS

A2

a $\dfrac{\text{total anticlockwise}}{\text{moment}} = \dfrac{\text{total clockwise}}{\text{moment}}$

b   total anticlockwise moment $= 800\,\text{N} \times 2\,\text{m}$
$= 1600\,\text{N m.}$

There are two parts to the clockwise moment; the moment due to Mary and the moment due to Rupesh:

$\dfrac{\text{clockwise}}{\text{moment}} = (500\,\text{N} \times 2\,\text{m}) + (600\,\text{N} \times y)$

where y is the distance of Rupesh from the pivot in metres. For the seesaw to balance:

$\dfrac{\text{total anticlockwise}}{\text{moment}} = \dfrac{\text{total clockwise}}{\text{moment}}$

$1600 = 1000 + (600 \times y)$
$1600 - 1000 = 600 \times y$
$600 = 600 \times y$
$y = 1\,\text{m}$

Rupesh needs to sit 1 m from the pivot.

c $\dfrac{\text{total anticlockwise}}{\text{moment}} = \dfrac{\text{total clockwise}}{\text{moment.}}$

$800\,\text{N} \times z = 500\,\text{N} \times 2\,\text{m}$

where z is the distance John needs to be from the pivot in metres.

$z = \dfrac{1000}{800}$
$= 1.25\,\text{m}$

John needs to sit 1.25 m from the pivot.

T2   Use the principle of moments. For the seesaw to balance:

total anticlockwise = total clockwise
     moment   moment

Always show all your working. Even if you get the final answer wrong, you may earn some marks for some part of your calculation.

Chapter 45

Flow
of Charge

What you should already know

☐ Electric current is the flow of charge.
☐ An ammeter is used to measure the current (flow of charge) in an electrical circuit.
☐ Components in an electrical circuit can be connected in series or in parallel.
☐ Current is not 'used up' by components in electrical circuits.
☐ The particle model of matter can be used to explain physical phenomena.

What you need to know

In an electrical circuit, the cell causes charged particles called electrons to flow around the circuit. This flow of charged particles (the current) can be increased by increasing the **voltage**. The voltage is a measure of how much electromotive force (e.m.f.) is applied to the electrons. The voltage can be increased by correctly connecting more cells in the circuit (to make a larger battery).

Look at the circuits below. There are two cells in circuit **B** so the current will be twice that of circuit **A**, which has only one cell.

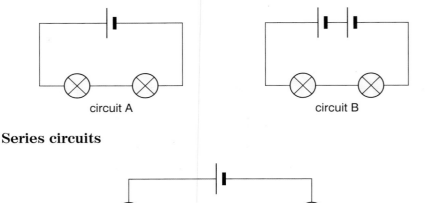

circuit A   circuit B

Series circuits

circuit C

The charge flows all the way round a series circuit. The same charge flows through each ammeter (there is nowhere else for the charge to go). Each ammeter in circuit **C** will show the same reading.

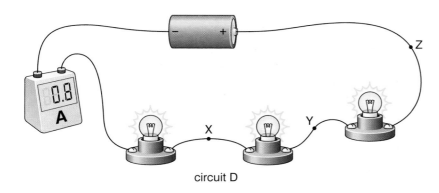

circuit D

The ammeter reading in circuit **D** is 0.8 A. If the ammeter is moved to position X or Y or Z, at each position the current will be 0.8 A. The current is the same at every point in a series circuit.

Bulbs, buzzers and other components make it harder for charge to flow round a circuit. They **resist** the current. The more **resistance** there is in a circuit, the more difficult it is for the charge to flow round the circuit.

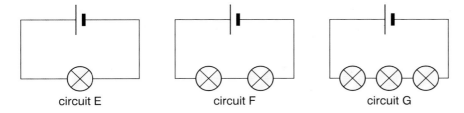

| circuit E | circuit F | circuit G |

There are twice as many bulbs in circuit **F** as there are in circuit **E**. The resistance in circuit **F** is twice that in circuit **E**, so the current in circuit **F** will be half the size of the current in circuit **E**.

Using the same reasoning, the resistance in circuit **G** is three times that in circuit **E**. Therefore, the current in circuit **G** is one third the size of the current in circuit **E**.

Parallel circuits

In parallel circuit **H**, the charge flowing from the battery splits into two parts at point X and joins back together again at point Y, before returning to the battery.

The current will split into equal parts if the bulbs have the same resistance. If the components in the branches of the circuit do not have the same resistance then the current will be greatest in the branch of the circuit that has components with the lower total resistance. This means that the branch of the circuit with the higher resistance will have the lower current passing through it.

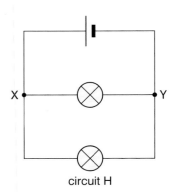

circuit H

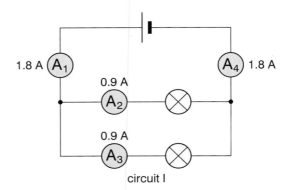

circuit I

In circuit **I**, the bulbs are identical. The ammeter, A_1 has a reading of 1.8 A. The current splits into two equal parts which means that A_2 and A_3 will both have a reading of 0.9 A. The current then recombines, so the reading on A_4 will be 1.8 A.

We can represent this by writing:

$A_1 = A_2 + A_3 = A_4$

In a parallel circuit, the current splits between the branches according to the resistance in each branch and joins together again in the return section of the circuit.

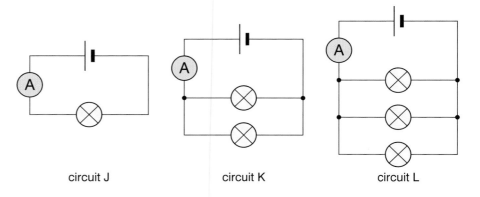

circuit J   circuit K   circuit L

The cells and bulbs in each of the circuits **J**, **K** and **L** are identical. It is easier for the electric charge to flow around circuit **K** than it is around circuit **J**. It may help to understand why this is so by thinking about cars driving along a motorway. If only one lane is open, the cars move slowly. If two lanes are open, the traffic splits between the two lanes and the cars can move more easily. When three lanes are open it is easier still for the cars to move. If we apply this model to electrical circuits, it suggests that the more branches there are in a parallel circuit, the lower the overall resistance to the flow of charge.

The resistance in circuit **K** will be half of that in circuit **J**. The current in circuit **K** will be twice as big as in circuit **J**.

The resistance in circuit **L** will be one-third of that in circuit **J**. The current in circuit **L** will be three times as big as the current in circuit **J**.

Check yourself

QUESTIONS

Q1 All of the bulbs and cells in each of the following circuits are identical.

What will be the reading on each of the ammeters labelled from A_1 to A_{10}?

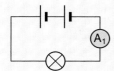 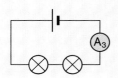

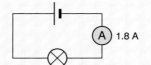 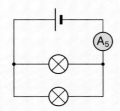

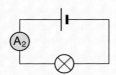 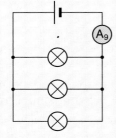

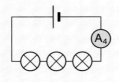

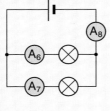

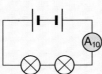

ANSWERS & TUTORIALS

A1 $A_1 = 3.6\,\text{A}$
$A_2 = 1.8\,\text{A}$
$A_3 = 0.9\,\text{A}$
$A_4 = 0.6\,\text{A}$
$A_5 = 3.6\,\text{A}$
$A_6 = 1.8\,\text{A}$
$A_7 = 1.8\,\text{A}$
$A_8 = 3.6\,\text{A}$
$A_9 = 5.4\,\text{A}$
$A_{10} = 0\,\text{A}$

T1 A_1 will be twice the original current because the number of cells has doubled.

A_2 is the same as the original current because the current is the same at every point in this circuit.

There are twice as many bulbs, so the resistance in the circuit has doubled. A_3 will be half the original value.

The resistance in the circuit has trebled, so A_4 will be one third of the original value.

The resistance in this circuit is half the original value because the current can travel along two paths, so A_5 will be twice the original value.

A_6 and A_7 are half of the value of A_8, because the current splits to travel along the two branches.

A_8 will be the double the original current for the same reasons as A_5.

The resistance in this circuit is one third of the original resistance because the current is split up over three paths. Therefore, A_9 is three times the original value.

No charge will flow because the two cells are connected with the voltage being applied in opposite directions.

1. Freckles are small patches of coloured skin.
The allele for freckles (a) is recessive to the allele for unfreckled skin (A). The diagram below shows a family where some of the people have freckles.

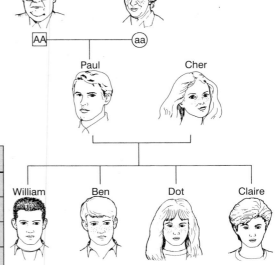

(a) Look carefully at the diagram and complete the table to show the genetic make-up (genotype) of William, Ben, Dot and Claire.

4 marks

family member	genetic make-up
William	
Ben	
Dot	
Claire	

(b) If Paul and Cher had another child, what would be the chance of it having freckles?

_____ *1 mark*

Explain your answer. You may use a diagram if you wish. *3 marks*

_____

_____

_____

2. The drawing shows the outline of a cell from the inner surface of the small intestine.

(a) Explain how the cell is adapted to make the absorption of the products of digestion more efficient. *1 mark*

_____

(b) In humans, glucose is formed by the digestion of a polymer of glucose. Give the name of the polymer. *1 mark*

_____

(c) Glucose is absorbed from the small intestine into the blood stream and is carried to the liver. Which part of the blood carries glucose? Tick the correct box. *1 mark*

plasma ☐   platelets ☐   red cells ☐   white cells ☐

(d) Glucose molecules cannot be stored in the body. They are converted into a compound which can be stored in liver cells.
(i) What is the name of this compound? _____ *1 mark*
(ii) Explain why glucose molecules cannot be stored in liver cells. *1 mark*

_____

3. (a) Egg white contains a protein called albumen.
A pupil carried out an experiment to investigate the digestion of three identical cubes of cooked egg white using the enzyme pepsin. She set up the experiment as follows.

Into beaker A, she put 50 cm^3 pepsin solution and a cube of egg white left whole.

Into beaker B, she put 50 cm^3 pepsin solution and a cube of egg white which had been cut into eight small cubes.

Into beaker C, she put 50 cm^3 pepsin solution and a cube of egg white which had been cut into sixty four tiny cubes.

She added 1 cm^3 hydrochloric acid to each beaker and placed the three beakers in a waterbath at 37 °C. The table gives the pupil's observations five hours later.

beaker	observations five hours later
A	a little of the egg white had gone from the edges of the whole cube
B	the cubes were about half their original size
C	only a few tiny fragments of egg white were left

    (i) Why was the cube of egg white which had been cut into sixty four pieces digested most quickly? _____ *1 mark*

    (ii) When protein is digested it is broken down into smaller molecules.
What name is given to these smaller molecules? _____ *1 mark*

(b) In another experiment, it was found that pepsin does not digest sucrose (sugar).
Explain why sucrose is not digested by pepsin.   *1 mark*

_____

(c) The graph below shows how quickly pepsin digests meat protein at different temperatures.

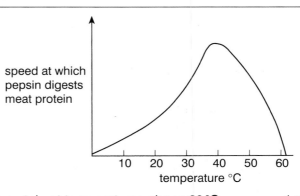

speed at which pepsin digests meat protein

temperature °C

Explain why pepsin does **not** digest protein at temperatures above 60 °C.   *1 mark*

_____

(d) Glands in the stomach wall produce mucus, hydrochloric acid and an inactive form of pepsin called pepsinogen. In the stomach hydrochloric acid reacts with the pepsinogen to produce pepsin.

    (i) Suggest **one** other purpose of acid in the stomach.   *1 mark*

_____

    (ii) Suggest **one** reason why pepsin is secreted in its inactive form.   *1 mark*

_____

    (iii) Suggest **one** purpose of mucus produced in the wall of the stomach.   *1 mark*

_____

    (iv) Bile from the liver makes the duodenum alkaline. Give **one** reason why the contents of the duodenum need to be alkaline.   *1 mark*

_____

4. (a) A pupil heated 1.24 g of copper carbonate strongly.
    The chemical reaction which took place is represented by the equation:

    $CuCO_3(s) \rightarrow CuO(s) + CO_2(g)$

    After the solid which remained had cooled, he weighed it.
    He found that its mass was 0.80 g.
    (i) Why did the pupil find a decrease in mass in this experiment?   *1 mark*
    _____

    (ii) He then heated the 0.80 g of solid again. When he weighed it after cooling,
    its mass was still 0.80 g. Explain why it had not changed in mass this time.   *1 mark*
    _____

    (b) (i) In another experiment, he burnt magnesium ribbon in air. He found that the mass of
    the powder formed was greater than the original mass of the ribbon. Explain this.
    _____ *1 mark*

    (ii) Write the balanced equation for the reaction which takes place when magnesium
    burns in oxygen. _____ *1 mark*

5. The metal chromium can be extracted industrially by **three** different chemical methods.
    The equations for these chemical reactions are shown below.

    $Cr_2O_3 + 2Al \rightarrow 2Cr + Al_2O_3$

    $2Cr_2O_3 + 3Si \rightarrow 4Cr + 3SiO_2$

    $2Cr_2O_3 + 3C \rightarrow 4Cr + 3CO_2$

    (a) What name is given to the extraction of a metal from its oxide in this type of
    chemical reaction?_____ *1 mark*
    (b) Use the equations to compare the reactivity of chromium with the reactivities of
    aluminium, silicon and carbon. Tick **one** box in each column in the table.   *1 mark*

	aluminium	silicon	carbon
more reactive than chromium			
less reactive than chromium			

6. An electrical current is a flow of charge.
    The diagram shows a circuit containing six identical bulbs.
    In which part of the circuit, A, B, C, D or E, is there:
    (i) the greatest flow of charge? _____
    (ii) the least flow of charge?   _____   *2 marks*

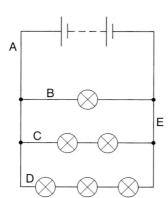

7. The diagrams below show four planks. The planks are pivoted in the middle and have boxes on them. All the boxes have the same weight.
Next to each plank write '**B**' if it is balanced or '**U**' if it is unbalanced.
If a plank is **unbalanced**, write which side goes **down**.
Write '**L**' for the left-hand side or '**R**' for the right-hand side. *4 marks*

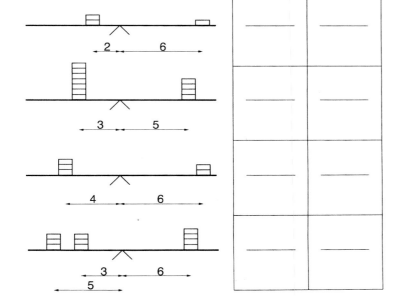

B balanced **or**	**R** right **or**
U unbalanced	**L** left
———	———
———	———
———	———
———	———

8. The graph shows the speed of a ball as it falls from a height and bounces from the floor.

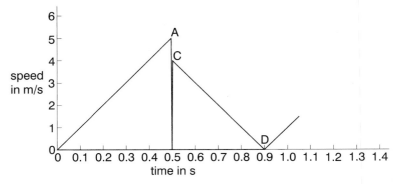

(a) The ball starts to fall and speeds up until it hits the floor.
   (i) For how many seconds does the ball fall before it first hits the floor? _____ *1 mark*
   (ii) Calculate the average speed of the ball during its fall. *1 mark*

   (iii) Calculate the height above the floor from which the ball was dropped. *1 mark*

(b) (i) What is happening to the ball in the time between points A and C on
      the graph? _____ *1 mark*
   (ii) In which direction is the ball moving between points C and D? _____ *1 mark*
(c) Calculate how high the ball bounces back up from the floor. *1 mark*

TEST ANSWERS

Level 4

Question	Answer	Mark	Examiner's comments
1 a (i) (ii) (iii)	mayfly nymph water beetle lymnaea	1 1 1	You should try to use the exact words from the key, e.g. mayfly nymph. In this case, using just nymph would get a mark but try not to take shortcuts – they may not pay off.
	TOTAL MARKS	3	
2	A Evernia C Usnea D Parmelia saxatilis	1 1 1	Try to copy the spelling accurately. Use the whole name given in the key. In this case, saxatilis would not be sufficient for the mark for lichen D.
	TOTAL MARKS	3	
3 a	digestive system	1	Pay attention to the instructions for the question 'Tick the correct box'. If you tick more than one box you will not be awarded the mark.
b	lowest box ticked	1	The question says 'Tick **one** box'. Do not be tempted to tick more than one. If you do not know the answer, you could guess and tick one box. You will not lose marks and you may guess the correct answer.
	TOTAL MARKS	2	
4	X lung Y heart Z kidney	1 1 1	Lines are given to write your answers on. Try to put your answers on the lines provided and only offer one answer for each labelling letter.
	TOTAL MARKS	3	
5 a	ovary B ovule C sepal D stamen A	1 1 1 1	Make sure you follow the instructions and only put ONE letter in each box.
b	makes pollen	1	You could answer that it puts pollen on the insect. You would not get the mark if you suggest part A 'sends pollen to other flowers'.
	TOTAL MARKS	5	
6 a	X on stigma P on any stamen	1 1	You can put the letters X and P directly onto the part shown on the diagram. If you want to use a labelling line always use a ruler to draw it and make sure the labelling line touches the part that it is meant to indicate.
b	S on ovary	1	Never try to hedge your bets by putting the letter in-between possible answers. You will not be awarded a mark unless your labelling is clear. Do not be afraid to guess if you really do not know or cannot work out the answer.
	TOTAL MARKS	3	
7 a (i) (ii)	liquid petrol or oil or diesel or paraffin or kerosene gas gas or natural gas or calor gas or butane or propane or LPG or petroleum gas or methane or camping gaz	1 1 1 1	You are asked to tick the correct box. If you tick more than one box you will not be awarded the mark. Write your example of a liquid fuel in the space provided, not elsewhere on the page, e.g. by the box you ticked.
	TOTAL MARKS	4	

8				Mark	
	solid	**liquid**	**gas**		
	✓			1	If more than one box is ticked no mark is awarded.
		✓	✓	2	If three boxes are ticked only one mark is awarded.
			✓	1	If more than one box is ticked no mark is awarded.
	TOTAL MARKS			4	

TEST ANSWERS

Question	Answer	Mark	Examiner's comments
9 a	It is an acid.	1	Tick only one box or you will not be awarded the mark.
b	bubbling *or* fizzing *or* effervescence	1	The gas given off is carbon dioxide. In a liquid the carbon dioxide forms bubbles and these are the bubbles seen.
c (i) (ii)	red *or* bright red indicators	1 1	This red colour is produced by all acids when added to red cabbage.
d (i)	acid can be poisonous *or* burn *or* is dangerous *or* harmful	1	'It will kill you' is not a suitable answer as this is not a certainty. It is certain that the acid is corrosive and this answer would be awarded a mark.
(ii)	(The answer should refer to the use of washing soda crystals with both liquids.) Any one from: • pour some of the liquid from each bottle onto washing soda; • add washing soda to a sample from each bottle. Any one from: • one bubbles and one does not; • one gives off carbon dioxide and one does not; • the acid bubbles or gives off carbon dioxide; • the water does not bubble or give off carbon dioxide.	1 1	When working with substances it is necessary to use a sample only. An answer 'Add washing soda to each bottle' is not awarded a mark. The question asks you to describe what you would see in each case. An answer 'it bubbles' is not acceptable as it is not clear which liquid it refers to. Always give specific detail in answers.
	TOTAL MARKS	**7**	

10 a (i) (ii) (iii)	It is an acid *or* acidic It is an alkali *or* alkaline purple	1 1 1	You have been given the colour of litmus in three different conditions; neutral, acid and alkali. To answer the question you must pay attention to the colour described and which condition it indicates.
b	neutralisation	1	You should not tick more than one box, otherwise the mark is not awarded. If you do not know the correct answer make a guess.
	TOTAL MARKS	**4**	

11 a (i) (ii) (iii)	soluble insoluble solution	1 1 1	The question needs you to use words given in the question. Follow the instruction carefully and write one word in the space in each question. If you do not know an answer make a guess from the words listed.
b	Any one from: • evaporate the water; • boil the water away.	1	Simply writing 'dry it' is not awarded a mark because it is not a precise answer. 'Distilling' is a method for getting the liquid back, not the solid.
c (i)	Any one from: • less coffee dissolves; • coffee is less soluble in cold water.	1	
(ii)	less than before	1	You should not tick more than one box otherwise the mark is not awarded. If you do not know the correct answer make a guess.
	TOTAL MARKS	**6**	

12 a	C	1	You must tick only one box. More than one tick will not be awarded a mark. The answer can be found by drawing a straight line from the bright light, touching the foot, and on to the screen.
b	Any one from: • the puppet stops the light; • the light cannot go through the puppet; • light travels in straight lines; • the light cannot go round the puppet.	1	There are two lines provided for your answer. Use words to describe how the shadow forms. You will not be awarded the mark if you only draw lines on the diagram as an answer.
c	Any one from: • it is very fast; • it is very high.	1	An answer 'faster than sound' is not awarded a mark. There is no reference to sound in the question for you to compare with.
	TOTAL MARKS	**3**	

13 (i) (ii) (iii) (iv) (v)	E B C A B and C	1 1 1 1 1	You must answer the question in the way it asks. In this case you are asked to write letters from the diagram. Where you are asked for one place you need to write one letter. If you write more than one letter in those questions you will not be awarded the mark. In part (v) you are asked for two places. Use two letters otherwise you will not be awarded the mark.
	TOTAL MARKS	**5**	

TEST ANSWERS

Question	Answer	Mark	Examiner's comments
14			The question asks you to tick the correct box for each circuit, i.e. each row needs one tick. More than one tick in a row will prevent the mark being awarded.

circuit diagram	buzzer on only	lamp on only	both on	neither on	Mark
A				✓	1
B		✓			1
C	✓				1
D				✓	1
E			✓		1

TOTAL MARKS 5

Question	Answer	Mark	Examiner's comments
15 a	(In each question both boxes must be correct for the mark to be awarded.) lamp ✗ motor ✗	1	Each question requires a tick or a cross in the box. If you leave any boxes blank, you will not be awarded the mark.
b	lamp ✗ motor ✗	1	
c	lamp ✗ motor ✓	1	
d	lamp ✓ motor ✗	1	

TOTAL MARKS 4

Question	Answer	Mark	Examiner's comments
16 a	the push of a jet engine on an aeroplane the weight of a book on a table the pull of a horse pulling a cart	1 1 1	You should only insert three ticks as the question asks. If there are more than three boxes ticked then take a mark off for each incorrect tick.
b	(Answers should indicate that the path of the ball is not straight.) Any one from: • it changes direction; • it does not go in a straight line; • it goes in a curve; • it goes up and comes down.	1	Try to describe your reasons clearly. Writing an answer 'gravity' is not awarded a mark because you are not answering the question. The force of gravity pulls the ball downwards, but you were asked how you can tell there is a force acting, not to name the force.
c	It makes the trolley go faster.	1	If you tick more than one box you will not be awarded the mark. If you do not know the answer then have a guess.

TOTAL MARKS 5

Question	Answer	Mark	Examiner's comments
17 a	A D E	3	You can write the letters in any order. Each correct letter gets a mark. Do not write more than three letters. If you do not know the answer then have a guess.
b (i) (ii)	gravity or weight air resistance or drag	1 1	Use accurate language. An answer 'wind' is not awarded a mark as it is not the same as air resistance.

TOTAL MARKS 5

Level 5

Question	Answer	Mark	Examiner's comments
1 a (i) (ii)	the uterus or womb the lung or lungs	1 1	Everyday words can be acceptable when they are specific, i.e. womb can only refer to one thing, the uterus. The lung is the organ. If you name parts of the lung such as an air sac it will not be awarded a mark.
b	transport of blood digestive or digestion	1 1	Moving blood or circulating blood would be acceptable answers. The blood also takes part in defence against disease and in keeping the body temperature controlled. Guts is not an acceptable answer. Intestines are only part of the system and it is therefore not a full enough answer.
c	Any one of the following answers: • gives support; • gives shape; • protects organs; • allows movement. Other acceptable answers include: • attachment for muscles; • produces blood cells.	1	You can see there is quite a range of answers possible. Do not be tempted to give more than one when the question asks 'Give **one** function of the skeleton'. If one of the answers is not correct you lose the chance of a mark.

TOTAL MARKS 5

T E S T   A N S W E R S

Question	Answer	Mark	Examiner's commemts
2 a	ovary *or* ovaries	1	
b	uterus *or* womb	1	
c (i)	placenta	1	The umbilical cord is not an acceptable answer as it only carries the blood to and from the placenta through which the food is passed.
(ii)	Any one of the following answers: • oxygen; • antibodies; • water.	1	'Air' is not a suitable alternative to oxygen. Much of the air is not oxygen and does not dissolve in the blood to be carried around the body.
2 d	reproductive system	1	Try to use the full phrase. In this case the answer reproductive or reproduction would be acceptable.

TOTAL MARKS   5

Question				Mark	Examiner's commemts
3					Where more than one thing is being asked for (e.g. name *and* function) be sure to give both. Only giving the name *or* the function will not be awarded a mark. Copy the phrases given accurately, i.e. do not change the words.

letter	name	function	Mark
A	flower or petal	to attract insects for pollination	1
B	leaf	to absorb light	1
C	root	to take up water	1
D	fruit or strawberry	to attract animals for seed dispersal	1

TOTAL MARKS   4

Question	Answer	Mark	Examiner's commemts
4 a	 X Y Z	1 1 1	The lines need to be drawn with a ruler so that they are clear. The end of the line should connect the letter to the part labelled. Try not to leave gaps between the line and the part it labels. The question asks for the stigma to be labelled. A labelling line to the style is not acceptable even though it supports the stigma. Be accurate.
b	stigma pollination fertilisation	1 1 1	The gap provided to write each word is generous. Do not be tempted to write more than one word/phrase given in the list.

TOTAL MARKS   6

Question	Answer	Mark	Examiner's commemts
5 a	water	1	Read tables carefully. All the information you need to answer the question is given in the table.
b	propanone	1	Propanone dissolves all three colours. Colours need to be dissolved before they will move up the chromatography paper.
c	yellow, Y	1	You should not tick more than one box otherwise the mark is not awarded. If you do not know the correct answer make a guess.
d	(One mark is for identifying that the same paints were used in picture 3 and picture 1, and the other is for identifying the differences between the paints used picture 3 and picture 2). Any one from: • the three paint colours are all the same in pictures 1 and 3; • the pattern of colours is the same in pictures 1 and 3; • the yellow, blue and green paints are the same in pictures 1 and 3. Any one from: • the yellow or green paint in picture 3 is different from that in picture 2; • only the blue is the same in pictures 2 and 3; • only the blue paint is the same in the three pictures.	1 1	

TOTAL MARKS   5

TEST ANSWERS

Question	Answer	Mark	Examiner's comments
6 a	filtration *or* filtering distillation *or* distilling	1 1	Use the two lines provided for your answers. Make sure you write the correct method against the correct number.
b (i) (ii)	sand and water dissolved salt and water	1 1	You should not tick more than one box otherwise the mark is not awarded. If you do not know the correct answer make a guess.
c (i) (ii) (iii)	(The correct positions of both red and blue spots are required for the mark.) blue, yellow, red yellow	1 1 1	If you draw more than two spots you are awarded no marks. Purple ink is made of red and blue dye and would produce two spots (one red and one blue). You only get the mark if all **three** inks are named, as the question asked.
	TOTAL MARKS	7	

Question	Answer	Mark	Examiner's comments
7 a	Any two from: • good electrical conductor; • good thermal conductor; • melting point above room temperature.	2	You are asked for **two** properties of magnesium. Choose **two** from the list provided and copy the spelling accurately. It does not matter what order you write them in.
b (i) (ii)	magnesium sulphide Any two from: • good electrical conductor; • good thermal conductor; • magnetic.	1 2	Magnesium sulphate is not a correct answer. Sulphates have sulphur and oxygen in them. The reaction in the question only involves magnesium and sulphur, not oxygen. You are asked for **two** properties that magnesium sulphide does not have. If you do not know make a guess from the list of answers provided.
	TOTAL MARKS	5	

Question	Answer	Mark	Examiner's comments
8 a	A Any one from: • highest frequency; • shortest wavelength; • most waves on oscilloscope screen; • lines *or* trails *or* waves are closest together.	1 1	Try to use accurate language. 'Waves go fastest' is not awarded a mark. There is no evidence for this in the question. The presence of the most waves means the highest frequency and does not describe the speed of the waves.
b	C Wave C has the largest amplitude	1 1	The space provided in the question indicates the detail of the answer required.
c	(The answer should be marked by considering wavelength, amplitude and number of waves separately.) Any two from: • a drawing of a wave showing three wavelengths; • amplitude less than the given trace; • each complete wavelength is half the wavelength of trace E.	2	Your drawing should be done as carefully as possible, e.g. a consistent wavelength and consistent amplitude. The original trace E has one and a half waves shown so a humming bird with twice the frequency would produce a trace with three waves shown.
	TOTAL MARKS	6	

Question	Answer	Mark	Examiner's comments
9 a	point E	1	You must tick only one box. If you tick more than one box you will not be awarded the mark. If you do not know the answer have a guess.
b	Marks are awarded for: • a continuous ray from the point to the eye; • straight lines to the mirrors at appropriate angles; • an arrow anywhere along the ray pointing from the tree to the eye.	1 1 1	You need to draw carefully. Use a ruler as the question asks, otherwise you will not draw straight lines for rays of light and could lose the marks. Make sure that the angles of incidence and reflection are equal.
c	Any one from: • move the bottom of the periscope towards the wall; • make it upright; • lift it higher.	1	An answer 'move it' is not precise enough. It could mean a movement in any direction.
	TOTAL MARKS	5	

TEST ANSWERS

Question	Answer	Mark	Examiner's comments
10 a (i)	The path must be drawn through the Sun, curving downwards at the East and West.	1	The Sun's apparent path across the sky is curved. An answer that is drawn with straight lines will not be awarded a mark. Light travels in straight lines but the source of the light, the Sun, appears to travel in a curved path.
(ii)	The arrow should point from East to West.	1	Do not be tempted to hedge your bets. If you put conflicting arrows showing different directions you will not be awarded the mark.
b	(One mark is for the Sun's path shown lower in the sky and one mark is for the shape of the path.) The curve should be: • drawn beneath the answer to part (a)(i); • reasonably parallel to your answer to part (a)(i).	1 1	An answer that is drawn with straight lines will not be awarded a mark. Light travels in straight lines but the source of the light, the Sun, appears to travel in a curved path.

TOTAL MARKS 4

Level 6

1	a (i)	Any one from: • holds cell together; • controls movement of chemicals in and out of the cell; • acts as a barrier; • allows active uptake. Other suitable answers include: keeps the cells shape.	1	The cell membrane does not protect the cell, that is one job of the cell wall.
	(ii)	controls the cell (An acceptable answer would be 'tells the cell what to do.')	1	If you describe the nucleus structure, e.g. contains chromosomes or genes, you would not be given the mark as these are not functions but descriptions of structure.
	b	The answers are pairs of responses with the structural difference described and explained for one mark each. **One pair could be:** Nerve cell is long... for taking information from one part of the body to another. **A second pair could be:** Nerve cell has branches (dendrites)... to pick up information from more than one cell or place. **A third pair could be:** Nerve cell has sheath around the long part... sheath acts as an insulator or speeds up conduction of impulses.	4	Only two pairs are required for a total of four marks.

TOTAL MARKS 6

2	a (i)	chloroplast	1	This word is given in the diagram. Copy the word carefully to make sure you are awarded the mark.
	(ii)	chloroplast	1	
		cell wall	1	Try and give the full names. Just saying 'wall' may not be credited. Use the words given in the diagram.
	b	**part of the cell** chloroplast nucleus cell wall cell membrane	1 1 1 1	Try to give the full name as given in the question. In this case 'wall' and 'membrane' can be marked correct.

TOTAL MARKS 7

TEST ANSWERS

Question	Answer	Mark	Examiner's comments
3 a	Any two from: • inheritance; • health of mother during pregnancy; • nutrition of mother during pregnancy.	2	The question asks for **two** reasons for low birth weight. The question provides **two spaces** for your answers. Try to put one reason in each space. Do not cram two into one space and do not give more than a total of two reasons.
b (i)	Any one from: • have same parents; • are similar genetically; • both developed under similar conditions in same womb.	1	Try to give your answers in as few words as necessary to be clear, e.g. they have the same parents. The twins are not identical (they are male and female) and so the answer 'they have the same genes' is incorrect.
(ii)	Any one from: • they are non-identical twins or of different sex • they will have different genes or have different genetic make-up; • they were in slightly different environments in the womb.	1	
	TOTAL MARKS 4		
4 a(i)	Any two from: • it is warmer; • the light is brighter. (Other possible answers are: • warmer, more light • the days are longer; • bigger leaves; • leaves start to grow; • more leaves.)	2	One common mistake is to use the word 'Sun' in answering this question. The Sun radiates light and also heats the objects it hits. Photosynthesis involves light and so light or sunlight are acceptable words to use. Simply saying 'Sun' is not sufficient.
(ii)	oxygen glucose	1 1	There are two spaces for your two answers. Always put one in each space. It does not matter in which order you write your answers.
b	photosynthesis or carbon dioxide uptake stops in autumn or starts in spring	1	An answer 'most photosynthesis occurs in summer' is an incorrect answer. There is more photosynthesis by evergreen trees in summer. Deciduous trees have no leaves in winter and there is no photosynthesis, unlike the evergreen trees.
c	respiration	1	
	TOTAL MARKS 6		
5 a	• oxygen *or* O_2 (is given out to the air) • water *or* H_2O (is taken from the soil) • carbon dioxide *or* CO_2 (is taken from the air)	1 1 1	Use the boxes provided for your answers. If you write elsewhere on the diagram it may not be clear which part you are referring to.
b	glucose *or* $C_6H_{12}O_6$	1	An acceptable answer would be 'sugar'.
c	chlorophyll	1	This is a difficult word to spell. Try to be accurate in your spelling. The word must at least be spelled as it sounds.
d	it absorbs *or* traps light	1	You need to use words accurately. The leaves absorb light but they do not attract it. 'Attract light' would be marked wrong.
e	Any one from: • more chlorophyll or chloroplasts near the upper surface; • to obtain maximum light for photosynthesis.	1	You only have one line to write on. Try not to repeat any part of the question.
	TOTAL MARKS 7		
6 a	Any one from: • more air or oxygen; • better mixing gives more combustion *or* more efficient burning.	1	Either air or oxygen are acceptable. Air contains oxygen that is needed for burning to take place.
b	(*methane*) + oxygen → carbon dioxide + water	2	Only put one substance in each answer space. On the right, you need to write the two products, carbon dioxide and water clearly, either side of the + sign.
	TOTAL MARKS 3		

TEST ANSWERS

Question	Answer	Mark	Examiner's comments
7 a (i) (ii)	zinc sulphate + copper brown	1 1	Zinc sulphide or zinc sulphur are incorrect answers. Use the colours given in the question.
b (i) (ii)	magnesium + copper sulphate → magnesium sulphate + copper silver grey brown	1 1 1	 Magnesium has been added in excess. Use the colours given in the question. Use the colours given in the question. Copper is used as a colour description and would be awarded a mark in this case.
c (i) (ii)	no reaction *or* nothing *or* none Any one from: • magnesium is more reactive than iron; • iron is less reactive than magnesium.	1 1	 Answers should refer to both magnesium and iron.
	TOTAL MARKS	7	

Question	Answer	Mark	Examiner's comments
8 a (i) (ii)	Any one from: • solid to liquid; • melting. Any one from: • liquid to gas *or* vapour; • evaporation.	1 1	The answer 'ice to water' is not awarded a mark. The question asks for the change of state. Ice and water are names specific substances but are not states. In the same way 'water to steam' is not an acceptable answer to part (ii).

b (i)

	solid	liquid	gas
close together	✓	✓	
far apart			✓
in a regular pattern	✓		
random		✓	✓

Mark: 3 — One mark is given for each correct column.
Two ticks are asked for in each column. If you put in more than or less than two you will not be awarded the mark.

(ii)

	solid	gas
move around slowly		
move around quickly		✓
only vibrate	✓	
do not move		

Mark: 1 — Both ticks are needed to be awarded one mark.

TOTAL MARKS 6

Question	Answer	Mark	Examiner's comments
9 a	oxygen	1	The answer 'oxide' is not awarded a mark because it is not the name of an element.
b (i) (ii) (iii)	sulphuric acid use a burning splint which lights the hydrogen and makes it go pop Any one from: • warm it; • heat it gently; • leave it to stand; • let the water evaporate; • make it more concentrated.	1 1 1	 A glowing splint is not the correct answer. This would be the test for oxygen and the splint would re-light. For crystals to develop, evaporation has to be slow. The answer 'heat it' is not precise enough as it could lead to too rapid evaporation or an unwanted chemical change.
	TOTAL MARKS	4	

TEST ANSWERS

Question	Answer	Mark	Examiner's comments
10 a	It is between the orbit of Earth and the orbit of Jupiter.	1	Tick one box only. If you tick more than one box you will not be awarded a mark.
b (i)	(An indication of any point within the limits shown below.) V	1 1	Try to draw your answer accurately. You are more likely to be awarded a mark if your answer is clearly drawn and labelled V as the question asks.
(ii)	Because the distance between Venus and the Earth changes.		
c (i)	(An indication of any point within the limits shown below.) J	1	Try to draw your answer accurately. You are more likely to be awarded a mark if your answer is clearly drawn and labelled J as the question asks.
(ii)	Because the distance between Jupiter and the Earth changes.	1	An answer 'because of air pollution' is incorrect. Pollution on Earth does not affect how much light is reflected from
	TOTAL MARKS	5	

Question	Answer	Mark	Examiner's comments
11 a	One mark is for: • storing energy by photosynthesis; The other mark is for one of: • the formation of oil from living things; • living things use energy from the Sun to grow; • oil is formed from the remains of living things.	1 1	There are two marks for this question and so your answer should contain two clear points.
b (i)	Because it cannot be replaced once it is used *or* because it takes a long time to form.	1	Try to be accurate in your answer. An answer 'it cannot be recycled' is not a true description of the fuel. The point is that the fuel will not be replaced (made again).
(ii)	coal natural gas	1 1	You are asked to tick two boxes. You will lose marks if you tick more than two boxes. If you do not know the answer make a guess.
	TOTAL MARKS	5	

Question					Mark	Examiner's comments
12	energy resource	directly from the Sun	indirectly from the Sun	not from the Sun		You need to tick one box in each row. If you tick more than one box then you will lose marks. If you do not know the answer then make a guess.
	nuclear			✓	1	
	hydro-electric		✓		1	
	solar	✓			1	
	geothermal			✓	1	
	oil		✓		1	
	TOTAL MARKS				5	

Question	Answer	Mark	Examiner's comments
13		1 1	The first mark is for the direction of the waves changing as in the diagram. The second mark is for a shorter wavelength, the lines being close together.
	TOTAL MARKS	2	

208

T E S T   A N S W E R S

Level 7

Question	Answer	Mark	Examiner's comments
1 a	Herbivore – any one from: • wood mouse; • aphid; • caterpillar. Omnivore – great tit	1 1	Animals that eat **only** plants are called herbivores. The great tit eats **some** plant material but also eats animals and so is an omnivore.
b (i)	less competition for caterpillars or aphids or food	1	You may have said 'more food' or 'more caterpillars', this implies less competition and would be awarded one mark. If there is less competition, the great tits could increase in number and not decrease. Any decrease must be due to some other factor such as predators eating them.
(ii)	weasels or stoats or sparrowhawks or predators eat more of them	1	
(iii)	Any one from: • sparrowhawks only eat blue tits and great tits; • stoats also eat wood mice.	1	
c	Any two from: • energy is lost as thermal energy or by respiration; • some material is not digested or is lost in waste; • some material is excreted.	2	Throughout your answers you should try to use scientific language correctly. 'Used up running around' is not as clear a description as 'lost by respiration' although it would be awarded a mark.
	TOTAL MARKS	7	

Question	Answer	Mark	Examiner's comments
2 a (i) (ii) (iii)	D A B	1 1 1	Follow instructions carefully. Your answer should be written in the spaces provided. Only one diagram should be identified for each food chain. If you are not sure, it is sensible to make a guess.
b (i) (ii)	respiration feeding	1 1	You are asked to tick the correct box. If you tick more than one box you will not be given a mark.
	TOTAL MARKS	5	

Question	Answer	Mark	Examiner's comments
3 a (i) (ii)	yellow respiration	1 1	Try to use the correct scientific word. You are asked to name the process. Giving a description of respiration only is not answering the question.
b (i) (ii)	purple photosynthesis	1 1	Try to use correct scientific vocabulary. You are asked to name the process. Giving a description of photosynthesis only is not answering the question.
c	Photosynthesis and respiration were happening at the same time or at the same rate.	1	
d	yellow	1	Do not tick more than one box. If you do not know the answer make a guess rather than leave a blank space.
	TOTAL MARKS	6	

Question	Answer	Mark	Examiner's comments
4	chloroplasts – to make food by photosynthesis waxy cuticle – to reduce water loss cilia – to remove particles from windpipe dendrites – to carry nerve impulses	1 1 1 1	The question requires that you draw lines connecting boxes. Use a ruler for clarity and make sure the lines actually touch the boxes you believe belong together. Never hedge your bets by drawing more than one line. If you change your mind make sure you clearly cross out the line to be ignored and then draw in the new line.
	TOTAL MARKS	4	

T E S T   A N S W E R S

Question	Answer	Mark	Examiner's comments
5 a	element compound Ar CO_2 N_2 H_2O Ne O_2	1	All six formulae are needed to gain the mark. The formulae are given in the question and it is important that your answers use the formulae accurately.

b	atom molecule
	Ar N_2
	Ne O_2
	          CO_2
	          H_2O
		1	All six formulae are needed to gain the mark. The order that the formulae are listed in is not important but they must be in the correct column.

c	Ne *or* neon	1	
d	*For the neon gas:* • up to ten randomly arranged particles spaced throughout the box (just one particle is acceptable but not an empty box.) • most of the particles are not in contact with each other. *For the liquid neon:* • the box is almost full of particles of neon, with more than half of them touching each other; • the particles are randomly arranged.	1 1 1 1	When drawing representations of a gas or a liquid it is important to take care and draw accurately. All the particles should look the same size and shape. In a gas, they are spread out widely with few being shown in the box provided in the question. The liquid will have particles filling the space in the box and the particles are shown touching even though they are free to move and are randomly arranged.

TOTAL MARKS   7

Question	Answer	Mark	Examiner's comments
6 a	• When water freezes it expands; • bits are forced off the sandstone *or* cracks are forced open.	1 1	You will notice that there are two marks for your answer. This implies that there should be two points in your answer. Always try to spot how many marks are available as this will give you an idea of how detailed your answer should be.
b (i)	Possible answers are: • expansion and contraction – due to rapid changes in temperature; • rocks split open – due to growth of plant roots; • rocks are pitted or cracked – due to wetting and drying.	 2	Again, this question has two marks awarded. Award one mark for the correct statement and one mark for the correct explanation. Answers may include processes which are sometimes classified as erosion.
(ii)	Acid rain *or* rain *or* pollutants – by reacting with substances in the rock.	1 1	When making your two points remember you are being asked about chemical changes. An answer 'wears away rock' suggests physical change and so is not awarded a mark.

TOTAL MARKS   6

Question	Answer	Mark	Examiner's comments
7 a (i)	the acid *or* rhubarb reacted with the steel	1	Your answer needs to refer to both reactants. An answer 'rhubarb is acid' is not awarded a mark.
(ii)	hydrogen	1	Use words for your answer unless a formula is asked for. While H_2 would be correct, H would not be awarded a mark because it is not the correct formula for hydrogen molecules.
b (i)	Any one from: • tin is less reactive than iron or steel; • tin is lower than steel in the reactivity series.	1	
(ii)	Any one from: • the steel reacts with the food *or* is corroded by the acid in the food; • the iron or steel will rust *or* react with the air outside the can.	1	The answer may focus on either the inside or the outside of the can.
c	aluminium is more reactive than iron *or* steel *or* tin	1	Your answer needs to compare the reactivity of aluminium with that of iron or steel. An answer 'aluminium is high in the reactivity series' does not give the comparison needed.

TOTAL MARKS   5

T E S T   A N S W E R S

Question	Answer	Mark	Examiner's comments
8 a	0.3	1	Pressure is force (or weight) divided by area, so $600 \div 2000$ will be awarded the mark.
	N/cm^2 (or $N\,cm^{-2}$)	1	There is another unit of pressure called a pascal (Pa). If this unit is used the answer must be 3×10^{-5} Pa to be awarded marks.
b	Any one from: • feet have a smaller area than the skis; • skis have area five times that of feet; • skis are bigger than feet.	1	
	TOTAL MARKS 3		

Question	Answer	Mark	Examiner's comments
9 a (i) (ii)	red red	1 1	
b (i) (ii)	black Any one from: • red ink absorbs green light; • red ink only reflects red light; • no green light is reflected from the ink.	1 1	You need to use scientific vocabulary. An answer 'there is no red in green' is not accurate enough.
	TOTAL MARKS 4		

Question	Answer	Mark	Examiner's comments
10 a (i)	Any one from: • the sheet is attracted to the electromagnet; • the sheet bends towards the electromagnet.	1	The sheet moves only towards the electromagnet while it is switched on. An answer 'it vibrates' is incorrect because the sheet would have to move towards and away from the electromagnet.
(ii)	Any one from: • it goes back to where it was; • it springs back; • it bends back; • it straightens.	1	Similarly to the above an answer 'it stops vibrating' is incorrect because it was not vibrating to start with.
(iii)	Any one from: • none *or* no difference; • it would still attract.	1	An answer 'it bends the other way' is incorrect. Connected in either way the battery produces a current and causes the electromagnet to attract the steel.
b (i)	higher pitch because the frequency of the vibration increases	1 1	An answer 'it vibrates more' for either part (i) or (ii) is not correct because it is not clear what it means. Vibrating more could mean a bigger amplitude which would make the sound louder but not higher in pitch.
(ii)	Any one from: • larger amplitude vibrations; • the sheet would bend more *or* further.	1	
	TOTAL MARKS 6		

Level 8

Question	Answer	Mark	Examiner's comments
1 a	William Aa *or* aA Ben aa Dot aa Claire Aa *or* aA	1 1 1 1	The order in which you write each pair of genes makes no difference, i.e. Aa is genetically the same as aA. Take care when filling in the table to ensure that you put the correct genes against the person you are considering.
b	50% *Either:* • Paul can pass on either A or a; • Cher can only pass on a; • Aa and aa offspring are possible in equal numbers. *or* A genetic diagram illustrating the same three points. It must be clear which gametes are produced by Paul and by Cher.	1 1 1 1	If you draw diagrams for your answer make sure they are clear. Use a ruler to draw lines connecting genes from one generation to the next: Paul Cher Aa aa A a a a Aa Aa aa aa
	TOTAL MARKS 8		

211

TEST ANSWERS

Question	Answer	Mark	Examiner's comments
2 a	(Answers should refer to microvilli and to the larger surface that they provide.) Any one from: • folds *or* projections *or* microvilli give a large surface area; • folds *or* projections *or* microvilli increase the rate of absorption.	1	To gain a mark you need to describe the adaptation AND the advantage it gives, e.g. 'projections give large surface area'. Simply describing the feature or the advantage will not gain the mark, e.g. 'increased rate of absorption' will not be awarded a mark.
b	starch (*or* glycogen)	1	
c	plasma	1	Tick only one box or you will not be awarded the mark. If you do not know the answer make a guess.
d (i) (ii)	glycogen they are soluble	1 1	Starch is stored in plants and therefore is not a suitable answer to this question about humans.
	TOTAL MARKS	**5**	

Question	Answer	Mark	Examiner's comments
3 a (i) (ii)	larger surface area Any one from: • polypeptides; • peptides; • amino acids.	1 1	You will not be awarded a mark for a general answer, e.g. 'monomers' would describe the product of breaking down any polymer and is not specific enough.
b	Any one from: • enzymes are specific; • enzymes only act on one type of substrate; • pepsin only digests proteins – sucrose is not a protein; • because of the shape of the molecules.	1	The question is specifically about the enzyme not digesting sucrose. An answer 'it is not a protein' is not precise enough because it is not clear if the answer is describing the sucrose or the enzyme.
c	enzymes become denatured *or* destroyed *or* deactivated	1	Enzymes are not alive but are produced by living things. An answer 'enzymes are killed' is not correct.
d (i) (ii) (iii) (iv)	Any one from: • kills bacteria or germs or micro-organisms; • provides the correct pH for the action of pepsin. pepsin could digest *or* damage the cells of the stomach protects the stomach wall from the action of pepsin *or* acid Any one from: • the enzymes in the duodenum work in an alkaline medium; • to neutralise acids from the stomach.	1 1 1 1	Each question asks for either one reason or one purpose. Do not offer more reasons than asked for because additional incorrect reasons will prevent a mark being given for your answer.
	TOTAL MARKS	**8**	

Question	Answer	Mark	Examiner's comments
4 a (i) (ii)	CO_2 *or* gas was given off Any one from: • no further reaction took place; • all the copper carbonate had already broken down; • CuO does not break down with heat.	1 1	An answer 'CO_2 is burned off' is not awarded a mark because CO_2 does not burn. Your answers need to be accurately given. An answer 'no more carbon to react with oxygen' is not awarded a mark. It is the carbonate that breaks down and not carbon that reacts with oxygen.
b (i) (ii)	the magnesium had combined with oxygen to form magnesium oxide $2Mg + O_2 \ 2MgO$	1 1	An answer 'magnesium combines with air' is not awarded a mark because it is not accurate enough. It is the **oxygen** in air that reacts with the magnesium.
	TOTAL MARKS	**4**	

TEST ANSWERS

Question		Answer	Mark	Examiner's comments
5	a	reduction	1	
	b	(table below)	1	All three ticks are needed to be awarded one mark. The question clearly asks for one box in each column to be ticked. If you do not know make a guess but use one tick in each column.

	aluminium	silicon	carbon
more reactive than chromium	✓	✓	✓
less reactive than chromium			

TOTAL MARKS 2

Question		Answer	Mark	Examiner's comments
6	(i)	A	1	You are provided with spaces on the paper for your answer. Write the letter in the space, not on the diagram.
	(ii)	D	1	

TOTAL MARKS 2

Question		Answer	Mark	Examiner's comments
7	a	U and R	1	The question asks for you to write a letter for each answer. Try to follow instructions.
	b	U and L	1	Both letters have to be correct to be awarded a mark.
	c	B	1	
	d	B	1	

TOTAL MARKS 4

Question		Answer	Mark	Examiner's comments
8	a (i)	0.5 s	1	Always give the units for your answer. Do show your working as it is easier for you or the marker to check the way you were thinking. In some questions you can be awarded marks for the working even if the answer is incorrect.
	(ii)	2.5 m/s *or* 2 m/s	1	
	(iii)	1.25 m *or* 1 m	1	
	b (i)	Any one from: • it is bouncing; • it is in contact with the floor; • it is changing direction; • it is changing speed.	1	You are given two lines for your answer. this is an indication of the extent of the answer wanted. Try not to write more than the space provides for.
	(ii)	upwards	1	An answer 'up and then down' is not awarded a mark. The ball is moving down from point D onwards
	c	0.8 m or 80 cm	1	Always give the units for your answer.

TOTAL MARKS 6

GLOSSARY

absorb To take in, e.g. some materials absorb water.

acid A solution with a pH value less than 7.

acid rain Rain which has a pH value less than 7 because it has dissolved pollutants from the air.

adaptation Any characteristic that enables the survival of an organism in its environment.

aerobic respiration A series of chemical reactions that use oxygen to produce energy from glucose in living cells.

air resistance The force produced by air particles when an object is moving through them.

alkali A solution with a pH value greater than 7.

alloy A solid mixture of two or more metals.

alveoli The air sacs in the lungs where gaseous exchange takes place.

amplitude The maximum deflection of a wave from its normal position.

angle of incidence The angle that a ray of light makes with the normal to a surface.

angle of reflection The angle from the normal at which a ray of light is reflected from a surface.

anther The part of the stamen which produces pollen.

atom The smallest part of an element that can take part in a chemical reaction.

balanced equation A precise summary of a chemical reaction using symbols and quantities.

base A compound that neutralises an acid to make a salt.

battery An energy source for electrical circuits.

biomass The body tissues of an organism.

boiling The rapid change of state from a liquid to a gas.

boiling point The temperature at which a liquid boils.

burning A vigorous reaction between a fuel and oxygen, producing heat and light.

carbohydrates A food group that includes starch and sugars.

carnivore An animal that eats other animals.

carpel The female part of a flower consisting of the stigma, style and ovary.

cell The building block of all life.
An energy store; can be joined to make batteries.

cell membrane The surface that surrounds a cell and holds everything inside. It also determines which materials can and cannot enter the cell.

cell sap The watery solution contained within cells.

cell wall A tough, protective outer layer of a plant cell.

chemical change A change which is difficult to reverse and where the products are different to the reactants.

chemical digestion The process of turning food into chemicals which can be used by the human body.

chemical formula Symbols used to show which and how many atoms of chemical elements make up a chemical compound.

chemical reaction A change where the products are different from the starting chemicals.

chemical symbol The letters used to represent chemical elements.

chemical weathering The breakdown of rocks caused by a chemical reaction.

chlorophyll The green pigment in plants which traps light energy for use in photosynthesis.

chloroplast Structures found only in plant cells which contain chlorophyll.

chromatography A separation method that relies on the different solubilities of substances in a solvent.

chromosome Coils of DNA found in all cell nuclei that carry the information needed to make an organism.

circuit A complete loop of electrical components and connecting wires around which electrical charge can flow.

classification Sorting organisms into related groups.

combustion The scientific name for burning a substance in oxygen to release energy.

compound A substance containing more than one type of atom chemically combined.

compress To squeeze something.

condensation A change of state from a gas to a liquid.

consumer An organism that eats a producer or another consumer. All animals are consumers.

contract Get smaller.

current A flow of electrical charge around a circuit.

cytoplasm The jelly-like part of a cell where many chemical reactions take place.

decomposition A reaction where one substance breaks down into two or more different substances.

diffusion The spreading out of gases and liquids caused by the particles moving randomly.

digestion Breaking down large, complex substances in your food, into smaller, simpler substances that can be absorbed into your blood.

dissolving When a substance forms a solution in a solvent. Dissolving is reversible.

distillation Separating a mixture of liquids by boiling one of them and then condensing it elsewhere.

DNA The substance responsible for transmitting genetic information.

dominant gene A gene that will always show as a characteristic, whatever other different genes for that characteristic are present.

electrical conductivity The extent to which a material will allow electrical charge to flow through it.

element A substance made from only one type of atom.

energy The ability to do work.

environment The area in which an organism lives or the surrounding conditions.

enzymes Chemicals in your digestive system that speed up the breakdown of food substances.

evaporation Changing state from liquid to gas at a temperature lower than the liquid's boiling point.

expand Get bigger.

fats The energy-rich food group contained within vegetable oils and dairy products.

fertilisation When male and female nuclei fuse to create a complete set of instructions for a new organism.

fetus A baby forming in its mother's uterus when cells start to become specialised.

fibre Mostly undigested plant material which helps food to move through your digestive system.

filament The stalk of a stamen.

filtering Separating an insoluble solid from a liquid by pouring the mixture through a filter paper. The filtrate passes through the paper but the solid residue is left behind.

filtrate The liquid that passes through a filter.

flower The reproductive part of a flowering plant.

food chain A series of feeding relationships.

food web A series of related food chains.

force A force pushes objects together or pulls them apart.

fossil fuels Fuels made from the fossilised remains of living things.

fractional distillation Separating a mixture of liquids using their different boiling points to boil one liquid off at a time.

freezing Changing state from a liquid into a solid.

frequency The number of waves that pass a point in a second. Frequency is measured in hertz (Hz).

fuel A material that burns to release energy.

gametes Reproductive cells with a single set of chromosomes capable of joining with another gamete of the other sex from which a new organism develops.

gas A state of matter. Particles in a gas move freely and are far apart from each other. A gas will fill its container and can be compressed easily.

gas pressure The force per unit area produced by gas particles hitting a surface.

gaseous exchange The process of oxygen moving into your blood from the air and carbon dioxide moving into the air from your blood via alveoli.

gene Part of a chromosome that carries the information for one tiny part of an organism.

genetic cross diagram A diagram showing the potential outcomes from genetic combinations.

genotype The genetic constitution of an individual.

geothermal energy Energy produced using the heat of the Earth's rocks.

glucose The sugar made during photosynthesis.

gravity The force of attraction between two objects.

greenhouse effect The trapping of light energy within the Earth's atmosphere by gases. This warms the Earth's atmosphere.

groups Collections of materials or living things which have similar properties.

guard cells Cells that open and close stomata.

habitat The area where an organism lives.

herbivore An animal that only eats plants.

hydroelectric power Electricity that is generated by moving water.

igneous rock Rock made from cooling molten rock (magma).

incident ray Ray of light moving towards an object.

indicator A substance that shows whether a solution is an acid or alkali by a colour change.

inheritance Passing on genetic information from adult to offspring.

insoluble Does not dissolve in a particular solvent.

insulator Any material that does not easily let heat or electrical charge flow through it.

invertebrates Animals that do not have a backbone.

joule The S.I. unit of energy.

key A set of questions or statements used to identify living things.

large intestine Part of your gut where water from food is absorbed into your blood.

laterally inverted An image with sides apparently the opposite way round to the sides of the object.

liquid A state of matter. A liquid's particles are free to move and close together. Liquids are difficult to compress and take the shape of their container.

luminous Something that gives out light.

machine A device used to do work.

magma Molten rock, from inside the Earth.

magnet A piece of iron that can attract other pieces of iron. Magnets can attract or repel other magnets.

magnetic field The area around a magnet where the force of the magnet can be detected.

magnetic field lines Lines drawn around a magnet to show where the magnetic field is.

mammals A class of vertebrate animals which incudes humans.

mass The amount of matter that an object is made of. Mass is measured in kilograms or grams.

mechanical digestion The part of the process of digestion which starts in the mouth causing the partial physical breakdown of food.

melting Changing state from a solid to a liquid.

melting point Temperature at which a solid melts.

metamorphic rock Rock formed when other rocks are heated and squashed in the Earth's crust.

microorganism An organism only visible using a microscope.

mitochondria The tiny mobile structures within cells where aerobic respiration takes place.

mixture Two or more elements or compounds that are not chemically joined together.

molecule Two or more atoms chemically joined together, the atoms could be the same or different.

moment The turning effect of a force; equal to the force multiplied by the distance from the pivot.

Moon The only natural satellite orbiting the Earth.

neutralisation The reaction between an acid and an alkali producing a salt and water.

newton The S.I. unit of force.

non-renewable energy source An energy source that cannot be replaced once it has been used.

normal A line at 90° to the surface of an object.

north seeking pole The pole of a bar magnet that points towards the Earth's magnetic north pole.

nuclear energy Energy produced when particles of uranium split.

nucleus The control centre of a cell.

offspring New animals or plants resulting from reproduction.

omnivore An animal that eats plants and animals.

opaque A description of materials which do not allow light to pass through them.

orbit The path an object follows as it moves around another object.

ore A rock that contains a useful mineral.

organ Part of an organism which is specialised for a particular function.

organ system A collection of organs which all have a role in one particular biological process.

oscilloscope A piece of equipment used to display a range of waveforms.

osmosis Diffusion of a solvent through a semi-permeable membrane.

ovary Part of the female reproductive system where female sex cells (ova in animals and ovules in plants) develop.

ovule The female sex cell of a plant.

ovum The female sex cell of an animal.

oxidation A reaction where a substance combines with oxygen.

oxide A compound of oxygen with another element.

parallel Two things extending in the same direction as each other and remaining the same distance apart.

particle model A useful set of ideas concerning a small body that helps us to understand some of the things that happen to substances.

petals Brightly coloured leaves of a flower.

pH A measure of the acidity or alkalinity of a liquid or solution of a solid.

photosynthesis The process by which plants make glucose from water and carbon dioxide using sunlight.

physical change The reversible change of a substance from one state to another.

physical weathering The breakdown of rocks caused by a physical process.

pitch How high or low a note is.

pivot The point on which something is able to turn.

pollen Grains that hold the male sex cells of plants.

pollination Transfer of pollen from the anther of one flower to the stigma of another.

primary consumers Animals which eat plants.

principle of moments The relationship between the forces on either side of a pivot.

producer An organism that traps energy to make glucose. Plants are the producers for most of the Earth's food chains.

products Substances made as a result of chemical reactions.

protein The food group that gives us the chemicals we need to grow and repair our bodies.

pure Containing only one type of particle.

pyramid of numbers A diagram showing the number of organisms at each level of a food chain.

radiation Any of the different types of electromagnetic wave.

random Without any pattern or organisation.

reactants Substances which react with each other.

recessive gene A gene which only shows its effect when it is received from both parents.

reduction The loss of oxygen during a chemical reaction.

reflect To bounce back from a surface.

reflected ray A ray of light reflected from a surface.

refraction When light changes direction as it passes into and out of a transparent object.

relay switch A switch in a circuit that, when it is closed, acts as the switch for another circuit.

renewable energy source An energy source that does not run out, such as wind, water or Sun.

reproduction Making offspring. Humans reproduce when they have babies.

resistance The opposition to the flow of electricity through a material.

respiration Releasing energy in cells through a chemical reaction.

reversible Can be changed back.

root hair cells Cells near the tip of a root that have hair-like extensions to absorb water.

saliva Produced by glands in the mouth, it wets food and contains amylase to start to digest starch.

salt The compound made when a metal displaces hydrogen from an acid.

secondary colour A colour made by combining two or more primary colours.

secondary consumers Animals that eat primary consumers.

sedimentary rock Rocks made when a sediment is squashed and becomes cemented together.

selective breeding Breeding your best animals or plants together to try to produce offspring with the characteristics you want.

semi-permeable membrane A thin layer which allows the solvent to pass through, but does not allow any dissolved substances to pass through.

series circuit A circuit in which all of the components are linked in one loop.

sex chromosomes The chromosomes that make you male or female.

sexual reproduction The process of producing new individuals as the result of the combination of both male and female genetic information.

shadows Dark patches made on a surface when an object stops light getting to the surface.

small intestine Part of the gut where digestion is finished and food particles are absorbed into your blood.

Solar System The complete collection of asteroids, planets and comets moving around the Sun.

solid A state of matter. In a solid, particles are in fixed positions. The particles cannot move around freely but they can vibrate. The particles are close together so solids cannot be easily compressed.

solute A substance that can dissolve in a solvent.

solution A mixture of a solute and a solvent in which the substances are not chemically combined.

solvent A liquid that dissolves a solute.

south seeking pole The end of a bar magnet that points away from the Earth's magnetic north pole.

specialised Adapted for a particular function.

species A grouping of organisms which can breed successfully.

sperm A male sex cell of an animal.

stamen The male parts of a flower (the anther and filament).

starch A carbohydrate made up of sugar molecules chemically joined together.

states of matter Solid, liquid and gas are the three states of matter. The state that a substance is in depends mainly upon its temperature.

stigma The sticky female part of a flower where pollen gets caught.

stomach The part of your gut where digestion of protein happens.

stomata Holes in the surfaces of leaves, mostly on the underside, used for the exchange of gases.

style The part of the carpel between the ovary and the stigma.

substance A material that only contains one type of particle. A substance is always pure because a pure material only has one type of particle.

Sun Our nearest star; the centre of the Solar System.

switch A component which is used to make and break an electrical circuit easily.

symbol equation A summary of a chemical reaction using symbols only.

tension The force produced within an object when it is being stretched.

thermal conductivity The measure of how easily thermal energy passes through a material.

thermal decomposition A reaction where one substance breaks down into two or more substances when it is heated.

translucent Allowing some light to pass through.

transparent A material that lets most light falling on to it to pass through.

trend A general pattern in data or behaviour.

Universal indicator A mixture of indicators which gives a definite colour change for each whole change of pH value from 1 to 14.

uterus The part of the female reproductive system where a baby develops.

vacuole Structures containing cell sap found in plant cells. Vacuoles help plant cells to stay rigid and the plant to stay upright.

variation The difference between individuals within a species.

vertebrate An animal that has a backbone.

villi Finger-like projections on the small intestine wall. Villi make the surface area much bigger so that more food substances can be absorbed into the blood.

virtual image An image that appears to exist but cannot be caught on a screen.

wavefronts Imaginary lines joining points at the same position on a series of waves.

wavelength The distance between the same point on two successive waves.

waves The movement of energy from one place to another without the particles of the medium being permanently displaced.

weight The pulling force of the Earth's gravity on an object. Weight tells you how heavy something is. Weight is measured in newtons (N).

white blood cells Cells in your blood that fight off invading microorganisms by engulfing them or making antibodies to kill them.

wind The horizontal movement of air over the Earth's surface.

wind energy Energy produced from the wind moving the blades attached to an aerogenerator.

word equation A summary of a chemical reaction using only words.

xylem Cells that are adapted for the transportation of water through a plant.

ACKNOWLEDGEMENTS

Published by Collins Educational
An *imprint of* HarperCollins*Publishers* Ltd
77-85 Fulham Palace Road
London W6 8JB

First published 1998

ISBN 0 00 323503 3

Ian Richardson and Steve Goldsmith assert the moral right to be identified as the authors of this work.

British Library Cataloguing in Publication Data
A catalogue record for this book is available from the British Library.

Edited by Mark Jordan
Production by James Graves, Anna Pauletti
Cover design by BCG Communications
Book design by Rupert Purcell and produced by Gecko Limited
Printed and bound in the UK by The Bath Press

Acknowledgements
QCA (SCAA) for permission to reproduce past Test questions
pp. 33–40, 75–79, 113–118, 153–157, 196–199
'Coca-Cola™', 'Coke' and the design of the contour bottle are registered trade marks of the Coca-Cola Company.

Photographs
Coca-Cola™ 58;
Hutchinson Library 158;
Mark Jordan 16, 42, 58, 70,103;
Andrew Lambert 17, 20, 26, 100, 101, 128, 137, 139, 159;
Microscopix Photo Library 89;
Science Photo Library 42, 48, 84, 125;
Paul Sterry 3,5,42,44;
Tony Stone Images 65, 70, 80;
Telegraph Colour Library 149.

Illustrations
Sally Artz
Roger Bastow
Harvey Collins
Richard Deverell
Gecko Limited
Sarah Jowsey
Ian Law
Mick Loates
Mike Parsons
Dave Poole

Every effort has been made to contact the holders of copyright material, but if any have been inadvertently overlooked, the Publishers will be pleased to make the necessary arrangements at the first opportunity.

INDEX

INDEX